The Age of Uncertainty

The Age of Uncertainty

John Kenneth
Galbraith

British Broadcasting Corporation
André Deutsch

For Adrian Malone
With admiration and gratitude

Published by the
British Broadcasting Corporation
35 Marylebone High Street
London W1M 4AA

ISBN 0 563 12887 9

and André Deutsch Ltd
105 Great Russell Street
London WC1B 3LJ

ISBN 0 233 96847 4

First published 1977

Printed in England by
Jolly & Barber Ltd, Rugby

Foreword
On The Age of Uncertainty 7

1. The Prophets and Promise of Classical Capitalism   11
2. The Manners and Morals of High Capitalism   43
3. The Dissent of Karl Marx   77
4. The Colonial Idea   109
5. Lenin and the Great Ungluing   133
6. The Rise and Fall of Money   161
7. The Mandarin Revolution   197
8. The Fatal Competition   227
9. The Big Corporation   257
10. Land and People   280
11. The Metropolis   303
12. Democracy, Leadership, Commitment   324

A Major Word of Thanks   343
Notes   345
List of Illustrations   349
Index   355

Foreword
On The Age of Uncertainty

One summer day in 1973, as the great Watergate uncover-up was the only thing otherwise occupying my mind, I received a call from Adrian Malone of the BBC in London. He wanted to know if I would do a television series on some unspecified aspect of the history of economic or social ideas.

The call came at an exceptionally opportune moment for me. Harvard professors are required by a custom that must reach back to the Pilgrims to tell how deeply they are in love with their teaching. Even those whose boredom is most visibly reciprocated by their minuscule classes speak feelingly at the Faculty Club of the depth of their devotion to this duty. The perpetration of this fraud I had been finding increasingly difficult. Once or twice I had caught myself looking at the ranks of eager young faces with mild revulsion. A terrible thing. I was thinking of retiring. Why not do so and try the vast, impersonal audience of television? There was, I had been told, no chance that you could hear the sets clicking off. What if a man dozed, a couple left? It had been a hard day, love had its claims, and anyhow I wouldn't know. After less than decent hesitation, I accepted. I sat down with the men — Adrian Malone, Dick Gilling, Mick Jackson, David Kennard — who were, for the next three years, to be my constant and truly esteemed companions in the enterprise.

We settled early on the title "The Age of Uncertainty" for the series. It sounded well; it did not confine thought; and it suggested the basic theme: we would contrast the great certainties in economic thought in the last century with the great uncertainty with which problems are faced in our time. In the last century capitalists were certain of the success of capitalism, socialists of socialism, imperialists of colonialism, and the ruling classes knew they were meant to rule. Little of this certainty now survives. Given the dismaying complexity of the problems mankind now faces, it would surely be odd if it did.

As our discussions continued, a further theme emerged. It began with the far from novel thought that ideas are important not only for themselves but also for explaining or interpreting social behavior. The ruling ideas of the time are those by which people and governments are guided. Thus they help to shape history itself. What men believe about the power of the market or the dangers of the state has a bearing on the laws they enact or do not enact — on what they ask of the government or entrust to market forces. So our treatment of ideas would fall very roughly into two parts: First, the men and the ideas, then their consequences. First, Adam Smith, Ricardo and Malthus, then the impact of their systems in Britain, Ireland and the New World. First, the history of economic ideas, then the economic history.

This would be the division within the early programs as in the early chapters of this book. But it would also be the sequence in the task as a whole. After a certain time we would shift from men to consequences, from ideas to institutions. The last of the great figures in economics with which I deal is Keynes. That does not mean that he is the last to deserve mention; it is only that those who followed were born too late. Neither they nor their friends should weep. Television is here to stay. Ideas and the resulting institutions were the two building blocks from which the series, and this book, were constructed, and both have their claim.

An enterprise for television such as this lends itself to an obvious and easy specialization. The substance would be mine; the presentation would belong to my colleagues of the BBC. Had this division been pressed, the results would surely have been sad. Effective presentation — intelligent planning, the search for the relevant scenes, the photography and direction — was only possible if my colleagues immersed themselves deeply and professionally in the ideas. This they did. And in doing so, they greatly influenced my thinking, added greatly to my information. The benefits carry over into this book. In turn, though it was generally less important, I suggested subjects and locations for pictures and occasionally how something might be given visual meaning.

My association with the BBC did not end with producers and directors. The British Broadcasting Corporation, as everyone must know, is a very great organization. In the world of responsible television there are the BBC and some others. Its genius lies in the quality of the people it attracts and also in the feeling of everyone — the talented cameramen, sound men, lighting men, production assistants, staff persons — that they have a deeply shared responsibility for the product.

Television, every author who encounters it realizes, is very different from writing. The discipline of time is relentless. An hour on Karl Marx may seem to some viewers very long; in relation to his long, intense, varied and prodigiously active life it is only a minute. The problem is not simplification; one can state a central point briefly and with accuracy and clarity, and one must expect to be held to account if he does not. The discipline of time manifests itself in the need to select — to concentrate on the main points and to choose even between these. And what the author selects will be intensely personal; no one should claim that what he chooses to say about Adam Smith, Ricardo, Karl Marx, Lenin or John Maynard Keynes or even the selection of these in preference to others reflects an immutable and objective wisdom. In television one cannot be comprehensive. One can only hope his selection is reasonably considered. The test one must propose with all available diplomacy and tact to his critics — those who, in the tradition of their craft, combine warm and unfailing generosity with deep perception — is whether he has added something that is accurate to knowledge.

In a television program, part of the story is carried by the pictures, part by the words. No one would think of publishing a book containing the pictures without the words, although such a proposition should be advanced cautiously. These are days when publishers will publish almost anything. Similarly no one should publish the words as written for the screen. A motion picture or television script is a mutilated thing, a form without a face. It must also be written in the knowledge that the viewer has only one chance. Perhaps for programs such as this there should, on difficult points, be provision for an instant replay at the viewer's discretion. But there isn't. The writer of a book, in contrast, assumes that the reader will, on occasion, allow his eye to travel back to see again what the author is saying or trying to say.

In preparing the series, I first wrote careful essays on each of the subjects to be covered. These were the basic material from which the television scripts were developed. From the original essays, amended by the scripts, I then wrote the book. On numerous occasions it goes beyond the ideas or events covered in the television programs. Happily one does not have to limit a chapter to what can be read in an hour — not yet. There are pictures here but they are to illustrate the story. The words were written to stand alone. I emerged from my three years with the BBC with an enhanced respect for television. But I do not wish to believe that the printed word is obsolete or obsolescent.

1.
The Prophets
and Promise of Classical Capitalism

On one of the last pages of his last and most famous book John Maynard Keynes — by wide agreement the most influential economist of this century — observed that ". . . the ideas of economists and political philosophers, both when they are right and when they are wrong, are more powerful than is commonly understood. Indeed the world is ruled by little else. Practical men, who believe themselves to be quite exempt from any intellectual influences, are usually the slaves of some defunct economist."[1] This was written in 1935. Thinking then of the oratory of Adolf Hitler, Joseph Goebbels and Julius Streicher which was at the time in full tide, and of Alfred Rosenberg and Houston Stewart Chamberlain from whose writings they drew their racial doctrines, he added: "Madmen in authority, who hear voices in the air, are distilling their frenzy from some academic scribbler of a few years back."[2] Then came his affirmation: ". . . the power of vested interests is vastly exaggerated compared with the gradual encroachment of ideas."[3]

Keynes provides the case for looking at the ideas that interpret modern capitalism — or modern socialism — and which guide our actions in consequence. Presumably we should know by what we are governed.

This is so even though Keynes overstated his point. For in economic affairs decisions are influenced not only by ideas and by vested economic interest. They are also subject to the tyranny of circumstance. This, too, is severe. In daily political discussion we think it greatly important whether an individual is of the right or of the left, liberal or conservative, an exponent of free enterprise or of socialism. We do not see that, very often, circumstances close in and force the same action on all — or on all who are concerned to survive. If one must stop air pollution in order to breathe or prevent unemployment or inflation in order to prove competence in economic management, there isn't much difference between what conservatives, liberals or social democrats will be forced to do. The choices are regrettably few.

Also we had best not close our eyes too completely to the idea of vested interest. People have an enduring tendency to protect what they have, justify what they want to have. And their tendency is to see as right the ideas that serve such purpose. Ideas may be superior to vested interest. They are also very often the children of vested interest.

The Source

The ideas that interpret modern economic life took form over a long span of time, as did the economic institutions that they seek to explain. But there is a convenient and generally agreed point at which one can begin. In the last half of the eighteenth century, economic life in Britain, and in lesser measure elsewhere in Western Europe and soon also in New England, was transformed by a succession of mechanical inventions. These were the steam engine and a series of remarkable innovations in textile manufacturing; the flying shuttle (which came early) was followed by the spinning jenny, water frame, spinning mule and power loom. Clothing was (as it remains) a major service to ostentation by the rich, an indispensable utility for the poor. The hand-spinning and weaving of cloth were infinitely tedious, costly processes; the purchase of a coat by an average citizen was an action comparable in modern times to the purchase of an automobile or even a house. The new machines took the manufacture of cloth out of the household and into the mills and made the product cheap — an item of mass consumption.

With the textile revolution went a more general instinct for technical change and a vast confidence and pride in its results. It was something like the great burst of confidence in technology and its wonders that followed World War II. With the Industrial Revolution went yet another in economic thought.

These ideas had a sense of the world to come but they were also — an important point — deeply influenced by the world that had always been. That was overwhelmingly the world of agriculture. Nor could it have been otherwise. Until then economic life, a tiny minority of the privileged apart, had meant supplying one's self and one's family with only three things — food, clothing and shelter. And all of these came from the land. Food, of course, did. So did skins, wool and vegetable fibers. And houses, such as they were, came from the nearby forest, quarry or brick kiln. Until the Industrial Revolution, and in many countries for a long time thereafter, all economics was agricultural economics.

The Landscape

Economists have recurrently tried to depict the economic system for the layman as a machine. Raw materials are fed into it; the workers turn it; the capitalist owns it; the state, the landlords, the capitalists and workers share its product, usually in an egregiously unequal way. One might have a better impression by thinking of the economic world as a landscape. Before the Industrial Revolution, it was overwhelmingly rural. The workers were mostly employed in agriculture. Income and power, two things that have usually gone together, were indicated by the size and magnificence of the dwellings in which people lived; those of the farm laborers were many and mean. The abundance of this labor and the relative scarcity of land favored the landlord. So did tradition, social position, law and education. The house of the landlord reflected this privileged status.

Exercising a further and major claim on both landlord and worker was the state. Power ran from the ruler to the landlord, from the landlord to the rural worker. As power flowed down, income extracted thereby flowed up. It's a rule worth having in mind. Income almost always flows along the same axis as power but in the opposite direction.

Neither the power of the state nor that of the landowners was plenary. In England by the time of the Industrial Revolution, by the workings of law and custom, tenant farmers and even farm workers had acquired certain minimal defenses against the power of their landlords. There were rules governing their compensation and expulsion that had to be respected. And at Runnymede in 1215, a great convocation had combined an historic commitment to human liberty with an even more immediate concern for the rights properly appurtenant to real estate. In consequence, the position of the large landowners had been substantially protected against the incursions of the King. England, however, was an advanced case. In France the peasants who worked the land were far less well protected from their landlords; both landless and landed were far more vulnerable to the ever more insistent claims of the King. So it was in most of the rest of Europe, and increasingly it was so as one moved east and to Asia. In India in the distant domain of the Moghuls — to whose gorgeous courts in the seventeenth century artistically and architecturally more primitive Europeans had begun finding their way — all land was considered to be owned in the manner of one great plantation by the Great Moghul himself.

The Founder

It would be reckless, maybe in these days even a trifle dangerous, to propose an ethnic theory of economists. All races have produced notable economists, with the exception of the Irish who doubtless can protest their devotion to higher arts.[4] But in relation to population no one can question the eminence of the Scotch, as properly they may be called. (Only in the last century did whisky wholly pre-empt our name.) The only truly distinguished competition is from the Jews.

The greatest of Scotchmen was the first economist, Adam Smith. Economists do not have a great reputation for agreeing with one another — but on one thing there is wide agreement. If economics has a founding father, it is Smith. He was born, or anyhow baptized, in the small port town of Kirkcaldy on the north side of the Firth of Forth in 1723. The father of the man whose name would ever after be linked with freedom of trade was a customs official.

The Founder: Adam Smith as professor.

Smith is remembered warmly but a trifle erratically in his native town. In 1973, I went for several golden days to Scotland to help celebrate the 250th anniversary of Smith's birth. It was June; when it does not rain, there is no countryside in all the world more tranquil and lovely than that around Edinburgh and across the Firth of Forth. But in the last century Kirkcaldy became the linoleum capital of the world; the industry has since declined but enough remains to project a particularly horrid smell. The air was better in Smith's time. As visitors, we were housed on the golf courses of St. Andrews some twenty miles away. One day I rode to the celebrations with a Kirkcaldy cab driver and James Callaghan, previously Chancellor of the Exchequer, as of this writing Prime Minister, and a friend. "I expect," Jim said to our driver as we were on our way, "that you're pretty proud hereabouts of being from the same town as Adam Smith? You know a good deal about him, I suppose?"

"Yessir, yessir," said the driver. "The founder of the Labour Party, I always heard."

Smith went to the good local school and on to Balliol. His impressions of Oxford were adverse; he later held that the Oxford public professors, as those with a salary were called, did no work. They got their pay anyway so why should they bother. The professors were a metaphor of his economic system.

Men — and women — do their best when they reap both the rewards of diligence or intelligence and the penalties of sloth. It was equally important that people be free to seek the work or conduct the business that would reward their efforts. What so served the individual, got him the most, then best served the society by getting it the most.

After Oxford, Smith went back to Scotland to lecture on English literature at Edinburgh. Here also he began his long friendship with his almost equally notable compatriot, the philosopher David Hume. In 1751, he was made a professor at the University of Glasgow, first of logic, then of moral philosophy. Scottish professors were paid partly in accordance with the number of students they attracted; Smith thought this a far better system. I remember thinking that Smith's view had application at Princeton when I taught there before World War II. Professors who were lazy or incompetent or merely dull and who were being deserted in droves by their students attributed their small classes to the importance of their subject and the attendant rigor of their instruction. They argued, accordingly, that their courses should be made a requirement for the degree. Though their argument was plausibly put, it seemed to me better that they be exposed to their empty classrooms.

Smith was also suspicious of those who laid claim to high principle in conflict with lower self-interest. He was greatly attracted by the American colonies, a subject on which he may have been instructed by his contemporary, Benjamin Franklin.[5] In one of the luminous passages in *Wealth of Nations* he observed that "the late resolution of the Quakers in Pennsylvania to set at liberty all their negro slaves, may satisfy us that their number cannot be very great."[6] In 1763, self-interest overcame high principle and captured Smith. He was offered a post as tutor to the young Duke of Buccleuch — a family which was then (as still) possessed of a vast land acreage of indifferent quality on the border. The post carried with it a good and secure salary and a pension at the end. Smith resigned his professorship and took his young charge off to the Continent on the Grand Tour. In the manner of young aristocrats the young man evidently survived this education without any historic effect. For Smith it was a very grand tour indeed.

The Men of Reason

The most notable of those Smith visited lived outside Geneva, almost exactly on the border between France and Switzerland. The archaeological ruins that once housed the financial enterprises of Mr. Bernard Cornfeld are only a few hundred yards away. The border location was chosen in both cases for the same reason — the need for international movement in advance of hostile authority. The occupant of the château was François-Marie Arouet, called Voltaire. One pleasant aspect of this visit must have involved the matter of language. Smith was having a wretched time with his French. Voltaire spoke excellent English. Voltaire always regarded England as an island quite literally of political liberty and freedom of thought, and he had lived there for more than two years (1726–1729) after a brief stay in the Bastille. His château, which stands on a small, tree-covered hill on large grounds, has been described as appropriate to a man of the Age of Reason — perhaps, in this respect, something like Jefferson's Monticello. This may be partly imagination; what is certain is that it is the house of a man of affluence. It's a munificent dwelling.

Voltaire was a man — perhaps *the* man — of reason. The word is one that scholars often hesitate to define for fear of seeming simple. Where things *are* simple, one should avoid making them complicated; there are other ways to display subtlety of mind. For both Smith and Voltaire reason required that one reach conclusions not by recourse to religion, rule, prejudice or passion; instead one brought the mind to bear fully and comprehensively on all the relevant and available information. Thus one made decisions. By this standard Adam Smith was also supremely a man of reason. He had a simply unlimited appetite for information. He gathered it, digested it and allowed it to guide his thoughts. These led him into new paths, made him a pioneer.

The Agricultural System

All of France was for Smith a major source of information and instruction. In 1765, he saw, as one still does, the rich land, the intelligent, patient and good-

Man of Reason: Voltaire receives visitors who seem appropriately nervous.

humored men who work it and the wonderfully varied products of the French soil. Only in France is the quality of the farm products — fruit, vegetables, cheese, wine needless to say — of different regions, even different villages, a major topic of interest and concern and also of scholarly dispute. At the time of Smith's odyssey, the agricultural faith of France was at its peak. It was reflected in the ideas of a fascinating group of economic philosophers known in the history of economic thought as the Physiocrats.

The Physiocrats held that all wealth originated in agriculture. Only there, as the gift of nature, did productive effort yield a surplus over cost. Trade and manufacture yielded no such gain. They were necessary but they were sterile. The surplus produced in agriculture — its "produit net" — sustained all other producers. Agriculture was *the* basic industry, the only basic industry.

There is proof here of Keynes's assertion that no economic idea is ever truly dead. For a time in my youth I served as research director for the American Farm Bureau Federation, the big, conservative farm organization, farm-supply cooperative and farm lobby, then at the height of its power. Each December our members met in convention. In the days that followed, the voice of physiocracy — the claim that agriculture is the source of all wealth — rang through the halls. I wrote some of the speeches. And the voice is not yet silent. When politicians campaign for the few farm votes that remain, the message of physiocracy may still be heard. "Yours, my friends, is the basic industry; the farmer is the man who feeds them all."

Smith met the Physiocrats at Paris and Versailles. The one who impressed him most and the most original of mind was François Quesnay, the physician, no less, to Louis XV. Quesnay was the friend of Madame de Pompadour, and she was his patron at the court.

Like most people without adequate occupation, the denizens of Versailles were always open to ingenious novelty. The French countryside was later glorified by Marie Antoinette's model village, Le Hameau, which can still be seen. The French rural economy was celebrated with similar ingenuity by Quesnay's famous *Tableau Économique*. The *Tableau* was an effort to show in quantitative terms the relationships of the principal parts of the economic system — to show how much product farmers, landlords, merchants received from each other and how much income they passed back to each other in return.

For a long time after Quesnay scholars dismissed the *Tableau* as an arithmetical curiosity; it was another French novelty, not to be taken more seriously than Marie Antoinette's village. Adam Smith had something to do with the rejection. His authority was great, and he thought economic scholarship was good only if clearly useful, a terrifying thought for modern economists. For Quesnay's calculations he saw no particular use.

Physician, Physiocrat: This is François Quesnay, physician to Louis XV, pioneer in quantitative economic relationships. His <u>Tableau Économique</u>, showing how income flows through the economic system.

A cottage in Marie Antoinette's <u>Le Hameau</u> at Versailles. In France agriculture was always both an industry and an art form.

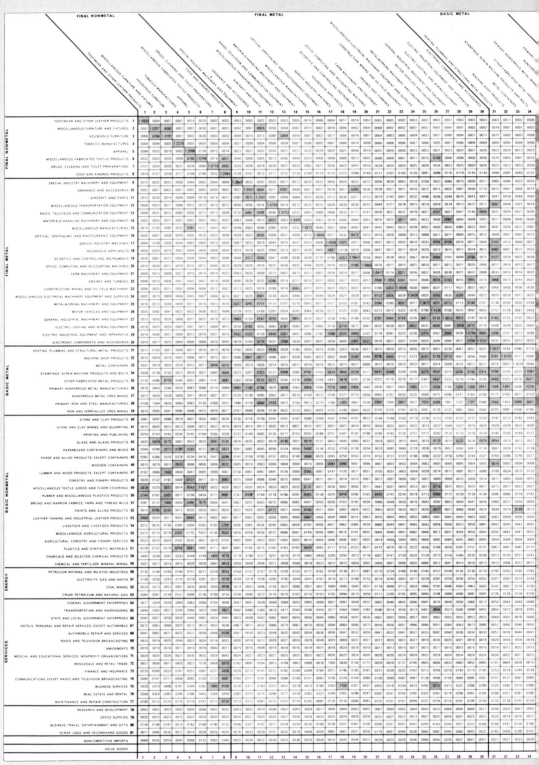

This great tabulation, in distant descent from **Dr. Quesnay**, shows what each **U.S.** industry gives to and receives from every other. In 1973, it won **Wassily Leontief** the Nobel Prize.

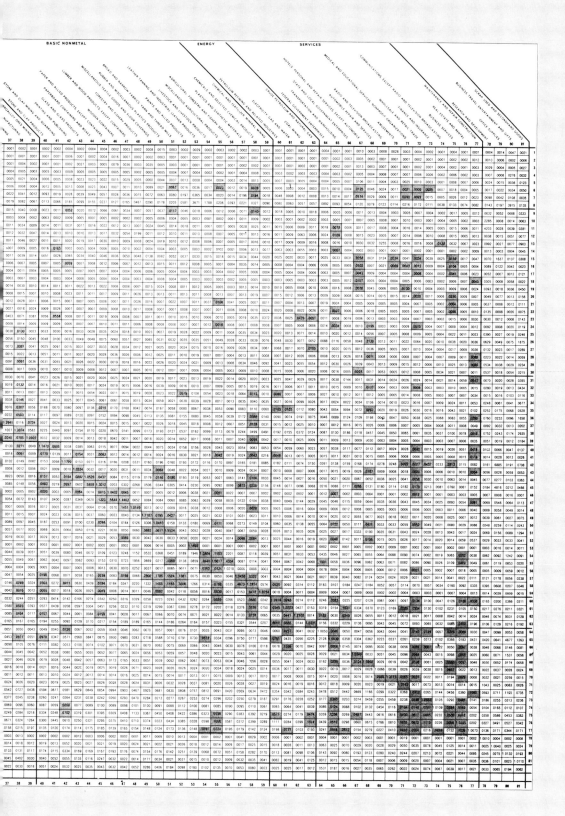

But in time Quesnay was redeemed. In 1973, Wassily Leontief, then of Harvard, received the Nobel Prize for his interindustry analysis, usually called the input-output system. The interindustry analysis shows in one great table what each industry (really each industrial category) sells to and buys from every other industry. Once compiled, it becomes possible then to calculate the effect of an increase in the output of automobiles (or weapons) on the sale of all other industries. It is an idea in distant but direct descent from Dr. Quesnay.

Another of the Physiocrats visited by Smith was Anne Robert Jacques Turgot. With his colleagues Turgot believed that public expenditure and therewith the burden of taxation on enterprise — or, as the Physiocrats saw it, on agriculture and the "produit net" — should be kept to a minimum. This should be done by limiting the power and function of the state.

In 1774, Turgot became Comptroller-General of France, and his task was to curb the extravagance of the French court and thus to reduce the burden on the "produit net."

He failed. A firm rule operated against him. People of privilege will always risk their complete destruction rather than surrender any material part of their advantage. Intellectual myopia, often called stupidity, is no doubt a reason. But the privileged feel also that their privileges, however egregious they may seem to others, are a solemn, basic, God-given right. The sensitivity of the poor to injustice is a trivial thing compared with that of the rich. So it was in the Ancien Régime. When reform from the top became impossible, revolution from the bottom became inevitable.

The Wealth of Nations

Long before Turgot was dismissed, Smith had taken the lessons of his travel back to Scotland. He was at work on his great book, and his friends had come to wonder if he would ever finish it. It was thought that he might be one of that great company of scholars, famous in the better universities to this day, which makes work on a forthcoming book (and conversation on its rigor and high scholarly merit) a substitute for ever publishing it.

Eventually, in 1776, he did publish it; the acclaim was immediate, and the first printing of *An Inquiry into the Nature and Causes of the Wealth of Nations* sold out in six months, a fact which would be more interesting if we knew the size of the printing. Distributed through, and sometimes all but lost in, the vast array of information which the book contained was the great thought that may well have originated with observing the Oxford professors. The wealth of a nation results from the diligent pursuit by each of its citizens of his own interests — when he reaps the resulting reward or suffers any resulting penalties. In serving his own interests, the individual serves the public interest. In Smith's greatest phrase, he is guided to do so as though by an unseen hand. Better the unseen hand than the visible, inept and predacious hand of the state.

These too are ideas that have lived in oratory. Let businessmen meet anywhere in the nonsocialist world, and the praise of self-interest — now usually modified to enlightened self-interest — also resounds.

Pins and the Division of Labor

Along with the pursuit of self-interest, the wealth of a nation was also enhanced by the division of labor. To this — broadly speaking, the superior efficiency of specialization — Smith attributed the greatest importance. Some of the gains in efficiency were from specialization by line of business and some from occupational specialization; some were from the fact that countries specialized in particular products or lines of trade. Some gains were from specialization within the industrial process. "The greatest improvement in the productive powers of labour, and the greater part of the skill, dexterity, and judgment with which it is anywhere directed, or applied, seem to have been the effects of the division of labour."[7]

Here is how Smith described the division of labor in his most notable case; in his pursuit of information he must have encountered the manufacture of pins and observed the process with his usual care:

One man draws out the wire, another straights it, a third cuts it, a fourth points it, a fifth grinds it at the top for receiving the head; to make the head requires two or three distinct operations; to put it on, is a peculiar business, to whiten the pins is another; it is even a trade by itself to put them into the paper . . .[8]

Ten men so dividing the labor, Smith calculated, could make 48,000 pins a day, 4800 apiece. One man doing all the operations would make maybe one, maybe twenty. It is still widely believed that the assembly line, with its attendant increase in labor productivity, was the invention early in the present century of Henry Ford.

The larger the market, the longer could be the production runs — pins or whatever — and the greater the opportunity for the division of labor. From this came Smith's case against tariffs and other restraints on trade and for the greatest possible freedom, national and international, in the exchange of goods, the widest possible market.

Freedom of trade, in its turn, enlarged the freedom of the individual in the pursuit of his self-interest. His scope became not national but international. From the combination of freedom of trade and freedom of enterprise came a yet larger production of what was most wanted — the most favorable social result.

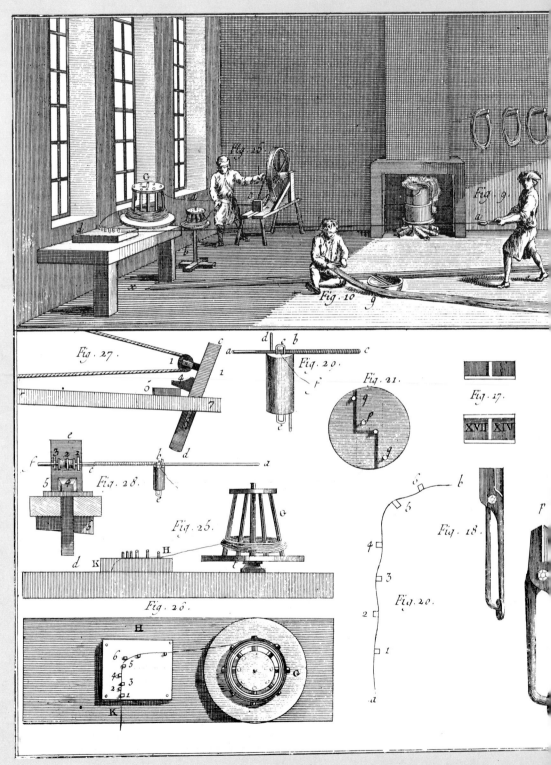

Many believe the assembly line was invented by Henry Ford. Diderot's <u>Encyclopaedia</u> shows one that assembled pins.

Combinations and Corporations

The ancient enemy of these freedoms was the state — the interventionist, mercantilist government which imposed tariffs, granted monopolies, burdened with taxes and, above all, sought to improve what, left to itself, was best. But the state was not the only threat, as almost all who cite Smith in modern times imagine. Businessmen were a major menace to their own freedom; their invariant instinct was to impose restraints upon themselves, and from this came another of Adam Smith's very trenchant observations: "People of the same trade seldom meet together, even for merriment and diversion, but the conversation ends in a conspiracy against the public, or in some contrivance to raise prices."[9]

Smith made another great point, which is also uncelebrated in modern business oratory. In fact, it will come to many as a shock: he was deeply opposed to joint-stock companies, now called corporations. Of the stockholders of these he said: ". . . [They] seldom pretend to understand anything of the business of the company; and when the spirit of faction happens not to prevail among them, give themselves no trouble about it, but receive contentedly such half-yearly or yearly dividend, as the directors think proper to make to them."[10] And of directors he added:

. . . being the managers rather of other people's money than of their own, it cannot well be expected that they should watch over it with the same anxious vigilance with which the partners in a private copartnery frequently watch over their own. Like the stewards of a rich man, they are apt to consider attention to small matters as not for their master's honour, and very easily give themselves a dispensation from having it. Negligence and profusion, therefore, must prevail, more or less, in the management of the affairs of such a company . . . Without an exclusive privilege . . . [joint-stock companies] have commonly mismanaged the trade. With an exclusive privilege they have both mismanaged and confined it.[11]

It is too bad that a visit by Adam Smith cannot be arranged to some forthcoming meeting of the United States Chamber of Commerce, the National Association of Manufacturers, the first merged meeting of the two or a gathering of the Confederation of British Industries. He would be astonished to hear heads of great corporations — or greater conglomerates or combines — proclaiming their economic virtue in his name. They, in their turn, would be appalled when he — of all prophets — told them their enterprises should not exist.

The Clearances

Adam Smith died in 1790, his last years made pleasant by his being the Commissioner of Customs in Edinburgh. This was a sinecure of which he disapproved, involving customs duties of which he disapproved, but again he was far too practical to refuse. He lies in a small burial ground just off the Royal

Mile in Edinburgh. His house is nearby. A few scholars come to visit but not many. Economists are generally negligent of their heroes. David Hume has a far grander monument a mile or two away, side by side with one of Abraham Lincoln which commemorates soldiers of Scottish origin who fought against slavery in the Civil War.

By the time Smith died, the changes of which he was the prophet were becoming visible in England and Scotland. And in both the countryside and in the towns. The Industrial Revolution was not a sudden, violent thing but it was the kind of revolution you could actually see.

People everywhere were being drawn from the country villages to the towns and to jobs in the mills. In Scotland they were also being abruptly expelled from the countryside in consequence of the rising demand for the principal industrial material which was wool.

The most spectacular example of this expulsion was in Sutherland. This, the northernmost of Scottish counties, is a vast expanse of rolling uplands; horizontally and vertically it makes up an appreciable part of the whole land area of Scotland. In summer it is green, lonesome and lovely, with the muted lighting of the far north. I was reminded, visiting there in the summer of 1975, of a comment of the late Richard Crossman: "No American really understands how much vacant space there is in Britain." At the beginning of the last century around two thirds of this particular space was owned by the Countess of Sutherland and her husband, the Marquis of Stafford.

Between 1811 and 1820, by common estimate they cleared some 15,000 Highlanders from their estates to make room for sheep. The Naver is a narrow black stream that runs north through the county for some thirty or forty miles to come out near Pentland Firth, some fifty miles west of Scapa Flow. Its thin and meager valley was then densely populated. Almost all the people were dispossessed.

At Strathnaver (as elsewhere) in May 1814, the operation assumed the definitive aspects of a final solution. In March the tenants had been given two months' notice to get out. But they were still around, for they had no place else to go. So the agents of the laird moved in with fire and dogs. They were especially careful to burn the roof timbers of the houses, for that meant, in this treeless land, that the houses could not be rebuilt, the people could not return. A few houses, it was later held, were burned without taking the precaution of evacuating the more aged and enfeebled inhabitants.

The sheep that took the place of the people returned far more revenue to the landlords — by a further estimate about three times as much. They had another advantage to the laird. The Cheviots moving over the hills were thought to do distinctly more for the landscape than the Highlanders. It could have been so.

Sutherland. "No American really understands how much vacant space there is in Britain."
The Clearances helped create this void.

Though cruel, the Clearances brilliantly illustrated a problem in economic development that persists unsolved to the present time. It is possible to have such a bad relationship between people and land — so many people, so little usable land — that development is impossible. Even the best result, given the number of people, is still bad. There is an equilibrium of poverty. So it is in much of India and in Bangladesh, Indonesia and other densely populated countries. No more land can be had. The Highland technique for reducing the population is no longer recommended. Birth control lends itself well to speeches but only slowly, when at all, to results. This is a problem to which I will return.

A Model Textile Town

By 1815 or 1820, there were factories, textile mills in particular, where, in principle, the dispossessed tenants could find jobs. But the male Highlanders did not take easily to the rhythm of the machine. Their stronger instinct was to migrate, most often to Canada. Nova Scotia was in fact, as in name, the new Scotland. Women and children were better and more pliable industrial material, though it was thought well to start the children young.

New Lanark, a half hour or so south and east of Glasgow in a deep valley by the Clyde — the water of a lovely falls turned the mills — was the scene of the most famous experiment in using children in industry. To this day the name, New Lanark, is associated in many people's minds, perhaps a bit vaguely, with enlightened humanitarian experiment. The mills and the houses and dormitories for the workers, erect and stern, survive unchanged.

The New Lanark experiment was initiated in the closing years of the eighteenth century by David Dale, a noted Scottish capitalist and philanthropist whose face in recent years has graced the notes of the Bank of Scotland. Dale's compassionate thought was to go to the orphanages of Glasgow and Edinburgh to rescue the miserable youngsters and give them both schooling and useful work. The cities, more than incidentally, would be relieved of the cost of their keep. New Lanark became the largest cotton mill in Scotland.

David Dale.

Once two thousand workers of all ages were employed. What was the town has now a population of eighty.

The atmosphere was of the highest moral tone. Each of the orphans was given an hour and a half of rigorous schooling each day. However, it was recognized that the mills must also return a profit; what is now commended as the work ethic had to be protected and encouraged. So the schooling was in the evening after a good, honest, thirteen-hour day in the mills.

No one should be too shocked. By the standards of the time New Lanark *was* a place of compassion and culture, if not exactly of rest. This was even more the case after 1799, when Dale's son-in-law, Robert Owen, took over. Owen was a philosopher, utopian socialist, religious skeptic and spiritualist. Reformers now came from all over Europe to visit New Lanark, to see for themselves this proof that industry could have a humane face. Under Owen, the Institution for the Formation of Character was built. It offered lectures for adults, singing and other recreation for the orphans, a nursery school for the very young. Public houses were closed and alcohol banned. In time, the work day for the children was reduced to ten and a half hours, and children under twelve were never employed. It's an indication of how things were elsewhere that this was considered lenient. Because of his compassion Owen was always in trouble with his partners. They would have much preferred a tough, down-to-earth manager who would get a day's work out of the little bastards.

The Indiana Footnote

New Lanark didn't wholly satisfy the utopian vision of Owen. So there was a sequel; this was New Harmony, Indiana, a cooperative elysium on the banks of the Wabash. Here Owen sought to make a completely fresh beginning; the new community would have no acquisitive genesis, no continuing capitalist taint. Its principle would be not Smith's self-interest but the far greater ideal of service to others.

Idealists did come to New Harmony, although the population was never more than a few hundred. So did an historic collation of misfits, misanthropes and free-loaders. Once there, they devoted themselves not to service but, more or less exclusively, to argument. While the discussions continued, so it was said, the pigs invaded the gardens. Harmony being lost, New Harmony failed. Free enterprise, the pursuit of self-interest, was thus saved in Indiana. It is my unhappy observation that idealists, including liberal reformers in our own time, are frequently less endangered by their enemies than by their preference for argument. Their righteous feeling, very often, is that everything should be sacrificed to a good row over first principles or a fight to the finish over who, if anyone, is to be in charge.

Building character at New Lanark. Owen's Institution for the Formation of Character in operation after ten and a half hours in the mills.

The mills today. Spare, silent, beautiful.

Ricardo and Malthus

If New Harmony was not in accordance with Smith's instruction, Britain was. A few months after Smith's death his position as a prophet was officially proclaimed. In a budget speech Pitt said of him that his "extensive knowledge of detail and depth of philosophical research will, I believe, furnish the best solution of every question connected with the history of commerce and with the system of political economy."[12] An economist could ask no more than that. None since in the nonsocialist world has had such a courageous endorsement.

Adam Smith offered more than counsel on public affairs. He offered what would today be called an economic model — a view of how the economic system works. Competition caused prices to be set in rough accord with the cost of production. The cost of production of an item, in turn, was the cost of reproducing, rearing and sustaining the labor that went into it.

Here were the germs of two ideas which were to grow and shape men's thought — and which still do. One was the labor theory of value. The other was that mankind would tend always to fall victim to its own fecundity — the never-to-be-repressed population explosion.

In the twenty-five years following Adam Smith's death, both ideas were taken up in London by two close friends, David Ricardo and Thomas Malthus. Ricardo is Smith's only serious contender for the title of founding father of economics; with him the great ethnic rivals of the Scotch arrive. Ricardo was Jewish. He was a stockbroker, a member of Parliament, a man of superb clarity of mind and terrible obscurity of prose. Malthus, a nonpracticing clergyman, was English.

Malthus, for much of his life, taught at Haileybury — the staff college, as we would now call it, of the East India Company. In the last century the East India Company was the source of income for Britain's greatest economists — besides Malthus, James Mill and his prodigious and luminous son, John Stuart Mill. None of them, it is interesting to note, was ever on the subcontinent, and this was not thought to be a handicap. James Mill produced a highly regarded history of the British in India. It included a devastating critique of the Hindu epics, which he deeply disliked, which he could not read in the original and which had not then been translated into English. The Mills, needless to say, were Scotch.

From Malthus came the Principle of Population. This held that, given "the passion between the sexes" (a most damaging thing that he sometimes thought might be subject to "moral restraint" and against which he suggested ministers might warn at marriage), population would always increase in geometric ratio — 2, 4, 8, 16 and so on. Meanwhile, at best, the food supply would increase only arithmetically — 2, 3, 4, 5. . . From this came the inevitable result: In the likely absence of moral restraint, population would be subject

Economics becomes the Dismal Science: David Ricardo, M.P.

The Reverend Thomas Robert Malthus.

only to the recurrent and ghastly checks imposed by famine or by war or natural catastrophe. Adam Smith, reflecting on the rewards from the freedom of trade, the resulting pursuit of self-interest and the division of labor, had a generally optimistic view of the prospects for man. Not Malthus. Nor was David Ricardo ever thought an optimist. It was with Malthus and Ricardo that economics became the dismal science.

The Ricardian View

Equally with his friend, David Ricardo foresaw a continuing increase in population, and Malthus's population became Ricardo's workers. Among the workers would be such competition for work on the one hand and for the food supply on the other that all would be reduced to bare subsistence. It was man's fate.

In an "improving society" this fate might be postponed, and, as a moment's thought will suggest, in the England of the nineteenth century this was a major qualification. But Ricardo's qualifications never caught up with his majestic generalizations. In the Ricardian world workers would receive the minimum necessary for life, never more. This was the iron law of wages. It led, among other things, to the conclusion that not only was compassion wasted on the working man but it was damaging. It might raise hopes and income in the short run. But it accelerated the population increase by which both were brought down. And any effort by government or trade unions to raise wages and rescue people from poverty would similarly be in conflict with economic law, be similarly frustrated by the resulting increase in numbers.

Different products of farms or factories required different amounts of Ricardo's minimally nourished labor. The amount of labor required established the relative value of things — again the labor theory of value. This, in turn, nurtured the distinctly pregnant thought that, since labor set the value of things, the whole product belonged to labor. Voiced in slightly different form by Marx half a century on, this proposal would shake the world.

Ricardo's world was still strongly rural. By the early decades of the nineteenth century, the Industrial Revolution was in the full thrust of change. However, in Ricardo's system the main figure was still the landlord. The same pressure of people on land that reduced wages had the effect of shoving up rents. In consequence, the more numerous the people, the richer were the landlords. They fattened, their people starved. And again nothing could be done about it; to return some of the rent to the farm workers would only cause their numbers to increase.

In Ricardo's world the state was receding in importance and power. It was the continuing lesson of Adam Smith that it should. Intervention by government would not, as noted, help the poor. But it would limit economic freedom and the pursuit of self-interest and thus make everything worse. David Ricardo was not, by his own lights, a cruel man. In a naturally cruel world he merely urged against contending in a futile way with the inevitable and for accepting the least bad. He did provide the rich with a very satisfactory formula for suffering the misfortunes of the poor.

There was a difference of opinion of much future importance between the two friends over what would happen to the handsome revenue accruing to the landlords. Ricardo held that it would either be spent or it would be saved and used for investment in land improvement, building, industrial development, in which case it would also be spent. He accepted a proposition made earlier by Jean Baptiste Say, the great French interpreter of Adam Smith. Say's Law held that production always provided the income to buy whatever was produced. What was saved was also spent, only in a different way, so there could never be a shortage of purchasing power.

On this point Malthus demurred. Perhaps the revenue might go unspent; perhaps there might, in consequence, be a shortage of purchasing power; perhaps, as a further consequence, the economy would, on occasion, falter and break down. There would be depressions resulting from a shortage of purchasing power as part of the natural order of things.

This too was a pregnant thought but it did not take. Ricardo's view, as Keynes was later to say, captured Britain as the Holy Inquisition captured Spain. For the next hundred years, until the decade of the Great Depression, Say and Ricardo ruled supreme. Men who said there could be a shortage of purchasing power did not know their economics; in fact, they were considered crackpots. Then, with John Maynard Keynes, Malthus's idea of a shortage of purchasing power became accepted doctrine. The most urgent task of government now was to compensate for the shortage, to offset the oversaving. Economics is not an exact science.

England and Ireland

One measure of an idea, though economists have not always thought well of it, is whether it works. In the very year that *Wealth of Nations* was published, 1776, imperial Britain was losing a territory of greater promise than all the rest of its lands combined. For Britain, Smith's idea — I do not exaggerate — was more than a substitute for the American colonies. Production and trade, now far less hampered than those of other countries, expanded wonderfully. These brought to the British nation all the wealth that Adam Smith had promised.

In the wars with Napoleon, Pitt used this wealth as a highly compassionate substitute for British manpower. Britain's continental allies had an abundance of men. Britain supplied the subsidies that supported and encouraged their valor. After Waterloo, trade and industry surged again. Ricardo was also affirmed. As prosperity expanded in these years, wages fell, as the Ricardian system had promised. Economists in that age were men of much prestige — more perhaps than now — and with reason.

Their ideas, especially those of Malthus and Ricardo, had another test during the first half of the last century. That was in Ireland, in those years fully a part of the kingdom but still John Bull's other island. The Irish test too, in its own way, was a triumphant validation.

No one could doubt the tendency of the Irish population; it was increasing geometrically. Within a mere sixty years, from 1780 to 1840, it first doubled and then very nearly doubled again. By 1840, there were 8 million on the whole island, compared with 4.6 million now.

In the preceding decades Ireland's food supply had also increased. There had been a green revolution based on the rapid expansion of the production of the potato. Nothing, when yields were good, fed so many people so well. But there was a lurking peril, to be noted in a moment, which made this food supply much more nearly arithmetic.

Ricardian landlords were also amply present in Ireland — or more often absent in England which was socially much more congenial and frequently also a safer place for a landlord to live. As the Irish population expanded, so did the competition for land and so did the return that was extracted by the absentee landlords. Grain was grown to pay the rent; potatoes were grown to feed the people. Even when people starved, the grain was sold and the rent was paid. Starvation might conceivably be survived. Eviction for nonpayment of the rent meant there would be nothing to live on forever.

The Malthusian climax is no gradual thing. As experience in India and Bangladesh in recent times has shown, it comes suddenly when something goes wrong — in those countries, the rains. In Ireland in 1845–1847, *Phytophthora infestans*, nurtured by the warm, moist Irish climate, first damaged the potato crop, then eliminated it. Much has always been attributed to the blight, as in India much is always attributed to drought or floods. Much more in Ireland should have been attributed to the losing race in earlier years of food supply with population and the losing contest of tenant workers with landlords.

Not only were the circumstances as Ricardo and Malthus foretold; the response of Westminster to the Irish disaster was as Ricardo would have recommended. As now would be said, it was from the book. The Corn Laws were repealed to allow the free import of grain. Though excellent in principle, this did not help those without money to buy grain, a category that included the entire starving population.

Indian corn — in the American language, corn — was imported for the purpose not of feeding the hungry but of keeping down prices. Low prices were also not helpful to people who had no money at all. In 1845, a program of public works was inaugurated. This was in conflict with the principle that the poor should never be helped, and in the following year, when it was greatly needed, it was abandoned. There was, it was said, no way of distinguishing between those who wanted a job in consequence of the crop failure and those who, as always in Ireland at the time, needed a job as a normal thing.

The custodian of the Ricardian tablets was Charles Edward Trevelyan, assistant secretary, meaning at the time permanent head, of the Treasury. Trade, he advised, would be "paralyzed" if the government, by giving away food, interfered with the legitimate profit of private enterprise. His Chancellor, Charles Wood, assured the House of Commons at a time when the hunger was severe that every effort would be made to leave trade in grain "as much liberty as possible."

On few matters in life is the gap so great as between a dry, antiseptic statement of a policy by a well-spoken man in a quiet office and what happens to people when it is put into practice. We've seen this often enough in our own time. In a Washington office during the Vietnam war it was a protective reaction. In Asia it was sudden, thunderous death from planes that could not even be seen.

Trevelyan's principles were enunciated in the old Treasury offices in Whitehall. There they were impeccable; in Ireland they meant starvation and death. In the manner of men in quiet offices Trevelyan was content. The laws of classical economics had clearly justified themselves. In a reflective letter in 1846, he wrote that the problem of Ireland "being altogether beyond the powers of men, the cure has been applied by the direct stroke of an all-wise Providence in a manner as unexpected and as unthought of as it is likely to be effectual."[13]

There is another tendency here. That is for the consequences of principled action, if they are very unpleasant, to be given divine sanction. Smith's unseen hand had become the hand of God — the hand of a rather ruthless God who couldn't have had much liking for the Irish.

The Escape

There was an escape hatch from the Great Hunger, the same one as from the Highland Clearances: that was the emigrant ship to America. It wasn't an escape from death; that too was a passenger on the ships. If you go thirty or forty miles down the Saint Lawrence River from Quebec, you come to Grosse Isle, a low, half-forested sliver of land with a scattering of decayed and decaying buildings. It is now a minor center for research on contagious animal diseases of the Canadian Department of Agriculture. In the famine years it was where the typhus-ridden ships from Ireland were required to stop to

One escape from Malthus and the famine. This is the fever hospital on Grosse Isle in the St. Lawrence where 5294 died. Cholera Bay is nearby.

unload their dead and dying. A tall shaft remembers 5294 people who died after they arrived on the island. Nor was typhus the only hazard; the memorial looks down on an inlet and beach, now deserted, not very beautiful, and interesting mostly for its name. It is called Cholera Bay.

But there was a brighter side. Perhaps in the New World the ultimate principles articulated by Adam Smith and David Ricardo were still valid. But their setting was very different. So, accordingly, was the result.

Here land was abundant and free. This being so, it conferred no power and no monopoly income on the landlord. No one could much squeeze a tenant or a farm worker if, the next day, he could thumb his nose gracefully at his landlord or employer and leave to take up a farm of his own. In America population might multiply as Malthus said, and it did. But the need for workers increased even more. So pay did not get worse, it got better.

In the treeless Highlands families had seen the precious roof timbers burned when they were told to go. This meant they could not rebuild. In the New World a few months later they were hacking farms from the forests. Trees were now the enemy. In America the settlers regularly sought the high land where the tree growth was the least dense. Only later did they move down to tackle the heavier forests on the richer valley floor. Ricardo had seen the pressure of population forcing settlement onto ever poorer land. Henry Charles Carey, an intelligent and exceptionally voluble American economist of the next generation, saw this new sequence and had the temerity to challenge the master. With increasing population and the general progress of the arts, ever better land was brought into use. He had seen it with his own eyes. He regretted that Ricardo had not.

On better land or worse, some of the immigrants were soon producing more food in a year than their parents had seen in a lifetime. And Irish construction crews, perhaps the best celebrated of the refugees from the Great Hunger, were building the railroads that would make this food available to the world. Malthusian pressure of population on food supply set in motion the great migration. And the migrants then solved the world's food problem, at least for a century.

Smith, Ricardo and Malthus might need revision in the New World. They were not, Smith especially, left behind. Self-interest and freedom of enterprise were a secular faith in the Old World. In the New World they emerged as religion. Fifty years after the Great Hunger this faith had filled a whole continent. In 1893, the children of those who had experienced the hunger and a few who remembered it gathered in Chicago for the great fair — a festival of celebration. Of the pessimism inherent in the ideas of Ricardo and Malthus it would have been hard to find much trace. But of the virtue of the ideas of free enterprise that wrought this miracle there was also not much doubt.

In the New World economics was revised by trees. Ricardo held that cultivation spread out from the best land. In the New World it often began with the worst — on the best land more trees had to be cut down before getting at it.

Smith Now

In the present century the world of Adam Smith has suffered heavy blows. Some of this has been from ideas, as Keynes suggested — from the revolutionary onslaught of Marx and the more gradual attack by those who see in the state the best hope for ameliorating the injustices and compensating for the inadequacies of modern capitalism. But more of the damage has been done by circumstances — the force that Keynes did not stress.

We've seen that the corporation was deeply inimical to Smith's world. So also was the union — something that Smith mentions mostly as he muses over how much more wicked combinations of workingmen are deemed to be as compared with those of merchants. War and the modern armed and technologically competitive state have also changed Smith's world, for governments of such a state cannot be inexpensive and small.

The tight control of births and the birthrate in the industrial countries is another change — one that strikes at the very heart of Smith's system and that of Ricardo and Malthus. And if improvement in income does not bring an eroding flood of births, it will be permanent; compassion is no longer self-defeating.

But while these changes are great, it is hard to believe that Adam Smith would have been much troubled. For his genius was less in his ideas than in his method. As we've seen, as a man of reason he informed himself as to circumstances and formed his ideas accordingly. The need to adjust to new circumstances and new information would neither have surprised nor troubled him. He would never have expected his ideas to apply in circumstances for which they were not intended.

2.
The Manners
and Morals of High Capitalism

The ideas of nineteenth-century capitalism did not encourage the notion of an egalitarian commonwealth. The landlords got rich; those who toiled on the land got poor, remained poor. And in time it became evident that the industrial capitalists could get rich beyond the dreams of landlords or, for that matter, of kings. In 1900, a good year for Andrew Carnegie, his steel mills brought him $25 million. That was before inflation and before the income tax. By 1913, John D. Rockefeller, a self-made man, had accumulated approximately $900 million, his net worth that year.[1] His friend and adviser, Frederick T. Gates, warned him of the terrible danger he faced:

Your fortune is rolling up, rolling up like an avalanche! You must distribute it faster than it grows! If you do not, it will crush you, and your children, and your children's children.[2]

However, Gates exaggerated. Rockefeller's son's sons seem still to be largely uncrushed by their assets.

Like the tenants on the land, the men employed in the steel mills and refineries mostly remained in that wholesome poverty that meant a hard life in this world but assured an easy one in the next. This last was not an idle thought. Many were so sustained, and nothing better expressed the hope than the exuberant verse left behind by an English charwoman — the legend has it, on her headstone:

> Don't mourn for me, friends, don't
> weep for me never,
>
> For I'm going to do nothing forever
> and ever.

The rich, by contrast, set more store by the pleasures of this world. There can be no doubt, I think, that the possession of money causes people to take a more favorable view of this world in comparison with the next. It is also sound strategy. There is that terrible needle through which the affluent must be threaded before they can emerge in paradise. Accordingly, if you are either rich or a camel, you should, as a purely practical calculation, enjoy life now.

In this chapter I would like to look at the enjoyments of the rich in the last century and the ideas by which these were sanctified. By what moral code did the rich live? How did it affect the acquisition and use of wealth? By what ideas did men defend their affluence? Remembering that ideas, like old soldiers (and certainly also old politicians), never die, we may be sure that these still influence our thoughts, our lives and our moral tone.

The Natural Selection of the Affluent

Of all classes the rich are the most noticed and the least studied. So it was, and so it largely remains. In the last century compassionate scholars looked thoughtfully into the conditions of the poor. Why were they poor? Was it sloth? Lack of ambition? Exploitation by cruel employers? Uncontrolled reproduction? The natural order of things? All of these explanations, especially the last, had their adherents. And the way of life of the poor was also studied. How were they housed? What did they eat? What were their amusements? With a delicacy appropriate to the age, how did they breed?

The rich, by contrast, were exempt from such attention. For the Victorians they were a proper subject of novels but not of social investigation. Poverty was something to study; wealth, though exceptional, was natural. Seventy years ago a man or woman of conscience might call on families in the slums of East London to find out how many people slept in a room. No butler would open the door to an investigator who was looking into sleeping habits in Mayfair.

A strong and even dominant current of social thought in the last century set the rich apart and held that they were, indeed, a superior caste. Of these ideas the rich themselves, not then a bookish lot, were often only dimly aware. They knew they were better but not why. These ideas depended a little on economics, a little on theology and a great deal on biology. One should begin their study by a stroll through a museum of natural history. The higher primates, in contrast with the slugs and snails or the dinosaurs and mammoths that never made it to the present, are the products of natural selection. Being the strongest, best adapted to their environment, they survived. And this same superior strength, this same capacity for adaptation explained the rich. Charles Darwin explained the ascent of man. Herbert Spencer, known to the world as the great Social Darwinist, explained the ascent of the privileged classes.

Spencer and Sumner

The life of Herbert Spencer, 1820–1903, an Englishman, philosopher and pioneer sociologist, coincided almost exactly with that of Victoria. It is to Spencer, and not to Darwin as often imagined, that we owe the phrase, "survival of the fittest." He was speaking not of survival in the animal kingdom but of survival in the rather more testing world, as Spencer saw it, of economic and social life. He was, however, explicit in his debt to Darwin:

. . . I am simply carrying out the views of Mr. Darwin in their applications to the human race . . . all [members of the race] being subject to the "increasing difficulty of getting a living . . ." there is an average advance under the pressure, since "only those who *do* advance under it eventually survive"; and . . . "these must be the select of their generation."[3]

Spencer was a highly prolific writer, deeply intellectual and exceptionally gloomy. His numerous books were influential in England but in the United States they were very little less than divine revelation. Across the United States in the forty years following 1860 — this was before paperbacks and almost before bookstores — a reported 368,755 of his volumes were sold. Spencer was American gospel because his ideas fitted the needs of American capitalism, and especially the new capitalists, like the celebrated glove, perhaps better.

These ideas couldn't, in fact, have been more wonderful. Never before in any country had so many been so rich or enjoyed their wealth so much. And in consequence of Spencer no one needed to feel the slightest guilt over this good fortune. It was the inevitable result of natural strength, inherent capacity to adapt. The rich man was the innocent beneficiary of his own superiority. To the enjoyment of wealth was added the almost equal enjoyment which came with the knowledge that one had it because one was better.

The ideas also protected wealth. No one, and especially no government, could touch it or the methods by which it was acquired or was being enlarged. To do so would interfere with the desperately essential process by which the race was being improved.

It might seem a problem for the rich that so many were so poor. This could trouble the conscience at least of the unduly sensitive. But Herbert Spencer took care of this embarrassment as well. To help the poor, either by private or public aid, also interfered disastrously with the improvement of the race. Here again one should let Spencer speak for himself:

Partly by weeding out those of lowest development and partly by subjecting those who remain to the never ceasing discipline of experience, nature secures the growth of a race who shall both understand the conditions of existence and be able to act up to them. It is impossible in any degree to suspend this discipline by stepping in between ignorance and its consequences, without, to a corresponding degree, suspending the progress. If to be ignorant were as safe as to be wise, no one would become wise.[4]

Charity remained something of a problem for Spencer. Obviously it acted to arrest the wholesome weeding-out process. But to forbid it was to infringe on the liberty, however misguided, of those who gave. In the end, he concluded that charity was permissible. While it was bad for those who received help, it was an ennobling thing for those who gave. Thus it was justified, at least for those who were so selfish as to seek their own ennoblement at the expense of the race.

Spencer, it will be evident, was a stern Messiah. Equally stern, as well as very numerous, were his American apostles. The most distinguished of these, a generation younger than Spencer, was William Graham Sumner. Sumner was a Yale professor of independent and rugged mind and perhaps the most influential single voice on economic matters in the United States in the second half of the last century. It was Sumner's great task to join the ideas of Herbert Spencer to those of Adam Smith and David Ricardo.

Sumner was an ardent Social Darwinist; he was fully as devoted as Spencer to improving the race. But he also saw in this process a more immediate amelioration that might help even the poor, might save them from being weeded out. For the struggle for survival was the whip on the back of the poor. It made them work hard against all their natural inclination. It was Adam Smith's self-interest in the peculiarly compelling form by which the poor could be persuaded. And the riches accruing to the rich caused them also to work hard in the common interest. From the combined efforts of poor and rich came production and wealth, and these, in turn, allowed more people than otherwise to survive. Sumner too should be heard in his own words. Here is his case for the rich:

> The millionaires are a product of natural selection. . . It is because they are thus selected that wealth — both their own and that entrusted to them — aggregates under their hands . . . They may fairly be regarded as the naturally selected agents of society for certain work. They get high wages and live in luxury, but the bargain is a good one for society.[5]

It was a sad day for the man of means when he could no longer send his son to Yale and know that he would be so instructed.

The Coming

As Jesus came eventually to Jerusalem, Herbert Spencer came eventually to America. The reception in the two cases was broadly the same. By the time of his journey in 1882, Spencer was no longer young — he was sixty-two — and not in the best of health. He was also averse to reporters and the press. His American tour, nonetheless, was the triumph that any observer would have expected. Everywhere he was greeted with reverence by men who saw in their own selection for affluence the strongest of proof that the race was being improved. Spencer was not, himself, wholly reassured. It was an era of exuberant pride in the American achievement. He was exposed to a bit too much of it. Once or twice he implied that, in the larger process of social evolution, the United States had lagged, was still in a slightly primitive stage. In Darwinian terms, Americans were still, maybe, with the higher primates.

Herbert Spencer: "I am simply carrying out the views of Mr. Darwin in their applications to the human race."

William Graham Sumner: "The millionaires are a product of natural selection."

Carl Schurz: "If Spencer's Social Statics had been better read in the South, the Civil War would not have occurred."

There were also sour notes at the last supper — the great final celebration at Delmonico's Restaurant, then at the very height of its fame as the watering place of the New York rich. Leaders in business, academic life, politics and even theology were present. The late Richard Hofstadter, a notable authority on the Social Darwinists and their time, has written of the evening with much joy. Spencer in his address said that Americans worked too hard. This was a chilling thought. Suppose the workingmen heard. However, his audience rallied, and so strenuous were the tributes that Spencer, although notably a vain man, was perceptibly undone. One speaker, Carl Schurz, said that if Spencer's *Social Statics* had been better read in the South, the Civil War would not have occurred. Henry Ward Beecher, the most famous of American divines and a man who, despite some aberrant tendencies that I will mention in a moment, considered his own salvation secure, said he looked forward to renewing his acquaintance with Spencer "beyond the grave."

No one at this happy gathering seems to have worried about a small but obvious point, which is how the Social Darwinists would bridge the generation gap. In those years John D. Rockefeller had himself formulated the doctrine for a Sunday school class in an exceptionally engaging way: "The American Beauty rose," he had explained to the young, "can be produced in the splendor and fragrance which bring cheer to its beholder only by sacrificing the early buds which grow up around it."[6] The same sacrifices occurred in business and accounted, *pro tanto*, for the splendor of a Rockefeller. "This is not an evil tendency in business. It is merely the working-out of a law of nature and a law of God."[7] The question, of course, was whether this same law of nature and of God would also explain the purely inherited splendor of John D., Jr., or yet later of John D. III, Nelson, Laurance, Winthrop and David. Surely, on the contrary, a Rockefeller inheritance, even more than a handout to the poor, would cool the struggle to survive, devastate the moral and physical tone of the legatees and justify a confiscatory inheritance tax that would save their efforts for society. A nasty problem.

No one should imagine that Spencer and Sumner are relics purely of the past. They still restrain the hand of the well-to-do individual when he is approached by a beggar. Perhaps it will damage the man's morale. Their doctrines still lurk in the inner cells of the Rockefeller consciousness. Or maybe only in those of their speech writers. Speaking in Dallas on September 12, 1975, to a convocation of committed conservatives, Vice President Nelson Rockefeller warned against the continuing dangers of compassion:

One of the problems in this country is that we have this Judeo-Christian heritage of wanting to help those in need. And this, when added to some political instincts, sometimes causes people to promise more than they can deliver.[8]

How the Fit Were Selected

We turn now to how the rich were singled out for their success. It brings us inevitably to the railroads. Nothing in the last century, and nothing so far in this century, so altered the fortunes of so many people so suddenly as the American or Canadian railroad. The contractors who built it, those whose real estate was in its path, those who owned it, those who shipped by it and those who looted it could all get rich, some of them in a week. The only people connected with the railroads who were spared the burdens of wealth were those who laid the rails and ran the trains. Railroading in the last century was not a highly paid occupation, and it was also very dangerous. The casualty rates of those who ran the trains — the incidence of mutilation and death — approached that of a first-class war.

The railroads got built. A great many honest men bent their efforts to their construction and operation; this should not be forgotten. But the business also attracted a legion of rascals. The latter were by far the best known, and they may well have been the most successful in enriching themselves. Spencer's natural selection operated excellently on behalf of scoundrels. Sometimes it tested one set against another.

A railroad allowed for an interesting choice between two kinds of larceny — robbery of the customers and robbery of the stockholders. The most spectacular struggle occurred in the late eighteen-sixties between rival practitioners of these two basic arts. At issue was the Erie Railroad, running from the New Jersey side of the Hudson River to Buffalo, in those days a deplorable and often lethal streak of rust. Cornelius Vanderbilt, who controlled the New York Central on the east margin of the river, wanted to own the Erie to ensure his monopoly of service to Buffalo and potentially to Chicago. Vanderbilt's commitment was to robbing the public. The enduring contribution of his family to spoken literature was the expression, "The public be damned."

One of his opponents was Jim Fisk, who died of gunshot wounds in 1872 at the rather early age of thirty-eight, and to the general regret of the better class of Americans who wished it had been earlier. Allied with him were Daniel Drew and Jay Gould, two other experienced larcenists, although Drew was by now a little past his best. Their commitment was to robbing the stockholders. Once an individual was in control of a railroad, there was a myriad of devices by which its cash and other assets could be siphoned off into his own pocket. Jay Gould was the acknowledged master of these techniques. Fisk, though not as highly qualified on detail, was far more colorful in the practice of fraud.

Control was the key to both forms of larceny. The struggle for the railroad came in 1867 and brought the kind of collision that in those days more often occurred on the tracks of the Erie itself.

The Erie Railroad: The cast.

Jim Fisk.

Jay Gould.

Daniel Drew.

Cornelius Vanderbilt:
Though he lost, it was
a battle, not a war.

Boss Tweed.

Vanderbilt's advantage was money; he had this, and with it he could hope to buy a controlling interest in the stock. But Drew and Fisk had an even greater advantage. They were in control of the railroad; and they had a printing press in the basement of the building that housed the railroad offices. In con-

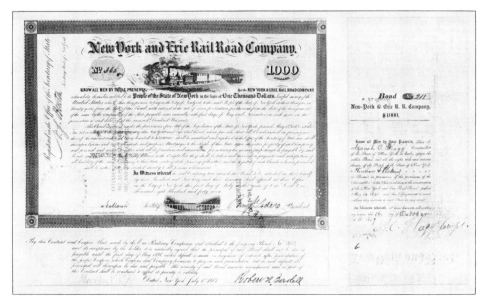

The shares.

sequence, they could print more stock than Vanderbilt could ever hope to buy and then enough more to ensure that they had the votes to keep themselves in power. This they proceeded to do. The strength of their position, it was said at the time, rested firmly on the freedom of the press.

Vanderbilt turned to the courts. There initially he had an advantage; he was in personal possession of George Gardner Barnard of the New York State Supreme Court. Barnard, though not a great jurist, was frequently described as the best that money could buy. Vanderbilt had bought him. In return, Barnard enjoined the publishing activities of what was called the Erie Gang and threatened them with jail. They responded by picking up the books of the railroad, not forgetting its cash, and fleeing across the river to Jersey City. Jim Fisk, a sensitive man, also took his mistress, a less than virginal woman named Josie Mansfield. There was a thought that Vanderbilt's men might try to kidnap these refugees back across the Hudson to Judge Barnard's jurisdiction. Accordingly, a defense force was recruited from the railway yards, a flag was hung out and the new headquarters in Taylor's Hotel was named Fort Taylor. The Erie war, as by now it was being called, was full on.

From Fort Taylor, Gould, Drew and Fisk counterattacked. In a breath-taking move they bought the New York State Legislature — or enough of it to

The shooting of Jim Fisk. He combined love
with the love of money, and for love he
died . . .

And is buried here.

have the stock they had printed made legal. Later they bought Judge Barnard away from Vanderbilt. More than money was involved; they also named a locomotive for him. And, a more important acquisition, they bought William Tweed, Boss Tweed, the head of Tammany Hall, and made him a director of the Erie. Vanderbilt now retreated. Peace, of a sort, broke out. Fisk was able to move the headquarters of the Erie back to New York and into the opera house, where he combined railroading with grand opera. His prospects seemed exceptional until he was shot by Edward Stokes. Stokes was a rival of Fisk for the love of Josie Mansfield, although, poor girl, it seems that she was more than willing to be nice to both. Fisk's body was brought back to Brattleboro, Vermont, whence he had launched his career, and the whole town turned out to give him a dead hero's welcome. He was buried there; four grieving maidens in stone still guard the burial plot. One of them seems to be pouring coins on his grave.

The Public Reputation

While the war for the Erie was at its height, the express from Buffalo one night was discovered, a little after the fact, to have lost four passenger cars on a curve. They had gone over a small precipice, and there was a painful fire when they landed. Coaches were of wood and heated by big potbellied coal stoves. Both the coaches and the passengers were a bad fire risk. A year or so later an engineer (engine driver to Englishmen) named James Griffin pulled his freight train into a siding to let the westbound passenger express go by. He dozed off, dreamed that the express had passed, then pulled out on the track and met the passenger train head-on. There was fire again; the casualties were again heavy.

As an even more normal occurrence, Erie freight cars jumped the tracks or didn't move because there was no serviceable locomotive to pull them. Since the principal purpose of the management was the rape of the stockholders, there was also, not surprisingly, continuing and articulate complaint from this quarter. Many of the stockholders were English, and none got a dividend. All of these things, along with the fact that the men who worked on the road often went unpaid, gave Drew, Gould and Fisk a bad name. As noted, they are still referred to in the history books as the Erie Gang. The public reputation of their families, though somewhat redeemed in later times, has never been high.

In contrast, the men who did in their customers fared far better in the public mind, and their families achieved high distinction. This was true of Vanderbilt. It was equally so in other fields of endeavor of Rockefeller, Carnegie, Morgan, Guggenheim, Mellon, all of whom made their money by producing cheap, suppressing competition and selling dear. All founded dynasties of the highest repute. All eventually became names of the greatest respectability. The point

The Natural Selection of the Rockefellers: John D. Rockefeller (left) held that men, like the American Beauty rose, were improved only by ruthless sacrifice — "a law of nature and a law of God." His law in operation:

John D., Jr.

Nelson.

David.

is an interesting and perhaps predictable one. To mulct investors — other capitalists — left a nasty taste permanently in the public mouth. Public predation — the mulcting of the people at large –– though criticized at the time, eventually acquired an aspect of high respectability, great social distinction. Even within their lifetimes many of its outstanding practitioners gained the reputation of being impeccably God-fearing men.

The involvement of capitalist predation with God in the last century requires a special word.

Natural Selection and the Church

God, as many have said, loves the poor, and that is why He made so many of them. It is one reason why poverty was regarded with equanimity in the last century and also, to some extent, is still. But in the last century there was, as well, the Ricardian thought that poverty was inevitable; it reflected the immutable working-out of economic law. And, as we've just seen, there was the further thought that, by natural selection, the poor were being weeded out. Given enough time, the undeserving poor, as George Bernard Shaw's Alfred Doolittle rightly called himself, would be gone.

This last doctrine was socially tranquilizing and otherwise admirable. But it posed an alarming problem for the devout. The doctrine derived from Darwin, and for all communicants of decently literal mind this involved a flat denial of scriptural truth. Man was created in God's image; he was not in descent from a monkey. Creation was not a thing of the ages; it took exactly six days because the Bible said so. Natural selection was a salutary remedy for the problem of poverty but the ideas from which it derived were in drastic conflict with religious belief. As late as 1925, the trial of John T. Scopes in Tennessee for teaching his high school class that Darwin's doctrines had truth would pit Clarence Darrow against William Jennings Bryan in one of the great judicial circuses of the age. It showed how sensitive was the nerve that mention of evolution touched.

Still, the stakes were high; if natural selection could be reconciled with Christian faith, the rich layman could indeed relax. Not surprisingly the effort was made, at the Plymouth Church in Brooklyn. The church still stands across the Brooklyn Bridge in what is now an unspectacular but decent neighborhood. Then, in the eighteen-sixties and seventies, it was becoming one of the richest parishes in the whole country, and Henry Ward Beecher, the man, no less, who had made the appointment to meet Herbert Spencer in heaven, was the pastor. The rich, the ambitious and the merely industrious were flocking to hear him in unbelievable numbers; Henry Adams guessed that no one had preached so influentially to so many since Saint Paul. In 1866, Beecher wrote Spencer that "the peculiar condition of American society has made your

The Reverend Henry Ward Beecher: "God intended the great to be great and the little to be little."

writings far more fruitful and quickening here than in Europe.''[9] Beecher was no man to resist a quickening.

His reconciliation involved a distinction between theology and religion. Theology, like the animal kingdom, was evolutionary. Such change did not contradict the Holy Writ. Religion was enduring. Its truths did not change. Darwin and Spencer belonged to theology; the Bible was religion. So there was no conflict between natural selection and the Holy Scripture. I do not understand this distinction, and it is fairly certain that neither Beecher nor his congregation did either. But it sounded exceptionally good.

Beecher had other good news for his affluent flock. God particularly loved sinners, for He greatly enjoyed redeeming them. So, by implication, one could go out of an occasional evening and sin. The ensuing repentance and redemption would then do wonders for God's morale. Beecher thereupon proceeded to follow his own advice. Robert Shaplen, the author of the definitive study of Beecher's private and litigious life and later one of the most authoritative reporters on Vietnam and the Vietnam war, has shown how faithful he was in this regard. Besides comforting his rich parishioners on the legitimacy of their wealth, Beecher comforted their wives — some of them at least — by taking them to bed. Eventually one, Elizabeth Tilton, was assailed by the thought that even though Beecher was being redeemed, her case was not so clear. So she confessed not to God as intended but to her husband, and he sued Beecher. The jury disagreed on Beecher's guilt. No one who has since looked at the evidence has had any similar doubt.

Earlier on, I mentioned that Beecher had told Spencer of his hope that they would meet again in heaven. There must be many, and I am one, who would prefer not to meet either.

Thorstein Veblen

There is a certain beguiling merriment in the ideas by which the rich justified themselves in the last century. The same is true of the way in which they spent their money. It's a field of study that I have always much enjoyed. But it would be quite wrong to imagine that this amusement is purely the product of hindsight — the perspective that time allows. By far the most amused and penetrating view of the American rich in their greatest days was by a contemporary observer. He wrote of them at the very peak of their power and ostentation. This was Thorstein Veblen. Veblen was the hero of my teachers at the University of California in the thirties. I was introduced to his books simultaneously with Alfred Marshall's *Principles*, the bible of economic orthodoxy in the last years of the last century and the first decades of this. Marshall has not been read for years; one can still turn to Veblen with delight.

The Veblen legend is of a poor farm boy, the son of Norwegian immigrants. He was driven through life by a gnawing sense of envy, a burning sense of injustice. (The etymology here is interesting: envy always gnaws; injustice always burns; it might be more accurate the other way around.) Veblen's Norwegian compatriots were many, frugal, worthy and poor. A few in this new land were profligate, idle and rich. This contrast Veblen could not forgive or accept. Thus his merciless books and tongue.

Thorstein Veblen was, indeed, the son of a poor Norwegian immigrant. When he was born in Wisconsin in 1857, life was still a struggle. But by the time he went off to college, his father, Thomas Anderson Veblen, was in possession of 290 acres of land in southern Minnesota as rich as any outdoors. Not a hundred working farmers in all of Norway were as affluent. The family was educated at nearby Carleton College, and they paid their own way. Thorstein, after trying Johns Hopkins, went on to study at Yale in 1882, the year of Spencer's Coming, with the farm still paying his way. At Yale he encountered and made a major impression on, of all men, William Graham Sumner. Spencer and Sumner would not be wrong in a world populated by Veblen's parents. Their life was hard but they were fit, and they survived handsomely, happily and honestly.

Thorstein Veblen wrote not out of envy but out of a sense of ignored superiority fortified by contempt. He did not regard the rich, those at the summit of what would now be called the WASP establishment, as being possessed of much intelligence, culture or charm. Their business success depended, at best, on a low cunning which was abetted by the very great advantage for accumulating wealth of being already rich. Being proud, pompous, intellectually obtuse and more than a trifle insecure, they were vulnerable to a particular kind of ridicule.

The rich have regularly invited the resentment of the less rich or the poor. Why should they have so much? What virtue justifies their higher income and station? This attack the rich can always stand. It proceeds from envy, and this affirms their superiority.

The Veblen weapon was far more refined; it was ridicule presented as the most somber and careful science. All primitive tribes had their festivals, rituals and orgies, some of them exceptionally depraved. Likewise the rich. Their social observances and rituals might be different in form and detail but their purpose was the same — self-advertisement, exhibitionism. And for every exhibitionist mannerism or enjoyment of the rich, Veblen came up with some deplorable barbarian counterpart. The Vanderbilts bound up their women in corsets, thus proving they were purely objects of enjoyment and display. The Papuan chief carved up the faces or breasts of his wives to the same end. The rich gathered for elegant dinners and entertainments. The counterpart ritual

Thorstein Veblen, 1857–1929.

of the aboriginal community was the potlatch or orgy. Veblen could do wonders even with a walking stick:

The walking-stick serves the purpose of an advertisement that the bearer's hands are employed otherwise than in useful effort, and it therefore has utility as an evidence of leisure. But it is also a weapon and it meets a felt need of barbarian man on that ground. The handling of so tangible and primitive a means of offense is very comforting to anyone who is gifted with even a moderate share of ferocity.[10]

Veblen himself lived a bemused, eccentric and very insecure life. American university presidents are a nervous breed; I have never thought well of them as a class. They praise independence of thought on all occasions of public ceremony, worry deeply about its consequences in private. They are paid above scale to suffer for the free expression of the less convenient members of the faculty but rarely believe they should have to earn their pay. However, in the last century they had some justification for their pervasive unease and self-pity. The successful businessmen, whose folk tendencies Veblen also examined, believed that the country should have centers of higher learning. It was only decent. Their offspring needed gloss. Also doctors and lawyers were essential. But they never believed that these academies should tolerate ideas inimical to property and men of property. They wanted professors who affirmed the conservative truths, treated wealth and enterprise with respect. This Veblen did not do; in consequence, he was always regarded as an ideal man for some other institution. During his academic life he moved from Cornell to Chicago, to Stanford, to Missouri, to the New School in New York. All were glad to see him go; it is now the pride of all that he was there.

His moves were facilitated, on occasion, by the fact that, though far from beautiful, he was inordinately attractive to women. He considered it a problem, and once, when rebuked by President David Starr Jordan, the president of Stanford, for the offense he was giving to middle-class morality, he asked resignedly what a man could do when they just move in with you. There is a legend that, when under consideration for a professorship at Harvard, he was warned by President Abbott Lawrence Lowell, who brought up the subject with embarrassment, for his was a world without sex or other sin, that some of Veblen's prospective colleagues were worried about their wives. It was an elaborately lighthearted hint that Veblen should promise, if appointed, to behave. Veblen replied courteously that there was no need to worry, he had seen the wives. I once investigated this story, and it seems, unfortunately, to be wholly untrue. Veblen, lonesome and sad at the end, died in 1929.

Conspicuous Consumption

Veblen's first and greatest book, *The Theory of the Leisure Class*, was published just before the turn of the century. With Henry George's *Progress and Poverty*, the great case for the single tax on land, it is one of the two American works of social comment from the last century which are still read and studied. It contains the germ of Veblen's basic economic idea, which was developed further in his later *The Theory of Business Enterprise*. This identified a conflict in economic life between industry and business — between those whose talent lay in the production of goods and those whose concern was not with making things but with making money. The money-makers, by restricting production to enhance profits, sabotaged (Veblen's word) the capacity of the producers to produce. It was an idea that won enthusiastic converts in the nineteen-thirties among a militant band of disciples committed to what they called Technocracy. Veblen's distinction between makers and moneymakers has not survived.

His enduring achievement was not in economics but in sociology — in his aforementioned examination of the social behavior of the rich. *The Theory of the Leisure Class* is centrally concerned with the deep sense of the superiority that is conferred on the rich by their wealth. But, to be enjoyed, this superiority must be known; accordingly, a major preoccupation of the rich is the carefully considered display of wealth. Two things serve this end — Conspicuous Leisure and Conspicuous Consumption. Both phrases, especially the second, were planted ineradicably in the language by Veblen. Conspicuous Leisure is the distinction gained by idleness in a world where almost everyone has to work, where nothing else so preoccupies the body and the mind. The rich man might work himself. But he gained much distinction from the conspicuous idleness of his women. Conspicuous Consumption was consumption designed exclusively to impress with the cost that was involved. Taste did not enter. Never after the publication of *The Theory of the Leisure Class* could a rich man spend with ostentation, abandon and enjoyment without someone rising to ridicule it as Conspicuous Consumption.

The Monument: Newport

How real was the culture of conspicuous wealth that Veblen described? Anyone who has doubts can go and see for himself. The place is Newport, Rhode Island. Most Americans have never seen these vast houses, do not know what they are missing. I've lived nearly all of my life a couple of hours' drive away and would be with the majority except for an accident of public life. In 1961, Prime Minister Nehru visited the United States and met President Kennedy in Newport. They passed along the waterfront in the presidential yacht, the *Honey Fitz*, to view the mansions. "I brought you this way, Mr. Prime Minister," the President said, "so that you can see how the average American lives." Nehru answered, to my special pleasure, that he had heard mention of the affluent society.

When the Newport houses were built around the turn of the century, a man's worth was, indeed, measured in simple, straightforward fashion by his wealth. Artists, poets, politicians and scientists did not dream of disputing the rich man's claim to pre-eminence, Hollywood had not been heard of, and television personalities were not even a gleam. But, as Veblen held, wealth, if it was to distinguish a man, had to be known. He couldn't walk around brandishing thousand-dollar bills or a statement of his net worth — although some tried. The Newport houses were not places of habitation, recreation, procreation. Their purpose was to proclaim the worth of the inmates.

The greatest of the houses was The Breakers, and it brings us back to the name that recurs in any discussion of the manners and morals of the rich. Commodore Vanderbilt was not only a creative and sanguinary entrepreneur who robbed the public with candor. He also headed a family that was notably conspicuous in its consumption. The Breakers cost the Vanderbilts, by one very early estimate, $3 million. The Commodore also adopted what became Vanderbilt University in Nashville, Tennessee. That, by comparison, cost him only $500,000, later raised to a million.

The Newport houses had a secondary function; they also affirmed the class structure of the society. A large army of servants was required to run these establishments. They were trained in the disciplined obedience and obeisance fitting to a subordinate. As Veblen observed:

It is a serious grievance if a gentleman's butler or footman performs his duties about his master's table or carriage in such unformed style as to suggest that his habitual occupation may be plowing or sheepherding.[11]

Practiced and servile behavior was, in turn, a constant reminder to those served of their superiority, of their membership in a privileged elite. It was also, more than incidentally, what brought this way of life to an end. It may be laid down as a broad and general rule that no one spends his life affirming the superiority of other people if he has any alternative. So, at the earliest moment possible, the servants got other jobs. The masters thought they were loved until the day one of their favorites farted loudly while serving dinner and the next day was gone. The very first manifestation of the classless society is the disappearance of the servant class.

The Ceremonials

Houses were not by themselves sufficient. In looking at the customs of barbarian tribes and the contemporary rich, which he saw as similar, Veblen concluded that neither a tribal chief nor a business tycoon could "sufficiently put his opulence in evidence" by relying on Conspicuous Consumption alone. Personal rituals and manners were also important; both chief and tycoon

Home and home away from home:
The Breakers: $3,000,000 to begin.

The Casino at Monte Carlo. "If a man dropped ten thousand or fifty thousand, he showed the audience that he was a man who could lose such sums."

Mrs. Stuyvesant Fish under full canvas.

Conspicuous Consumption: Of and by dogs.

needed to be "connoisseurs in creditable viands of various degrees of merit, in manly beverages and trinkets, in seemly apparel and architecture, in weapons, games, dances, and the narcotics."[12] Veblen concluded also that "drunkenness and other pathological consequences of the free use of stimulants" were valuable indications of "the superior status of those who are able to afford the indulgence" and that "infirmities induced by over-indulgence are among some peoples freely recognized as manly attributes."[13]

The ceremonies at which wealth was displayed — "costly entertainments such as the potlatch or the ball"[14] — were of particular importance in the competition for esteem. The person seeking distinction invited his friends and competitors to his feasts, orgies or other entertainments. These were the very people he most needed to impress, those upon whose good opinion his own standing depended. His guests were thus the unwitting instruments of his effort to establish his superiority over them. Naturally when his guests had a ball or potlatch, they showed him how much they could spend and so got their own back.

To be certain of attendance, it was thought wise to introduce an element of novelty, even of eccentricity, into the ceremonials. One example, soon after the turn of the century, was the inspiration of Mrs. Stuyvesant Fish. She staged a major party not ostensibly for her neighbors but for their dogs. Not without difficulty, while exploring the anthropology of Newport, my colleagues of the BBC recreated this entertainment. No one watching the event could have any doubt that, as Veblen argued, the festivals here differed only in form, not at all in kind, from those in Borneo or New Guinea or on Christmas Island.

Publicity

Next only to consuming in a suitably conspicuous way, the greatest pleasure of the rich was in reading about themselves and in imagining that others did so too. This occupation is still much enjoyed by the affluent. We speak wonderingly of a *shy* millionaire; it's because they are so rare. The late Mr. Howard Hughes built one of the greatest reputations of our time almost exclusively out of not being seen. Half of the pleasure in the dogs' dinner just mentioned was in thinking how amazed the masses would be in reading about it. The society columns of the modern newspaper can be understood only as one appreciates the pleasure they give those who are mentioned, the envy it is hoped that such mention will arouse in those who are ignored.

For making sure that the denizens of Newport were publicized to the enjoyment of all, the indispensable resident was James Gordon Bennett, Jr., who owned the *New York Herald*. William Randolph Hearst is usually thought to be the founder of the American yellow press; in fact, as Samuel Eliot Morison held, it was Bennett's father. The purpose of a newspaper, he had

James Gordon Bennett, Jr.: Journalist and faithful son. The purpose of a newspaper, his father said, is "not to educate but to startle."

proclaimed, is "not to educate but to startle."[15] His son agreed, and his *Herald* had plenty of room in its columns for the activities and depravities of Newport, for it did not go in heavily for public affairs. "We shall support no party," his father had also proclaimed, ". . . care nothing for any election or any candidate, from President down to a Constable."[16] When the rich showed signs of being dull, Bennett sent Stanley into Africa to find Livingstone and another expedition into the Arctic to find the North Pole. But Newport was his base.

The Riviera

A troublesome problem of affluence in the last century was an inconvenient and even perverse feature of the class structure. Wealth a man could get. But wealth was greatly improved by being old, and this age was not so easily acquired. In their earliest manifestation the Vanderbilts, Astors, Whitneys, not to mention the Rockefellers and Fords, were all rather crude and were so regarded. Only in the subsequent generations did these families become first civilized, then distinguished. There was the companion circumstance that industrial wealth, until it is exceptionally well-aged, is inferior to landed or even mercantile affluence. In the last century a titled Englishman of modest means, even an impecunious and venereal Polish count, was often the equal of a Whitney or a Rockefeller. Among Americans, Lowells, Cabots and Coolidges were much better. Their wealth had aged.

A further and much neglected feature of wealth is the problem posed by its more sensuous use and enjoyment. The poor and people of modest income have always believed that the principal delights of the rich are in such sensuous consumption — in food, alcohol and expensive, varied and reliably available fornication. Given some extra money, the poor man's instinct is for a good meal, a bender or an imaginatively obliging woman. So it must be for all. These were not, in fact, negligible pleasures for the rich in the last century. The Victorians were prodigious eaters and devout, two-handed drinkers, and many went off each year to a continental spa — most often Carlsbad — with two sets of clothing, one set to wear over and another to wear home after losing a few dozen pounds. Nothing was so discussed as the state of one's liver, an organ uniquely important for the large-scale consumption of alcohol. Sex may well have ranked ahead of horsemanship as a source of masculine pleasure and a measure of accomplishment.

But there are physical limits to the amount of food and drink that can be ingested, and there are similar, although more variable, limits to the time that can be spent actively in bed. And with the passage of time, the consequences of excessive eating and drinking — vast bulk, chronic drunkenness, a grossly debased appearance — ceased to be admired and became subject to rebuke. Similarly, sexual promiscuity, once considered the greatest of the delights of wealth, eventually became a mass recreation and even a branch of physical therapy. The sensuous enjoyments of the rich ceased to be a source of admiration and distinction, and they ceased to be the exclusive pleasure of the rich. Much of the enjoyment had always consisted in having that of which others were deprived.

The Riviera, in the last century, had many advantages of scenery and climate and much less traffic and pollution than now. "A sunny shore," the late Adlai Stevenson once wrote to a friend while paying a visit there, "where shady characters from underdeveloped countries consort with overdeveloped women." But its much greater advantage was in the way it solved all of the problems of the affluent just mentioned. Not surprisingly, James Gordon Bennett, Jr., the indispensable citizen of Newport, also had a villa at Cap Ferrat. With him he took his gift for publicizing the playtime of the rich. The Paris *Herald*, which he founded, recorded the movement of the American rich into European society, and an item in the social column of the very first issue brought the news that "Mr. William K. Vanderbilt will return from London . . . on Wednesday." As ever a Vanderbilt.

But the Riviera was pre-eminently the resort of the European aristocracy, and from this came its major service. Daughters of the American rich could here be traded for the esteem that went with older landed wealth or title, or sometimes merely the title. By this single simple step the new wealth achieved the respectability of age. And the anciently respectable got money, something they could always use. So inevitable was this bargain that they were negotiated by the scores, and brokers — often impoverished women of imagined social rank — appeared to make the deals. The resulting flow of dollars would have been a recognizable item in the American balance of payments, had a payments balance then been calculated. By 1909, by one estimate, 500 American heiresses had been exported for the improvement of the family name, along with $220 million.[17]

The greatest, or nearly the greatest, of the English families in this age were the Churchills; their palace, Blenheim, is one of the grandest of English houses; the title, Marlborough, is the most honored in British history. It was natural, therefore, that a Duke of Marlborough should marry Consuelo Vanderbilt for an initial payment of $2,500,000. More was later invested in repairing Blenheim, which was run down, and in a great new London house. In all, the Marlborough connection cost around $10 million. The results, however, were excellent. The robber–baron connotation was almost completely excised from the Vanderbilt family tradition. All descendants and even, *ex poste*, all antecedents, including the Commodore, became people of the highest repute.

Less was invested in making respectable the far more awkward name of

Consuelo Vanderbilt and parent: She brought distinction to Vanderbilt, solvency to Marlborough.

Anna Gould and Count Boni de Castellane: The Goulds paid less and got less. Compare the faces.

Gould, and, as might be expected, much less was accomplished. Only about $5,500,000 was paid to marry Anna, daughter of Jay Gould, to the Count Boni de Castellane, a figure far inferior in grandeur to a Duke of Marlborough. Partly in consequence of trying to do it on the cheap, the Goulds achieved only a very modest grandeur.

Winston Churchill was the son of a somewhat similar union — that of Lord Randolph Churchill with the American, Jennie Jerome. This, however, seems to have been the limiting case where love was an operative factor.

Gambling

The Riviera's other service to the rich came from the casino at Monte Carlo. This derived from its incomparable efficiency for doing what, as Veblen had shown, the rich most sought and needed — advertisement of the existence and extent of their wealth.

The sociology of gambling is little understood. Most people think that men and women gamble to make money. And, without doubt, some do. But many also gamble to lose money. In the last century this was very important. Men and women of the highest fashion — those whose judgments determined, above all, an individual's social rank and repute — assembled of a night at the Société des Bains de Mer. Richly accoutered, they moved around the tables, through the adjacent salons. Never before or since was there such an audience for the man who wanted to prove that he had money to burn. If he was rich, he could not lose. If he dropped ten or fifty thousand, he showed to this audience that he was a man who could lose such sums. If he won, it did him no damage.

To build a big house required a modicum of taste. For suitably expensive entertaining, one needed some entrée to society and also, as a starter, a few friends. A yacht, before radio, meant isolation from the world and one's affairs. Also it had another drawback: it was only for the supremely rich. The great J. P. Morgan is remembered for two aphorisms, neither quite deathless. He asserted before a congressional committee that influence on Wall Street depended on character, not money — a proposition that has never gained complete acceptance. And he told an acquaintance who wanted to know what a yacht would cost to operate that if he had to ask, he couldn't afford it.

But the casino solved all problems. You could lose whatever you could afford. And this required no taste, no entrée, no social grace, no friends, nothing but the money.

The Manners and Morals of the Modern Rich

What of the modern rich? The problem of finding distinction has greatly changed. Nowhere in the United States (to which my own studies have mostly been confined) does wealth and its conspicuous display any longer serve by itself. The modern politician now ranks well above the man of wealth as a person of distinction. No Washington or New York hostess would consider it the slightest source of dignity to get a mere millionaire for dinner. Any decently high and honest political figure is infinitely superior. Such is the distinction conferred by public office that men of great wealth gladly pay large sums to be ambassadors to small countries. Television performers, journalists, artists with minimal standards of personal deportment and hygiene, in-tellectuals of conservative or harmlessly radical beliefs far outrank the modern millionaire in esteem. In consequence, the man of wealth must either seek association with such people or try for achievement himself in these or related fields. Otherwise he will be almost totally overlooked.

There are some regional differences in practice in this regard. In Boston and New England generally, affluent males affect plain, often repellent attire, large but rather shabby dwellings. Women dress similarly, feature a utilitarian or athletic appearance according to personality or taste. Esteem is then sought by association, however innocent, with music, art, philanthropy or, in appli-cable cases, intellectual effort or harmless public service. Mere wealth does nothing for a family except as it makes them an object of attention for those collecting money for charitable or political causes.

New York is much the same. But there, by many women of means, extrava-gant attire is still thought a useful way of attracting attention. Eccentrically furnished apartments of considerable discomfort are also thought useful. In the New York suburbs large houses, boats and entertainment that avoids excessive reliance on a servant class still confer some distinction within the particular subculture. But, although these residual obeisances survive, they are far from being sufficient. A reputation for knowledgeable association with the arts or public issues is essential for anyone of the slightest ambition. In recent decades no slight damage has been done by rich New Yorkers, many of them lawyers, who have sought esteem through association with the field of foreign policy. Not unnaturally they have shown an unfortunate attachment to foreign leaders and potentates who share their own commitment to personal enrichment. However, the support of liberal politicians and radical causes of an adequately innocuous sort can also be a significant source of distinction.

In Texas, where wealth is relatively new and hence has a high novelty quotient, a family's position is still influenced by the extent and cost of its possessions — by the assessed value of the house, the acreage of the ranch, the size, speed and furnishings of the airplane and the visible cost of the grooming and caparisoning of the horses and women. Much store is set by barbecues and similar fiestas at which these possessions are displayed and admired. It is the logical consequence of these folk habits that the world's most notable market for costly consumer artifacts is in Dallas, Texas. With age this too will change.

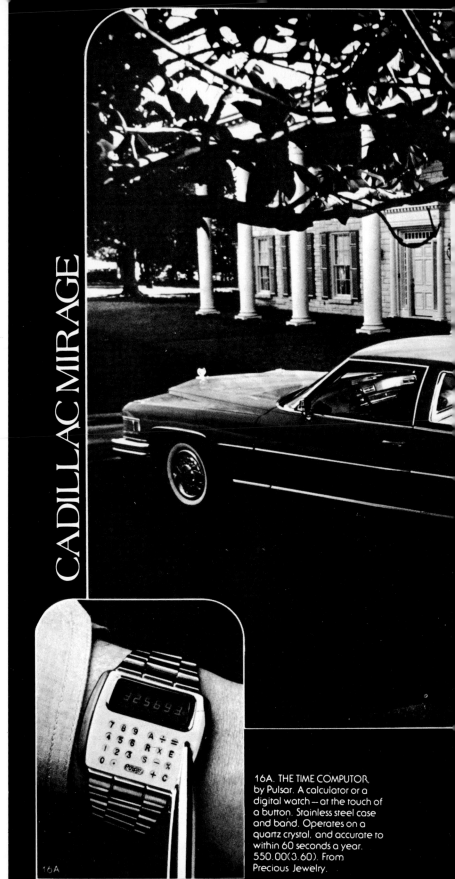

CADILLAC MIRAGE

Consumption can still be conspicuous in Texas.

16A. THE TIME COMPUTOR, by Pulsar. A calculator or a digital watch — at the touch of a button. Stainless steel case and band. Operates on a quartz crystal, and accurate to within 60 seconds a year. 550.00(3.60). From Precious Jewelry.

16A

THE GENTLEMAN'S TRUCK

The best of two worlds combines in the dynamic design of the Cadillac Mirage.
A unique vehicle incorporating both luxury and utility, with all the expected craftsmanship
of the Cadillac tradition. The Mirage is a town and country coupe: sleek enough
ferry passengers to the Opera Ball, rugged enough to carry feed and supplies to the most
remote corner of the ranch or farm, comfortable enough for the most extended tours,
and professional enough for the serious sportsman. Our limited edition
Mirage features custom enamel in the Neiman-Marcus signature color as shown,
special interior trim package, sports style wire wheel covers, and carpeting of mouton
throughout. The Cadillac Mirage shown is available only through Neiman-Marcus.
Allow eight weeks for delivery. 17A. 24,500(X).
For further information, call AC 214/741-6911, ext. 1225.

73

A narrow and largely imaginary line divides what is admired as elegance from what is condemned as ostentatious display — conspicuous consumption.

Such change has already overtaken Southern California, suburban Los Angeles in particular, where Moorish revival houses, swimming pools, exquisitely clipped lawns and slightly eccentric automobiles were once a source of major esteem but which, though still necessary, are no longer sufficient. An adequately publicized association with figures of substantial notoriety in television, motion pictures, politics or crime — in the late sixties and early seventies high figures in the Nixon Administration were especially valuable — is now essential.

Have the manners and morals of the moneymakers improved? — a question, alas, that everyone will ask. As to the manners, there is no doubt; Vanderbilt, Jim Fisk, Jay Gould showing up at one of the Texas fiestas just mentioned would be thought very coarse. Even a modern oil man would shudder to hear a Vanderbilt tell the public to be damned. In our day the most ruthless predator must present himself as a public benefactor, speak admiringly of his primary concern for serving the people of a free society. He makes money but that is a passive consequence of the free enterprise system. It is not his primary concern. Regular bathing is obligatory. No one can chew tobacco. Thus have the manners of modern capitalism improved.

As to the advance in morality as opposed to manners, one can be less sure. I.O.S., Vesco, Poulson, Sindona, Hoffman, C. Arnholt Smith and the Real Estate Fund of America, though possibly more sophisticated in accelerating the separation of widows, orphans and fools from their money, are not, most will think, a quantum step up to righteousness from Erie.

Vanderbilt and the Erie Gang bought judges. In recent times the great U.S. corporations have bought politicians at home and abroad or, in any case, paid for them. In the last century Pavel Ivanovich Chichikov traveled over Russia buying dead serfs — Gogol's Dead Souls. He bought them from landlords and used their ownership as security for loans from a bank. In the nineteen-sixties in Los Angeles one Stanley Goldblum created souls that were equally ethereal, insured their lives and sold their policies (and the premiums these theoretically would earn) to more substantial insurance companies at a handsome profit. While it lasted, he was greatly esteemed. The stock of Equity Funding Corporation boomed; men of repute joined its board. The moral improvement even on early Russian enterprise is not clear.

My own thought is that if men are sufficiently concerned to acquire money, their behavior will reflect that preoccupation and be much the same, whatever the time or place. Out of moral sense, caution or conscience — conscience being, as Mencken once said, "the inner voice which warns us that someone may be looking" — most, it may be expected, will remain within the law. But a largely stable minority will be impelled to step over the line into forthright rascality.

The rascality will not vary much as to form from one period to the next. Popular opinion and popular fiction to the contrary, this is not a line of work that attracts the highly innovative mind. The man who is admired for the ingenuity of his larceny is almost always rediscovering some earlier form of fraud. The basic forms are all known, have all been practiced.

The manners of capitalism improve. The morals may not. But, equally, they do not get worse.

Karl Marx at 49.

3.
The Dissent of Karl Marx

Adam Smith, David Ricardo and their followers affirmed as the natural order an economic society in which men owned the things — factories, machinery, raw materials as well as land — by which goods were produced. Men owned the capital or means of production. Spencer and Sumner gave this the highest social and moral sanction. Thorstein Veblen mused over and was amused by the result. But even Veblen did not dissent. Though a merciless critic of the high capitalist order, Veblen was not a socialist or even a reformer.

The massive dissent originated with Karl Marx. In considerable measure he used the ideas of Ricardo to assail the economic system which Ricardo interpreted and described. I've used the word massive to describe his onslaught. If we agree that the Bible is a work of collective authorship, only Mohammed rivals Marx in the number of professed and devoted followers recruited by a single author. And the competition is not really very close. The followers of Marx now far outnumber the sons of the Prophet.

Marx lies in Highgate Cemetery in London where he was buried on March 17, 1883. As with Smith's grave it is a place of only minor pilgrimage — the pilgrims are mostly delegations from the Communist countries on official business in London. Until about twenty years ago Marx's grave was in an obscure corner, almost unmarked. Now it lies at no great distance from that of Herbert Spencer. It would be hard to think of two men who are taking less pleasure in the company of each other.

The Universal Man

The world celebrates Karl Marx as a revolutionary, and for a century most of the world's revolutions, serious or otherwise, have invoked his name. He was also a social scientist, many would say the most original and imaginative economist, one of the most erudite political philosophers of his age. The late Joseph Schumpeter, the famous Austrian (and Harvard) economist, iconoclast and devout conservative, introduced his account of Marx's ideas with the statement that he was a genius, a prophet and, as an economic theorist, "first of all a very learned man."[1]

Marx was also a brilliant journalist, and all American Republicans, including Mr. Gerald Ford and Mr. Ronald Reagan, both highly prominent as I write, may note with suitable pride that, during an exceptionally meager time in his life, he was sustained by the *New York Tribune* and was described by its editor as its most esteemed as well as best-paid correspondent. The *Tribune*, with the *Herald* another parent of the *Herald Tribune*, was, for generations, the organ of the highest Republican establishment. Marx had another involvement with Republicans. After the election in 1864, he joined in congratulating Lincoln warmly on the Republican victory — and on the progress of the war: "The working men of Europe," he said, "felt instinctively that the star-spangled banner carried the destiny of their class." [2]

Marx was also an historian, a man for whom history was less a subject to be studied than a reality to be lived and shared. Paul M. Sweezy, the most distinguished of present-day American Marxists, has said that it is this sense of history that gives Marxist economic thought its special claim to intellectual distinction. Other economists have heard of history; Marxists make themselves and their ideas a part of history.

Finally, Marx was a major historical event. Often it can be imagined that if someone hadn't lived, someone else would have done his work. The innovating force, to recur to a familiar point, was not the individual but the circumstance. No one will ever suggest that the world would be the same had Marx not lived.

Marx, as an historian, would expect one to begin with his history.

Trier

It begins in Trier, or Trèves, at the head of the Moselle Valley. When Marx was born there in 1818, the surrounding countryside must have been the loveliest in Europe. Many would say that it still is. The valley is filled with towns out of the Brothers Grimm. Above are the vineyards. And beyond the rim of the valley are gently rolling farmlands, much of which is still farmed in the thin, inefficient but vividly contrasting strips that remain a common feature of Rhineland agriculture. Delegations come from the Communist countries to Trier as they do to Highgate. From the West, travelers come to drink the wine. The local tourist office reports that only the most occasional visitor asks about Marx. A largish store in the town features a variety of merchandise and the family name. The pleasant and spacious house in which Marx was born still survives.

There was much in this small town — it then had a population variously estimated at from 10,000 to 15,000 — to stimulate a feeling for history. Once, as Augusta Trevorum, it was called the Rome of the North. The German tribes regularly erupted southward on the Latins, a habit they did not break until the middle of the present century. Augusta Trevorum was the principal bastion against this aggression. The Porta Negra, the great black gate from the

Birthplace in Trier: Marx was born in this pleasant house on May 5, 1818. It's a place of minor pilgrimage from the Communist lands. Western tourists are rarely aware of its existence.

Roman wall, stands to this day as the most impressive Roman relic in what was northern Gaul.

Trier is now, of course, part of Germany; in 1818, it was only recently so. When Marx was born, French occupation had just given way to Prussian rule. The change was a matter of prime importance for the family of Heinrich Marx. The Marx family was Jewish; numerous of Karl Marx's ancestors had been rabbis. The French had been comparatively liberal to the ancient Jewish community of the town. Prussia was not. As an officer of the High Court and the leading lawyer of the town, Heinrich Marx could not be a Jew. So he and later his family were baptized as Protestants. It was, most scholars now agree, a purely practical step, one that did not involve any rejection of the social and intellectual traditions of Jewish life. As to religion, by the time Karl Marx was born, it was no longer thought very important by his family. Their mood was by now strongly secular.

His Jewish antecedents were, nevertheless, to be wonderfully useful to Marx's enemies in later times. Anti-communism could be combined with anti-Semitism. This was a fine start for anyone with an instinct for rabble-rousing, and Hitler and the Nazis found it especially valuable. But many others made use of it.

However, there would also be a lurking suspicion that Marx was himself anti-Semitic. After all, he had been baptized. More important, some of his writing was very hard on Jews. This was partly a literary convention; the word Jew in the last century was used extensively as a synonym or metaphor for the avaricious businessman. But it takes effort not to read some racial animus into his writing.

Marx was also an atheist. This was an age when most people took religion very seriously, when its active practice was a badge of respectability. And Marx was not a passive but an active atheist. One of his most famous phrases described religion as the opiate of the people. It taught them to acquiesce patiently in hardship and exploitation when they should rise up in angry revolt. A similar thought, we've seen, stirred the soul of the Reverend Henry Ward Beecher, though with very different results. Religion helped people to suffer patiently and unprotestingly their assigned economic lot in this world, however meager that might be, and this was one of the things Beecher thought good about it. It obviously matters greatly how a proposition is phrased; Beecher's formulation was a lot more acceptable to the devout than that of Marx.

Karl Marx never cultivated popularity but where religion was concerned, he obviously excelled. To be Jewish, open to the charge of anti-Semitism and openly hostile to Christianity as well as all other faiths, was to ensure adequately against religious applause.

The Young Romantic

Marx was a deeply romantic youth. He wrote poetry, much of it unreadable — or so his family thought — and idealistic essays (some of which have survived) on nature, life and the choice of a career. A career should be where one "can contribute most to humanity . . . and glowing tears of noble men will [then] fall on our ashes."[3] While still in his middle teens, he affirmed his love for Jenny von Westphalen.

Jenny was the daughter of the leading citizen of the town, Baron Ludwig von Westphalen. Baron von Westphalen, obviously a rather remarkable man, was an intellectual and a liberal, and he had taken a great liking to the young Marx. They walked together on the banks of the Moselle, and he introduced his young friend to romantic poetry and also to the notion that the ideal state would be socialist, not capitalist; be based on common property, not private property.[4] This was heady conversation for a German aristocrat to be offering a young lad of the town. It is not suggested that Marx's socialism began with these talks but they do explain how it was possible for him, though not without social strain, to marry into this family.

At seventeen, Marx was sent down the Rhine to Bonn to the University. This was then a small academy of a few hundred students, very aristocratic in tone. Marx was still a romantic; his interests now extended to include drinking and duelling. Even by the relaxed academic standards of the time, he was rather idle. His father complained both of his high living costs and his almost complete failure to maintain communications with his family. But after a year he moved on from Bonn to Berlin. This was in 1836, and it was much more than a change in universities. It was a move into the very mainstream of German, even European, even Western intellectual life.

Berlin and Hegel

The romantic years were now at an end; the years of Hegel began. Not only was Berlin a far more serious place than Bonn but Marx was now surrounded by the disciples of Georg Wilhelm Friedrich Hegel. These young men, the young Hegelians, took themselves and their scholarly mission very seriously indeed. Recurrently in history intellectuals have been so impressed with their unique vision of truth that they have seen themselves fated to change how all men think. This was one of those moments.

What is not so easy to describe is the change the young intellectuals sought. Hegel is not a very accessible figure for the Anglo-Saxon or American mind; certainly I have never found him so. Once, years ago, I was greatly comforted by a story told me by Arthur Goodhart, the Oxford law professor and onetime Master of University College. It concerned a night in 1940 when, as a member of the Home Guard, he was deployed with a fellow professor, a distinguished

Georg Wilhelm Friedrich Hegel, 1770–1831.

philosopher at the university, to guard a small private airstrip near Oxford. They may well have been the two most improbable soldiers in the annals of British military history. But they marched back and forth in a light mist, one with a rifle of Crimean vintage more or less, the other with a fowling piece. Occasionally, being professors, they stopped to converse. Toward dawn, during one of these pauses, Goodhart's fellow soldier lit his pipe and said, "I say, Arthur, do you suppose those wretched fellows aren't coming? I did so want a shot at them. I've always detested Hegel."

Marx's lifetime associate and ally was Friedrich Engels. The best short summary of what Hegel meant to both of them comes from him: "The great merit of Hegel's philosophy was that for the first time the totality of the natural, historical and spiritual aspects of the world were conceived and represented as a process of constant transformation and development and an effort was made to show the organic character of this process."[5]

An organic process of transformation and development would become the central feature of Marx's thought. The moving force in this transformation would be the conflict between the social classes. This would keep society in a condition of constant change. Once it had developed a structure that was seemingly secure, the structure would nurture the antagonistic forces that would challenge and then destroy it. A new structure would then emerge, and the process of conflict and destruction would begin anew.

Thus, in the real world at the time, the capitalists — the bourgeoisie — were challenging and destroying the old and seemingly immutable structure of feudalism, the traditional ruling classes of the old aristocratic system. In gaining power, the bourgeoisie would nurture the development of a class-conscious proletariat from the exploited, propertyless and denationalized workers. In time, the proletariat would move against the capitalists. The capitalists, including the bourgeois state, would be overthrown. The workers' state would be the next new structure.

By all Hegelian law, the process should continue. Perhaps the workers' state, by the nature of its productive tasks, would be highly organized, bureaucratic, disciplined. It would need scientists, other intellectuals. And it would nurture artists, poets, novelists for whose work the literate masses would now have a large demand. These artists would then begin to assert themselves. Their opposition to the bureaucracy would become acute. Thus the next conflict, one that is far from invisible in the countries of Eastern Europe and the Soviet Union. However, Marx did not allow Hegel to take him so far. Nor do modern Marxists as they look at their dissident scientists, novelists, poets. Rigorously applied to modern Communist society, Hegel could be quite a problem.

Hegel's ideas did not come easily to Marx. Their acceptance, or more likely the experience of serious study itself, involved him in emotional crises, weakened his health and, it appears, brought him to the edge of a physical breakdown. For a time he left the city and went to the small village of Stralau outside Berlin to recover. Each day he walked several miles to attend his lectures — and wrote in surprise at how good it was for his health. It was a lesson he would soon forget. For much of his life he would be in poor health, the result of singularly unwholesome living. Much of the world's work, it has been said, is done by men who do not feel quite well. Marx is a case in point.

It is tempting to see in modern Berlin the dramatically visible manifestation of the transformation which was Marx's great preoccupation. The place to view it is the Wall. On one side is West Berlin; this is the embattled outpost of the capitalist world. On the other side is the next stage; there the triumphant masses. For years all excessively articulate visitors to Berlin have been seeing precisely this, although those viewing the Wall from the West have usually spoken of democracy, not capitalism, and few have conceded the inevitability of the transformation unless it be out of weakness. Still, the contrast is accepted; Marx has had an enormous success in the rhetoric of the Wall.

I've long believed, alas, that in highly organized industrial societies, capitalist or socialist, the stronger tendency is to convergence — that if steel or automobiles are wanted and must be made on a large scale, the process will stamp its imprint on the society, whether that be Magnitogorsk or Gary, Indiana. If so, the Wall is not a place of historic confrontation; rather, as those on each side become aware of their higher commitment to the mass production of goods and to the vast and intricate organization that this requires, it will become progressively less important. It is hard, visiting West and East Berlin, to believe that this is not already happening. The preoccupation with the production of goods and the practical productive arrangements are becoming more, not less, alike.

In 1841, Marx left Berlin. Henceforth he would be part of the Hegelian process — one of the prime instruments of its transformation. A new factor would also now begin to influence his movements. Hitherto they were relaxed and voluntary. Henceforth, for years, they would be sudden and compelled. Germany, France and Belgium would all unite in the belief that Marx was an excellent resident for some other country. For a man pursued by the police, another insufficiently recognized point, there are two sources of solace and protection: one is to be innocent of the crime. The other is to be righteous in committing it. Marx was always to have this second and greater support.

Cologne and Journalism

Marx went to Cologne. Like Trier, Cologne is also in the Rhineland, and, like Trier, it was also then recently redeemed from France and somewhat more liberal for the experience. In France it was said that what wasn't prohibited was permitted. Prussia followed a sterner rule: what wasn't permitted was prohibited. In Cologne Marx became a journalist. The paper was the brand-new *Rheinische Zeitung*; it was well-financed and by, of all people, the burgeoning industrialists and merchants of the Rhineland and the Ruhr. Marx was an immediate success; he was first a highly valued correspondent and very soon the editor. None of this was surprising. He was intelligent, resourceful and extremely diligent and in some ways a force for moderation. He also enforced high standards. Revolution was much discussed. The word "communism," though still indistinct as to meaning, was now coming into use. Marx said that numerous of the resulting contributions were:

. . . scrawls pregnant with world revolutions and empty of thought, written in a slovenly style and flavoured with some atheism and communism (which these gentlemen have never studied) . . . I declared that I considered the smuggling of communist and socialist ideas into casual theatre reviews was unsuitable, indeed immoral . . .[6]

Marx would still be a force for editorial good in dealing with highly motivated writers of the left today.

Under Marx's editorship the *Rheinische Zeitung* grew rapidly in circulation, and its influence extended to the other German states. It became also of increasing interest to the censors who reviewed the proofs each night before it went to press. They reacted adversely to Marx on many things; the most important collision was over dead wood. I must acknowledge my debt on numerous matters to David McLellan's recent and very lucid biography of Marx, and they include the story of this conflict.[7]

From ancient times, residents of the Rhineland had been accustomed to go into the forests to collect fallen wood for fuel. Like air or most water, it was a free good. Now, with increasing population and prosperity, the wood had become valuable and the collectors a nuisance. So the privilege was withdrawn; wood now became serious private property. The cases seeking to protect it clogged the Prussian courts. Some eighty to ninety percent of all prosecutions were, it is said, for theft of dead wood or what was so described. The law was now to be yet further tightened — the keepers of forests would be given summary power to assess damages for theft. In commenting on this power, Marx asked:

. . . if every violation of property, without distinction or more precise determination, is theft, would not all private property be theft? Through my private property, do not I deprive another person of this property? Do I not thus violate his right to property?[8]

In these same months of 1842, Marx also came to the support of old neighbors, the winegrowers of the Moselle Valley. They were suffering severely from competition under the *Zollverein*, the common market that the German states had recently adopted. His solution was not radical — more free discussion of their problems — and he came to this also with rather labored caution:

To resolve the difficulty, the administration and the administered both need a third element, which is political without being official and bureaucratic, an element which at the same time represents the citizen without being directly involved in private interests. This resolving element, composed of a political mind and a civic heart, is a free Press.[9]

Marx also criticized the Czar and urged a more secular approach to divorce. Prussia was Prussia: here was a man supporting wood collection and free discussion and criticizing the Czar. A line had to be drawn. In March 1843, the *Rheinische Zeitung* was suppressed. Marx went to Paris. First, however, on June 19, he went to Kreuznach, a resort town some fifty miles from Trier. There, in a Protestant and civil ceremony, he married Jenny von Westphalen. It can be said without exaggeration that for no woman since Mary did marriage portend so much. A few months earlier Jenny had written her future husband urging him, come what may, to keep clear of politics.

Birth of a Socialist

For Marx, Paris was the beginning of a new life. The streets of Paris were then, as so often, the nursery of revolution. Many of the revolutionaries at this time were German, refugees from Prussian censorship and repression. Many, of course, were socialists. Their influence on Marx during his stay in Paris was very great.

The Marx family lived at various addresses on rue Vaneau — for the longest time at number 38, now a small hotel-boardinghouse. A sign in the entrance hallway tells of the most famous tenant, as does, most willingly, the proprietor. André Gide lived in recent times at one end of the street. Stavros Niarchos now has an apartment just a few doors away. One imagines that the neighborhood has come up a bit since Marx's day.

Once settled in Paris, Marx went ahead with his next journalistic enterprise, the editing of the *Deutsch-Französische Jahrbücher*, the German-French Yearbooks. This was really a magazine but by calling it a book, he hoped to avoid censorship. The reference to France in the title was also a gesture. Though he was in Paris, Marx's thoughts were on Germany, and it was for Germany that the Yearbooks were written. Rue Vaneau was a convenient location for Marx's editorial activities, for his co-editor, Arnold Ruge, was a near neighbor.

A review in the very first issue of the Yearbooks led to another collision with the censors. Again it sounds rather innocuous — also complicated, labored, with distinct elements of wishful thinking:

Jenny Marx: "For no woman since Mary did marriage portend so much."

Friedrich Engels.

The emancipation of Germany is the emancipation of man. The head of this emancipation is philosophy, its heart is the proletariat. Philosophy cannot realize itself without transcending the proletariat, the proletariat cannot transcend itself without realizing philosophy.[10]

But again the Prussian police showed themselves to be very sensitive men. This was dangerous stuff. The first double-issue of the Yearbooks was confiscated at the border. There could now be no German readers, and since there never were any French contributors or readers, the publication was obviously in trouble. Marx, by this time, was also quarreling with his fellow editor, Ruge. So the first issue of the German-French Yearbooks was the last.

In the next weeks, however, something far more important happened. Friedrich Engels was passing through Paris; the two men had met briefly once before; now at the Café de la Régence, once frequented by Benjamin Franklin, Denis Diderot, Sainte-Beuve and Louis Napoleon, they met and talked, met again and formed what was to be one of the world's most famous partnerships. Engels would be Marx's editor, collaborator, admirer, friend — and financial angel. His name would forever, and all but exclusively, appear in association with that of Marx. "Our complete agreement in all theoretical fields became obvious," he later wrote, "and our joint work dates from that time."[11] Engels always considered himself a junior partner, and so, without doubt, he was. But that does not lessen his role. Had he not been the junior partner, much for which his senior partner is known would not have been done.

Like Marx, Engels was a German. And like Marx, he was a member of the upper middle class. All of the early revolutionary leaders (it is hard to think of any exceptions at all) were middle-class intellectuals. Only in hope and oratory did they come from the masses.

However, the Engels family — textile manufacturers in the Ruhr and, in an early way, a multinational enterprise — was much wealthier than that of Marx. Engels would spend most of his life in England, in Manchester, where he combined revolutionary thought with the supervision of the local branch of the family firm.

Relieved of his editorial duties, Marx settled down for a period of serious reading and study, perhaps the most intense of his life. Numerous of the ideas which were to dominate his later years are thought to have taken form in this period. No one should imagine, although some do, that socialism began with Marx. By this time it was under the most intense discussion. Saint-Simon and Charles Fourier had preceded Marx. So had Robert Owen whom we've already encountered. Louis Auguste Blanqui (who spent most of his life in prison), Louis Blanc, P. J. Proudhon, all Frenchmen, and the Germans, Ferdinand Lassalle and Ludwig Feuerbach, were contemporaries. All, and especially the Germans, were sources of Marx's thought.

Marx, during these years, was not only gathering ideas but considering the role of ideas themselves. For John Maynard Keynes ideas were the motivating force in historical change. Marx, while not denying the importance of ideas, carried the proposition a step further back. The accepted ideas of any period are singularly those that serve the dominant economic interest:

... intellectual production changes its character in proportion as material production is changed. The ruling ideas of each age have ever been the ideas of the ruling class.[12]

I have never thought Marx wrong on this. Nothing more reliably characterizes great social truth, economic truth in particular, than its tendency to be agreeable to the significant economic interest. What economists believe and teach, whether in the United States or in the Soviet Union, is rarely hostile to the institutions — the private business enterprise, the Communist Party — that reflect the dominant economic power. Not to notice this takes effort, although many succeed.

Taking form, also, in these years were Marx's views on the process by which capitalism itself would be changed. Sir Eric Roll, a remarkably eclectic English student of Marx — he has been a professor, a senior civil servant, an accomplished international negotiator who led the negotiations for both the Marshall Plan and the EEC, a banker, a member of the Court of the Bank of England and a respected writer on the history of economic thought — many years ago gave the most succinct summary of the motivating influence in capitalist change:

It had to be some contradiction in the system which produced conflict, movement and change ... This basic contradiction of capitalism is the increasingly social, cooperative nature of production made necessary by the new powers of production which mankind possesses and (as opposed to this) the individual ownership of the means of production ... [From this comes the] inevitable antagonism ... between the two classes whose interests are incompatible.[13]

The notion of contradiction and inevitable conflict was leading Marx to its consequences. As a result, he was forming his ideas on communism and beginning to identify himself with the ultimate vision of the classless society.

With all else, he continued writing. His preoccupation was still with Germany, and his new outlet was *Vorwärts (Forward)*, the organ of the German refugee community in Paris. But the censors were still on guard. Once again one must read what he said:

... Germany has a vocation to social revolution that is all the more classic in that it is incapable of political revolution. For as the impotence of the German bourgeoisie is the political impotence of Germany, so the situation of the German proletariat ... is the social situation of Germany. The disproportion between philosophical and political development in Germany is no abnormality. It is a necessary disproportion. It is only in socialism that a philosophical people can find a corresponding activity, thus only in the proletariat that it finds the active element of its freedom.[14]

One yearns for policemen who could be aroused today by such prose. But, reliably, the Prussian police were aroused. They complained to the French; to harbor such a writer was not a neighborly act. They asked for a friendly, fraternal gesture of repression. Guizot, the French Minister of the Interior, was obliging in such matters and issued an order for Marx's expulsion. That was on January 25, 1845. On twenty-four hours' notice the Marx family — there was now a baby girl — departed for Brussels. *Vorwärts* was also closed down.

The Communist Manifesto

The Communist Manifesto was composed by Marx with the help of Engels in the next rather peaceful and happy years in Belgium. The *Manifesto* was an organizing document, a brochure for the League of the Just (soon to become the Communist League) which Marx was now actively promoting. It is, incomparably, the most successful propaganda tract of all time. There was also, in comparison with Marx's early writing, a quantum advance in the impact of the prose. What before had been wordy and labored was now succinct and arresting — a series of hammer blows:

The history of all hitherto existing society is the history of class struggles. Freeman and slave, patrician and plebeian, lord and serf, guild-master and journeyman, in a word, oppressor and oppressed, stood in constant opposition to one another, carried on an uninterrupted, now hidden, now open fight, a fight that each time ended either in a revolutionary reconstitution of society at large, or in the common ruin of the contending classes.

. . . The executive of the modern State is but a committee for managing the common affairs of the whole bourgeoisie . . .

The bourgeoisie, by the rapid improvement of all instruments of production, by the immensely facilitated means of communication, draws all, even the most barbarian nations, into civilisation. The cheap prices of its commodities are the heavy artillery with which it batters down all Chinese walls . . .

It [the bourgeoisie] has created enormous cities, has greatly increased the urban population as compared with the rural, and has thus rescued a considerable part of the population from the idiocy of rural life . . . during its rule of scarce one hundred years, it has created more massive and more colossal productive forces than have all preceding generations together. . . .

[Initially] the proletarians do not fight their enemies [the great bourgeoisie or capitalists], but the enemies of their enemies, the remnants of absolute monarchy, the landowners, the non-industrial bourgeoisie, the petty bourgeoisie.

The Communists disdain to conceal their views and aims. They openly declare that their ends can be attained only by the forcible overthrow of all existing social conditions. Let the ruling classes tremble at a communistic revolution. The proletarians have nothing to lose but their chains. They have a world to win. Working men of all countries, unite! [15]

The Communist Manifesto:
Its crescendo tones still
sound when modern
politicians are moved to
proclaim their faith.

Manifesto of the Communist Party.

KARL MARX and FREDERICK ENGELS.

A SPECTRE is haunting Europe—the spectre of Communism. All the Powers of old Europe have entered into a holy alliance to exorcise this spectre; Pope and Czar, Metternich and Guizot, French Radicals and German police-spies.

Where is the party in opposition that has not been decried as communistic by its opponents in power? Where the Opposition that has not hurled back the branding reproach of Communism, against the more advanced opposition parties, as well as against its re-actionary adversaries?

Two things result from this fact.

I. Communism is already acknowledged by all European Powers to be itself a Power.

II. It is high time that Communists should openly, in the face of the whole world, publish their views, their aims, their tendencies, and meet this nursery tale of the Spectre of Communism with a Manifesto of the party itself.

To this end, Communists of various nationalities have assembled in London, and sketched the following manifesto, to be published in the English, French, German, Italian, Flemish and Danish languages.

I.
BOURGEOIS AND PROLETARIANS. (a)

The history of all hitherto existing society (b) is the history of class struggles.

Freeman and slave, patrician and plebeian, lord and serf, guild-

(a) By bourgeoisie is meant the class of modern Capitalists, owners of the means of social production and employers of wage-labour. By proletariat, the class of modern wage-labourers who, having no means of production of their own, are reduced to selling their labour-power in order to live.

(b) That is, all *written* history. In 1847, the pre-history of society, the social organization existing previous to recorded history, was all but unknown. Since then, Haxthausen discovered common ownership of land in Russia, Maurer proved it to be the social foundation from which all Teutonic races started in history, and by and bye village communities were found to be, or to have been, the primitive form of society everywhere from India to Ireland. The inner

Even more durable than the political impact of *The Communist Manifesto* has been its effect on political style. Its assertive, uncompromising, thrusting mood has become part of the consciousness of all politicians, including those for whom the name of Marx is anathema and those who identify it only with Hart, Schaffner and men's suits. In consequence, when American Democrats or Republicans, British socialists or Tories, Frenchmen of the right or left decide to tell the people of their purposes, the crescendo tones of the *Manifesto* sound in their ears and presently in those of the public. The prose so contrived is, invariably, a terrible thing.

The *Manifesto* is not without its contradictions. There is none, as some might suppose, in Marx's praise of capitalism and its accomplishments, his call for its extinction. These are different stages in the historical process. Nor, as pedants have suggested, is there any real conflict between his call for revolution and his claim that it is inevitable. One can always try to advance the inevitable. But there was a great and intensely practical conflict between his immediate program and his hope of revolution. The program in the *Manifesto* is, by all modern standards, mostly a collation of reformist measures. The demands are for:

> Ending of private ownership of land.
> A progressive income tax.
> Abolition of inheritance.
> . . .
> A national bank with a monopoly of banking operations.
> Public ownership of railroads and communications.
> Extension of public ownership in industry; cultivation
>   of idle lands.
> Better soil management.
> Work by all.
> Combination of agriculture with industry;
>   decentralization of population.
> Free education.
> Abolition of child labor.
> Education along with work.[16]

In one way or another in the advanced capitalist countries quite a few of these things — ending of the private ownership of land, decentralization of population and a public monopoly of banking are the major exceptions — have been done. And these reforms have helped take the raw edge off capitalism. Thus they have had the effect of postponing that "forcible overthrow of all existing social conditions" for which Marx called. In such fashion did Marx work against Marx. The internal revolution came in those countries — Russia, China, Cuba — where the reforms Marx urged were never known.

Revolution — Of a Sort

A revolution did come on the heels of the *Manifesto*. In the Italian states, France, Germany and Austria, governments now tottered and crowned heads fell, some to rise again in a few weeks. This was in 1848, the year of revolutions, a year that is still connected in the minds of many people with Marx and the *Manifesto*, neither of which, in fact, had an appreciable influence on events. When the revolution came, the words of the *Manifesto* were still all but unknown. It was, however, the first revolution that could be identified, however indistinctly, with the aims and aspirations of the workers — with the proletariat as a class. So it was watched closely by Marx, especially as it developed in Paris. And it had a profound effect on his view of the nature of revolution. For that reason the events in Paris require a closer look.

Every great event has its geographical epicenter — that of the American Revolution was the few city blocks around Carpenters' and Independence Halls in Philadelphia; that of the great French Revolution was the Place de la

1848 was the year of revolutions: Paris.

Berlin.

Vienna.

Prague.

Bastille; that of the Revolution of 1848 was the Luxembourg Gardens. The setting had something to do with causes and participants, neither of which were much to Marx's taste. In the years before 1848 in France there had been a severe depression and much unemployment. Businessmen suffered as well as the workers. The crops had also been bad and bread prices very high. Then, in 1847, crops were very good and prices fell. So now the peasants took a beating. Almost everyone was being punished; the market, which is much loved by conservatives, was playing a very revolutionary role.

In particular, the circumstances greatly encouraged a dangerous line of thought now coming into circulation. It was that private production of goods might not be the only possible form of economic organization. This was the influence of Saint-Simon, Charles Fourier, Louis Blanc and others mentioned above. In circulation, also, was the compelling notion that every man had the right to a job; the reference was to *the right to work*.

In the United States, the phrase, the right to work, now stands for opposition to unions, for the principle that no person should have to join a union to hold a job. It is heard by conservatives with approval, or at least with a pleasant sense of nostalgia, and never by a devout liberal without a distinct shudder. A state with right-to-work laws, even though they are unenforced, is, in trade-union matters, a very retarded place indeed. Time changes everything. In 1848, the right to work was a truly radical thought.

The uprising in February 1848 united highly disparate groups, something that did not encourage Marx. There were the workers who wanted work and income. They were joined by businessmen, mostly smaller entrepreneurs, who wanted freedom of enterprise and a chance to recoup the losses suffered in the preceding years of depression. And, initially, there was support from the peasants who wanted better prices. The leadership was mostly by men who wanted freedom of expression — freedom from censorship and the attentions of the police. By most standards, the leaders were conservative. As the symbol of revolution, the red flag was rejected in favor of the tricolor. The tricolor was thought less damaging to business confidence and the public credit.

The revolt was quickly successful. The Tuileries Palace was occupied. Louis Philippe found it convenient to depart. The Luxembourg Palace was brought into use as the seat of a commission to study means for rescuing the workers from their poverty. This device was not yet a transparent stall.

The concern with the workers brought the focus on the Gardens. The assemblage there was, or has been called, the first congress of workers in history. It was also, more than incidentally, a means for segregating and keeping under control the most troublesome and dangerous participants in the revolt. It was one thing to be liberal, republican, romantic. It was another thing to question private property, be for workers' rights, higher pay, a twelve-hour day. Let there be a revolution but let it not be irresponsible.

The word revolution comes easily to the tongue; revolutions are always being threatened. If we knew how hard it is to have one, we might use the word less, and conservatives might fret less about the danger. They are far, far safer than they know.

Three conditions are absolutely essential. There must be determined leaders, men who know exactly what they want and who also know that they have everything to gain and everything to lose. Such men are rare. Revolutions attract men who have an eye for the main chance.

The leaders must have disciplined followers, people who will accept orders, carry them out without too much debate. This too is unlikely; revolutionaries have a disconcerting tendency to believe they should think for themselves, defend their own beliefs. There is opportunity and attraction for windbags. These cannot be allowed. Such men will be crushed while they debate.

And, above all, the other side must be weak. All successful revolutions are the kicking in of a rotten door. The violence of revolutions is the violence of men who charge into a vacuum. So it was in the French Revolution. So it was in the Russian Revolution in 1917. So it was in the Chinese Revolution after World War II. So it was not in 1848.

In the Luxembourg Palace the leadership was weak and the talk was long. It was of government workshops in which men would produce cooperatively for the common good; it didn't matter much what or at what cost. Or it was of public works, a great underground canal across Paris, in which imagination took the place of engineering. Wages were, indeed, raised. But this and associated relief measures had the effect of raising taxes and giving the peasants the impression that they were paying for the revolution. Meanwhile no real thought was given to seizing the instruments of power — guardsmen, police, soldiers. These are extremely important people in the moment of revolutionary truth.

This moment of revolutionary truth came in the early summer days of 1848. On June 23, the workers decided to leave their revolutionary ghetto and assemble at the Pantheon a few hundred yards away. From there they marched to the Place de la Bastille to enforce the much-discussed demands on the provisional government. The government was not without resources, and it had been viewing the workers with increasing alarm.

The workers succeeded in getting to the Place de la Bastille and in building a formidable barricade. The first attack by the National Guard was repelled, and some thirty guardsmen were killed. The romantic tendencies of revolutionaries now asserted themselves. Two handsome prostitutes climbed to the top of the barricade, raised their skirts and asked what Frenchman, however reactionary, would fire on the naked belly of a woman. Frenchmen rose to the challenge with a lethal volley.

Presently the barricades were stormed and the workers overcome. Prisoners were taken, and initially they were shot. Then, it is said, out of consideration for the neighbors who objected to the noise, they were put to the bayonet instead. The massacre extended to the Gardens. In another thoughtful gesture, again according to legend, these were kept closed for several days until the blood was washed or cleaned away. Already by 1848, people were becoming conscious of the environment.

Marx was not greatly surprised by this outcome. The bourgeois leadership of the revolution did not inspire his confidence. And as far as the workers were concerned, the timing and sequence were wrong: first, there had to be the bourgeois revolution, then the socialist triumph. Later in the year Marx noted that the revolution, symbolically at least, had succeeded in the matter of the flag. "The tricolour republic now bears only *one colour*, the colour of the defeated, the *colour of blood.*"[17]

Elsewhere in Europe even the monarchies survived. Concessions were made to the bourgeois power but not to the workers. Before 1848, to speak generally, the old feudal classes and the new capitalist class were in conflict. Thereafter they were united, with the capitalists gaining in real, if not visible, power. This union would be secure for another sixty-five years — until the great ungluing of World War I.

To London

The year 1848 did bring great personal changes for Marx. The Belgians were more liberal than their neighbors but just as nervous; they decided that even they could not harbor so dangerous a man. By now Marx was at the head of the police lists, a celebrated name in all the dossiers.

For the moment the revolutionary mood had its effect. On almost the day he was expelled from Brussels, he was invited back to France. And he was able to go from there to Cologne to revive the *Rheinische Zeitung*, now become the *Neue Rheinische Zeitung*. His first loyalty was still to the German workers.

However, the revived paper was, financially speaking, a shoestring operation. And it existed only because of the uncertainty of the conservative and counterrevolutionary forces as to whether they had the power to suppress it. Once they saw the feebleness of the revolutionary threat, they moved in again. Marx was still, in some ways, a voice for moderation. He had warned strongly against reckless, adventurist action by the workers that could only lead to disaster.

Nevertheless he had once more to move. Only two countries were still available, England and the United States. Marx gave thought to going to the

United States, and it is interesting to speculate on his future and that of the Republic had he done so. But he didn't have the money. So he went to London. This was his last move; he lived in London for the rest of his life.

Marx crossed the Channel on August 24, 1849. Though he had the experience of several lifetimes behind him, he was, incredibly, only thirty-one. Before him lay three further tasks: the first was to put in final form the ideas that would guide the masses to their salvation; the second was to create the organization that would bring and lead the revolution; the third was to find the means by which he and his family could eat, be housed and survive. Each of these tasks interfered sadly with the others but, in the end, all were accomplished.

The financial help came from Engels and from other friends. There was an occasional inheritance windfall from Trier, and there was the *New York Tribune*. (In 1857, when times were lean, the *Tribune* fired all of its foreign correspondents but two. Marx was one of the two who were kept.) But Marx was always a terrible hand with money. Where before his movements were at the behest of the police, now they were at the behest of landlords and creditors. Thus the migrations — from rooms in Leicester Square to a flat off the King's Road in Chelsea, to 64 Dean Street in Soho, to number 28 further up the street. Children came, six in all, and three of them died in the squalid, crowded rooms in Soho. (There was, additionally, an illegitimate son.) The uncertainty, the sudden moves and the squalor were Jenny Marx's marriage portion. She accepted it, one gathers, with infinite good nature.

The Prussian police maintained their interest in Marx. In 1852, a police spy infiltrated Marx's rooms and sent back a lucid account of the Marx ménage. It is a valuable contribution to history from the files and holds forth hope as to what, one day, the CIA may offer:

As father and husband, Marx, in spite of his wild and restless character, is the gentlest and mildest of men. Marx lives in one of the worst, therefore one of the cheapest, quarters of London. He occupies two rooms. The one looking out on the street is the salon, and the bedroom is at the back. In the whole apartment there is not one clean and solid piece of furniture. Everything is broken, tattered and torn, with a half inch of dust over everything and the greatest disorder everywhere. In the middle of the salon there is a large old-fashioned table covered with an oilcloth, and on it there lie manuscripts, books and newspapers, as well as the children's toys, the rags and tatters of his wife's sewing basket, several cups with broken rims, knives, forks, lamps, an inkpot, tumblers, Dutch clay pipes, tobacco ash — in a word, everything topsy-turvy, and all on the same table. A seller of second-hand goods would be ashamed to give away such a remarkable collection of odds and ends.

When you enter Marx's room smoke and tobacco fumes make your eyes water so much that for a moment you seem to be groping about in a cavern, but gradually, as you grow accustomed to the fog, you can make out certain objects which distinguish themselves from the surrounding haze. Everything is dirty, and covered with dust, so that to sit down becomes a thoroughly dangerous business.[18]

Marx's house at 41 Maitland Park Road. They moved here from "the evil, frightful rooms" in Soho which Jenny Marx said "encompassed all our joy and all our pain." This neighborhood was better then.

In 1856, seven years after coming to London, a small inheritance enabled the family to escape, as Jenny Marx wrote of them to a friend, "the evil, frightful rooms which encompassed all our joy and all our pain."[19] They moved with vast delight to a suburban villa in Hampstead, a brand-new real estate development. There were more financial troubles but the worst was over. Although the myth is to the contrary, in later years in London Marx had a very satisfactory income by the standards of the time.

In the thirty-odd years that he lived in England, Marx had something more important even than income, although income is rarely a secondary matter for those who do not have one. This was nearly complete security in thought and expression. The governments under which Marx had previously lived had the greatest difficulty in seeing why he should be so favored.

On arriving in London, the practical problems of his life notwithstanding, Marx plunged immediately into political work. He attended meetings; highly disreputable characters gathered in his squalid quarters to consider the strategy and tactics of revolution. In 1850, the Austrian Ambassador made an official protest to the British government. Marx and his fellow members of the Communist League were engaging in all kinds of dangerous discussions, even debating the wisdom or unwisdom of regicide. The Ambassador received a superbly insouciant reply: ". . . under our laws, mere discussion of regicide, so long as it does not concern the Queen of England and so long as there is no definite plan, does not constitute sufficient grounds for the arrest of the conspirators."[20] However, as a conciliatory gesture, the British Home Secretary said that he was prepared to give the revolutionaries financial assistance for emigrating to the United States. Regicide could not be practiced there. However, in the following year, when a joint request came from Austria and Prussia for the transportation of Marx and his friends, it was rejected.

In London Marx had one other resource that has been more celebrated. That was the library of the British Museum.

Das Kapital

In the British Museum Marx read and wrote. He wrote, in particular, his enduring testament, the three volumes of *Das Kapital*.

No one, least of all the person who attempts it, can be satisfied with a short characterization of the conclusions of this vast work. And no modern Marxist will ever be satisfied even by a much lengthier effort. It has long been the acknowledged right of every Marxist scholar to read into Marx the particular meaning that he himself prefers and to treat all others with indignation. This is especially the case if Marx's words are taken literally, as he may have meant. The decently subtle mind always discerns a deeper, more valid, less vulgar meaning. Still, the effort must be made.

The Reading Room of the British Museum. Marx worked here, as later also did Lenin.

David Ricardo, it will be recalled, gave the world (or gets credit for giving, for there were precursors) the labor theory of value, the proposition that things exchange in accordance with the amount and quality of the labor required in their manufacture. And with the labor theory of value went the iron law of wages, the ineluctable tendency of wages to reduce themselves to the lowest level that still sustained life and perpetuated the race. Given anything more, the workers proliferated. The price of the means of subsistence — food, in the main — was bid up. Wages were bid down. The landlords did well; workers were kept at, or returned to, the level at which they just survived.

Where Ricardo left off, Marx began. It is David Ricardo's unique position in history that he was an innovating force in both capitalist and socialist thought. For Marx the value that labor gave to a product was divided between the worker and the owner of the means of production. What workers did not get was surplus value. This surplus value accrued not as in the case of Ricardo primarily to the landlord but to the bourgeoisie, to the capitalist. Wages were now kept down by unemployment, by an industrial reserve army always waiting and eager for jobs. Should that labor be brought into employment and wages rise, this would reduce profits, precipitate an economic crisis, later variously to be called a panic, a depression, a recession or, in the days of Richard Nixon, a growth correction. The requisite unemployment and wage level would thereby be restored.

From the surplus value accruing to the capitalists would also come investment. This would grow more rapidly than the surplus; thus capitalism would suffer a declining rate of profit. Finally, out of the surplus value would come the wherewithal by which the large capitalists would gobble up the small — the process of capitalist concentration. In consequence of this concentration, individual capitalists would grow stronger but the system as a whole would be ever more attenuated, ever weaker. This weakness, in combination with the falling rate of return and the increasingly severe crises, would make the system progressively more vulnerable to its own destruction. Confronted by the angry proletariat it created, a force fully aware of its exploitation, disciplined by its work, there would come the final attack and collapse:

Along with the constantly diminishing number of the magnates of capital, who usurp and monopolise all advantages of this process of transformation, grows the mass of misery, oppression, slavery, degradation, exploitation; but with this too grows the revolt of the working class, a class always increasing in numbers, and disciplined, united, organised by the very mechanism of the process of capitalist production itself. The monopoly of capital becomes a fetter upon the mode of production, which has sprung up and flourished along with, and under it. Centralisation of the means of production and socialisation of labour at last reach a point where they become incompatible with their capitalist integument. This integument is burst asunder. The knell of capitalist private property sounds. The expropriators are expropriated.[21]

So the capitalist world ends. By such words the police might well have been aroused, for by now Marx was endowing his great events with great phrases. His capitalist was given the satisfaction of knowing that his end came not with a whimper but with a bang.

The International

The first volume of *Capital* — in the German original, *Das Kapital: Kritik der Politischen Oekonomie von Karl Marx*, Erster Band, Buch 1: "Der Produktions process des Kapitals" (Hamburg: Verlag von Otto Meissner) — was published in 1867. The second two volumes, with a claimed readership many times the real, were not published in Marx's lifetime. They were prepared for the press from notes and manuscripts by the ever-faithful Engels and could not have been completed by anyone else.

One reason for the delay was the early poverty and struggle. Another was scholarship; as his friends observed, Marx was incapable of writing anything until he had read everything. Yet another was the endless swirl of discussion, debate and polemic in which Marx lived. What he disliked he described with great pleasure and no instinct for understatement. Thus he described a well-known London daily:

By means of an artificially hidden sewer system all the lavatories of London spew their physical filth into the Thames. By means of the systematic pushing of goose quills the world capital spews out all its social filth into the great papered central sewer called the *Daily Telegraph*.[22]

Thus Adolphe Thiers, President of the French Republic, following the defeat and fall of Napoleon III:

A master in small state roguery, a virtuoso in perjury and treason, a craftsman in all the petty stratagems, cunning devices, and base perfidies of parliamentary party-warfare; never scrupling, when out of office, to fan a revolution, and to stifle it in blood when at the helm of state.[23]

But the most important reason was that in these years Marx was laying the foundations for the revolution which he hoped and occasionally allowed himself to believe was imminent. The instrument of revolution would be an organization that would link together in common purposes and action the workers of all the industrial countries — those proletarians who, as Marx powerfully averred, knew no motherland. Now known as the First International, the organization was born in London on September 28, 1864, at a meeting attended by some 2000 workers, trade unionists and intellectuals from all over Europe. A governing council was selected, of which Marx, naturally, became secretary. Its first task was to produce a statement of principles and purposes; this was done, and Marx was appalled by the verbosity, illiteracy and general crudity of the result. So, knowing the subject to be irresistible, he got the members discussing rules. He then attended to the

Membership card in the First International.

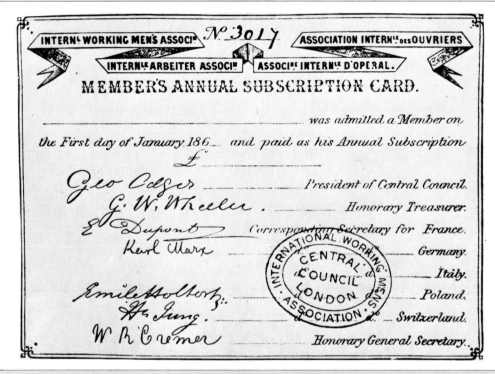

Leaders of the First International.

principles. The result, his *Address to the Working Classes*, is another famous document in the history of Marxist thought:

. . . no improvement of machinery, no application of science to production, no contrivance of communication, no new colonies, no emigration, no opening of markets, no free trade, nor all these things put together, will do away with the miseries of the industrial masses. . . .

. . . to conquer political power has therefore become the great duty of the working classes.[24]

And, once again, the call: "Proletarians of all countries, unite."

The International had individual members and affiliated trade unions and other organizations. In the next years it grew in membership and influence. Notable Congresses were held, especially in 1867 in Lausanne and in the following years in Brussels and Basel. The resolutions — calling for limitations on working hours, state support for education, nationalization of railways — were not very revolutionary. Reform was again showing itself to be the nemesis of revolution.

Revolution had another nemesis. That was nationalism. In 1870, Bismarck, who had once made overtures to Marx to put his pen at the service of his fatherland, went to war with Napoleon III. In a prelude to the vastly greater drama of August 1914, the proletarians of the two countries showed themselves far from being denationalized; instead they rallied to the defense, as they saw it, of their respective homelands. Then, as later, nothing was so easy as to persuade the people of one country, workers included, of the wicked and aggressive intentions of those of another. The First International, already split by disputes, was outlawed by Bismarck and soon by the Third Republic. Its headquarters was moved to Philadelphia, not a place of seething class consciousness; there, a few years later, it expired. In 1889, as a union of working-class political parties and trade unions, it rose again — the Second International. This Marx did not live to see.

Paris Again

But if the war was the nail in the coffin of the International, it also gave Marx a moment of hope. For where revolution is concerned, war in modern times has worked with double effect. It has been extremely efficient for mobilizing the proletarians of the world into opposing armies, defeating the dream of the internationally unified working class for which Marx (and those to follow) hoped. But it has been equally efficient for discrediting, at least temporarily, the ruling classes that conducted it — a tendency by no means confined to the countries suffering defeat. This now happened in France.

On March 1, 1871, the Assembly of the Third Republic met. The overthrow of Napoleon III was affirmed, and the legislators acquiesced in the peace terms. The Prussian army made its triumphal march down the Champs

Élysées. Outrage at the incompetence of the old rulers, knowledge that the wealthy had departed Paris, offended pride, the experience of hunger and hardship, all combined to bring revolt. It began on Montmartre when the troops of the Republic sought to secure guns which were in the hands of the Parisian National Guard whom, rightly, they did not trust. There were echoes, most of them soon suppressed, in Marseilles, Lyons, Toulouse and other cities. Only in Paris was power truly taken — the Paris Commune of 1871.

It lasted but a few weeks. On May 21, the troops of the Republic entered the city, and on May 28, after a week of street fighting, the revolt was over. The rule of the Commune had been confused, purposeless and often bloody. When Thiers had shot prisoners, the Communards had shot hostages, including, in the final days, the Archbishop of Paris. The repression in the aftermath was exceedingly cruel. Such of the leading Communards as were spared execution (or did not escape France) were sent to populate New Caledonia.

The war, the siege of Paris and the Commune were reported with much of the avidity with which all modern disasters are now enjoyed. Again Paris events were followed closely by Marx, and by now such was his fame that when there was bloodletting by the revolutionaries, it was attributed to him. The Red Terrorist Doctor. This time, in contrast with his doubts of a quarter century earlier, he was optimistic as to both leadership and aims. It is not clear why he should have been. Much of the leadership of the Commune was middle-class in both origin and outlook. The aims were incoherent. The opposition had the power that comes out of gun barrels. The requirements for successful revolution were again far from complete.

When it was all over, Marx sent a final reflective and saddened Address to the Council of the dying International — *The Civil War in France*. It is one of the most eloquent of Marxist tracts:

Working men's Paris, with its Commune, will be for ever celebrated as the glorious harbinger of a new society. The martyrs are enshrined in the great heart of the working class. Its exterminators history has already nailed to the eternal pillory from which all the prayers of their priests will not avail to redeem them.[25]

The Commune and the Communards have not been forgotten. But neither have they ever been wholly enshrined in the great heart of the working class. Though now eloquent, Marx was still not above some wishful thinking.

Thus ended the first revolution that was to use, seriously, however inaccurately, the root word of communism. It was the only one Marx was to see.

Death and Life

After the Paris revolt Marx lived on for another twelve years. He continued his work; he also remained the high, though not the undisputed, judge of what

Paris after the Commune. The destruction along the Champs Élysees was impressive even by modern standards.

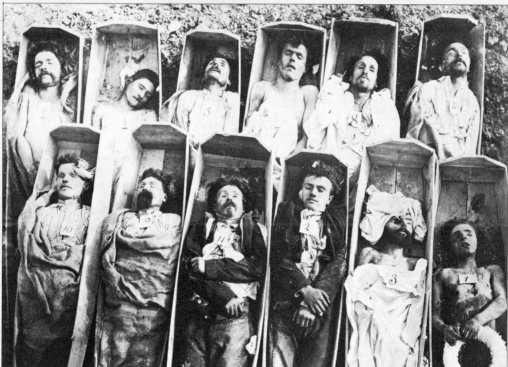

Communards after the Commune.

was right and what was error in socialist thought. One of these judgments brought the most enduring of his phrases. In the years following the Franco-Prussian War, the working class in Germany grew rapidly in political strength. Again the aftermath of war. Not one but two working-class parties emerged, and in 1875, they met at Gotha in central Germany to merge and agree on a common program. The result was extremely displeasing to Marx: the program offended deeply against Marxist principles, and once again reform replaced revolution. His *Critique of the Gotha Programme* held, with much else, that after the workers had taken power, the scar tissue remaining from capitalist habits and thought would have first to disappear. Only then would come the great day when society would "inscribe on its banners: from each according to his ability, to each according to his needs!"[26] It is possible that these last twelve words enlisted for Marx more followers than all the hundreds of thousands in the three volumes of *Capital* combined.

His last years were not a happy time for Marx. His health was bad and not improved by the abuse to which he had long subjected himself in matters of food, sleep, tobacco and alcohol. (He was a prodigious consumer of beer.) On frequent occasions he was forced, in the fashion of the time, to retire to a spa for the cure. Several times he went to Carlsbad in what was then Austria and is now Czechoslovakia where the police watched over him along with his doctors and reported principally on the very satisfactory way that he kept to his prescribed regimen. In 1881, his wife Jenny was found to have cancer and that December she died. A few months later she was followed by their daughter Jenny, the first and most beloved of Marx's children. Distraught and very lonely, Marx too ceased in any real sense to live. On March 13, 1883, with Engels at his bedside, he died. Not since the Prophet has a man's influence been so little diminished by his death.

4.
The Colonial Idea

The ideas of which we have been speaking so far had application in the last century only to a small corner of the world. They were important for Western Europe and for the United States. They had little meaning or relevance for India, China, the Middle East, Africa, Latin America or Eastern Europe. This part of the world was without capitalists, without proletarians, without much industry. Overwhelmingly the people were farmers or landlords; much was a feudal society still awaiting the progressive onslaught of capitalism of which Marx spoke. Much of this world was, directly or indirectly, a colonial dependency of one or another of the industrial countries. The independence of China was more nominal than real. Latin America, although released from Spain, was under both the economic influence and (through the Monroe Doctrine) the protection of the United States. In the rest of the poor lands independence was an invitation to rescue by what no one hesitated to call the civilized countries.

Colonialism being so general a phenomenon, one would have expected the great economists to have considered it at length, produced a major justification of its purposes and a detailed consideration of its methods. They did nothing of the sort.

Adam Smith was interested in the subject as in everything else. But he was mostly concerned to warn against efforts by the mother country to monopolize trade with its possessions. It should make no attempt to do this either for trade in general or for specific — they were called enumerated — commodities such as tobacco, molasses, whale fins and, for a time, sugar. For the rest he was content to condemn the East India Company and all its works. "Such exclusive companies, therefore, are nuisances in every respect; always more or less inconvenient to the countries in which they are established, and destructive to those which have the misfortune to fall under their government."[1] He had earlier concluded that: "Under the present system of management, therefore, Great Britain derives nothing but loss from the dominion which she assumes over her colonies."[2] In a modern British or American university such stalwart conclusions might be thought a sign of inferior scholarship.

Anyone would expect that Malthus, who taught the future servants of the East India Company, would draw, for his pessimistic evidence, on the huge, poor and prolific population of India. There is, however, only passing reference to Hindustan in his great *Essay on The Principle of Population*. Most of his case for the relentless tendency of population growth comes from his observations in Europe and America. Ricardo, in his *Principles*, confines himself to some mild corrections of Adam Smith. There might, he argued, be some selfish advantage for the mother country in exclusive trading privileges with its colonies. James Mill, like Malthus, was supported by the East India Company, and he devoted much of his life to his great *History of British India*, a book to which all historians of economic thought advert and which few have read. He too abhorred the company's trading monopoly; otherwise his case for colonialism is political and administrative, not economic. He looked forward to the day when "India will be the first country on earth to boast a system of law and judicature as near perfection as the circumstances of the people would admit."[3] John Stuart Mill, who, like his father and Malthus, was supported by the company, did not get around to colonial questions until the last pages of his *Principles*. There he contented himself with urging government-assisted emigration where population was excessive and empty lands needed people. The recent famine, he noted, had made this intervention unnecessary in the case of Ireland. The great scholars of classical capitalism took colonialism for granted and concerned themselves with the conditions for progress in the advanced countries. The colonial world earned attention only as it affected that progress.

Marx and Imperialism

Marx, in contrast, did make the colonial world an organic part of his system. He saw the rush for colonies as a way of gaining markets for capitalist production. Thus it postponed for a little the still inevitable crisis and collapse of capitalism. But, like earlier economists, Marx's primary interest was the advanced capitalist state itself. It was here that the climactic struggle between bourgeoisie and proletariat was coming. This was the focus of all Marx's passion.

The colonial world, in contrast, had no bourgeoisie, no proletariat. So for it the climactic struggle was far in the distance. It was capitalism that would transform production in these countries and develop a disciplined revolutionary proletariat. So in the colonial world capitalism was something to be urged — a progressive force. If, as in India, colonialism helped to break down the feudal structure and nurture capitalism, that was progressive.

In what was once called the colonial world and is now the Third World, no one has greater standing as a prophet than Marx. Nothing is so reviled as colonialism; capitalism has also a very poor press. There would be astonishment and some discomfort were Marx to accept an invitation to address the General Assembly of the United Nations.

The Colonial Mission

The nature of our discussion of the colonial ideas follows from what has just been said. It was not, for the great figures in economics, the subject of a developed doctrine. The ideas governing colonialism were merged into the experience itself, and they changed somewhat as the experience changed. To appreciate these ideas, we must go not to the books but to the practice and the way this was explained and justified.

It follows from what has just been said that this part of our discussion, and accordingly this chapter, have some of the character of a digression. They take us out of the main current of ideas and events in the development of capitalism and socialism to look at a special phenomenon, one that was not satisfactorily integrated into the main course of economic history. But digression is also an unsatisfactory word, for it suggests something less important. We must not forget that the colonial world far exceeded in population and extent the industrialized world that colonized it.

The ideas that interpreted capitalism, at least in its early stages, were reasonably candid. The ideas that justified colonialism have never been candid. There is nothing remarkable about this. On many matters men sense that the underlying reasons for action are best concealed. Conscience is better served by a myth. And to persuade others one needs, first of all, to persuade one's self. Myth has always been especially important where war was concerned. Men must have a fairly elevated motive for getting themselves killed. To die to protect or enhance the wealth, power or privilege of someone else, the most common reason for conflict over the centuries, lacks beauty.

The case of colonialism is the same. The real motives, were they stated, would be altogether too uncouth, selfish or obscene. So where colonization has involved people — where it has not meant merely the appropriation and settlement of unused lands — the colonialists have almost always seen themselves as the purveyors of some transcendental moral, spiritual, political or social worth. The reality has as regularly included a considerable component of pecuniary interest, real or anticipated, for important participants. Those who have questioned the myth have been lucky to be considered merely wrong; far more often they have been thought unpatriotic or traitorous.

Colonial rule, the government of one people by another and geographically or ethnically distant power, has had another great constant. Sooner or later it always comes to an end. Usually the end is bloody, both for those leaving and those remaining behind. Always the departure is less the result of the rising power of the colonial people than the diminishing interest of those who leave. All modern empires — Spanish, British, French, American, Portuguese, most likely Dutch and Belgian — could have been kept if the people of the metropolitan country had thought it worthwhile to do so. But none was as willing to expend blood and treasure to keep the colonies as it had been to win them. Also, an important point, the people of these countries were no longer willing to suspend disbelief as to their purpose in being there. They would no longer accept the myth of righteous purpose as opposed to the lower facts of pride, prestige or the pecuniary interest of those who had committed themselves and their money to the colonies.

One final feature of colonialism must be stressed. To this day in the United States, the other onetime colonies of Britain, Latin America, Africa and Asia, much that happens and more that does not happen can be explained by the colonial experience — by the way the land was held, the way the economy was developed or not developed, the justice or injustice of the colonial rule. No memory is so deep and enduring as that of colonial humiliation and injustice. But, it must also be added, nothing serves so well as an alibi. In the newly independent countries the colonial experience remains the prime excuse whenever something goes wrong. In these countries much does go wrong. So, in this respect too, colonialism remains a lively source of myth. Once the myth was made by those who colonized. Now by those who were colonized.

To the East

Mention colonialism, and the first image is of a great thrust westward by Europeans into the New World. In fact, the first great colonial enterprise of Western Europeans was to the eastern Mediterranean. It began nearly nine hundred years ago with the First Crusade; it continued for an incredibly long time. Had the Crusades begun in the year of American independence, they would still be very actively under way. Were they under the auspices of the Pentagon, it would still be heard that, in the Holy Land, there was light at the end of the tunnel. However, in more skeptical quarters there would be emerging doubt as to the ultimate success of the enterprise.

The Crusades are important for the singular and enduring importance of myth. The myth was of men of the highest religious purpose, the most selfless sense of commitment. The purpose was to redeem Jerusalem from the infidel and to save the Eastern Christians in Constantinople from the Turks. A crusader to this day is a man who is ruled by basic moral or spiritual force; in politics no one is viewed with more unease than "a crusader type." The less avowed motive of the Crusades was the acquisition of land and other property. Preaching the First Crusade in Clermont in 1095, Pope Urban II was candid enough to say that good real estate was available for the Christian taking in the Holy Land. This was a deeply inspiring thought to the younger and landless sons of the Frankish nobility. Later scholars have suggested that the Holy Father had also in mind to find "a job for the unemployed brigandage of Europe."[4] Better to have them in Asia than at home.

At Constantinople, the motives were deeply mixed: These were the eastern Christians to be saved. The looting was remembered forever.

We do know that the looting of Constantinople in 1204 by the Fourth Crusade — the city that the men of the Cross were initially sent to save — was one of the most impressive operations of its kind in history and designed to make the inhabitants yearn for the Turks. Even the improving myth was cast aside for the moment. Pope Innocent III was moved to say: "The Latins have given an example only of iniquity and of works of darkness."[5] Certainly it was not an act of Christian beneficence.

The First Crusade rather quickly achieved its most distant goal. Jerusalem was won. So was the real estate that reinforced the commitment to the Cross. Then there were reverses. In less than a century both Jerusalem and the land were lost. There now came yet later Crusades, and now also the reports that with a little more effort, a few more men, all would be won. The losses continued, and, when another century had passed, the invaders had been forced back to a few footholds along the Mediterranean shore. Though the land was gone, the pride of the Westerners was still engaged. It was thought important, as was later suggested in Vietnam, to retain enclaves. These would also be good for trade.

Of the enclaves, Acre, in what is now northern Israel, was the most important. On May 18, 1291, it too came under assault. Things were much as in Saigon seven hundred years later. A blood bath was promised for all the surviving defenders, with the difference that the validity of this promise was not in doubt. And to have planned the evacuation would have been to concede defeat. So when hope was gone, there was the same anarchic rush to escape. Space, as later, was sold to the highest bidder; fortunes changed hands during the course of that single night. Passage out was by ship, not helicopter.

The Fiscal Aspect

The younger sons were not the only ones interested in property. The sword arm of the kings of Jerusalem, and of the later Crusades, was the military orders, the armed monks. Of these there were three — the Knights of the Order of the Hospital of St. John of Jerusalem, known as the Hospitallers, the Poor Knights of Christ and the Temple of Solomon, known as the Templars, and the later Teutonic Knights. The military orders were especially notable for their combination of motives. They were devout, disciplined and exceedingly ruthless in their service to the crusading cause. They were also exceptionally committed to the acquisition of wealth, and increasingly so with the passage of time. The Templars, the *Poor* Knights of Christ and the Temple of Solomon, the most austere of the Orders, became highly accomplished international bankers. Their interest revenues were admired by all the early financial world.

Acre today.

The Hospitallers, a slightly more relaxed convocation, had, before becoming a military force, rendered care to pilgrims to the Holy Land. Their military architecture, which stands to this day, is one of the wonders of the medieval world. Krak des Chevaliers on a mountain in western Syria has been called the most nearly perfect castle ever built. I visited it in 1955. What I saw through a blinding rainstorm fulfilled every expectation. The Hospitallers who escaped from Acre came to Rhodes. The Palace of the Grand Master there is also one of the superbly graceful sights of the island. (I once visited it and spent the better part of a week recording a television discussion — with, among others, the late John Strachey — in the great courtyard. The program was not a success; it developed at the end of the week that the sound apparatus had not been recording.) For the next two and a half centuries the Hospitallers were the policemen of the eastern Mediterranean, combining this function with service to the Lord and occasional lapses into piracy. Again the undisclosed but deeply real admixture of motives, and among the holiest men in the service of the cause.

The long shadow of colonialism has been mentioned. No shadow is so long as that of the Crusades. It remained in the memory of Islam that men had come from afar, with religious purpose and sanction, to occupy Jerusalem but also to take up the land and engage in other secular pursuits. The fear persisted that one day they would come back. It was inevitable that any who did return would be viewed with the utmost hostility, and especially so if they claimed anything that seemed remotely like religious sanction. Thus it did not matter too much whether those returning were Christians or Jews. The shadow of the Crusades is still over Israel.

The Spanish Achievement

Had the Crusaders been exclusively concerned with protecting or regaining Christian lands from Islam, they could have found work closer to home. Not many years after the fall of Jerusalem to the Arabs in 637 and long before the Turks threatened Constantinople, Moslem armies had moved along the southern shore of the Mediterranean and then across the straits into Spain — into Europe itself. Then, as the crusading spirit waned in the East, so did the power of the Moors in the West.

It tells something of the strength of the colonial idea that in the same year that Spain freed herself from the Moors, *her* colonial masters, she launched the most spectacular of all colonial ventures herself. Christopher Columbus was in Seville that year — 1491 — on a sales trip; he had come to persuade Queen Isabella to back his voyages but could not get her attention until she had finished with the Moors. Immediately that he did, the building of Spanish America was under way.

The Spanish Empire was a remarkable creation. That of the Romans took centuries to build. Likewise that of Britain. Within a very few years of the voyages of Columbus, Spain was in possession of a major share of the American continent. By the middle of the sixteenth century Peru, a vice-regality of the Spanish Crown, was being administered on a parity with Spain herself. Spaniards thought of it almost as they might think of Holland. Oregon, Washington and British Columbia, only a little more remote but out of the Spanish orbit, remained anonymous, trackless wilderness for another three hundred years.

With Spain, the colonial idea took definite and explicit form. To rescue souls was a strongly avowed purpose. As Adam Smith observed, "The pious purpose of converting . . . [the inhabitants] to Christianity sanctified the injustice of the project."[6] But economic purpose was now also openly proclaimed. No one doubted that the purpose of the colonies was to enrich the colonists and the Spanish realm.

The effort being Spanish, there was no reason to share these rewards. Accordingly, the colonial trade was monopolized by Spain. Mercantilism, the notion that trade must be managed by the state, and the idea above all that Adam Smith attacked, had its classic expression in the Spanish Empire. Land, mines and inhabitants in the Americas were to be worked exclusively to enrich their Spanish masters.

There was recurrent conflict between the two purposes, although also a fairly adept reconciliation. The conquest of the Americas by Spain was so fortunate as to attract the interest of one of the greatest historians of all time, William Hickling Prescott. His *History of the Conquest of Mexico* and its companion, *History of the Conquest of Peru*, I think of as two of the most completely engrossing books I have ever read. (Prescott was nearly blind for much of his life, the result of being hit in the eye by a bread crust thrown during a juvenile scuffle when he was an undergraduate at Harvard. He was so highly regarded in Spain for his scholarship that, risking the hazards of nineteenth-century shipping, the Spanish scholars sent great boxes of valuable documents, laboriously-made copies of original manuscripts, from Spain to Boston for his perusal and use.) Prescott had respect for the religious motive in Spanish colonialism. The Dominicans, he tells admiringly, ". . . devoted themselves to the good work of conversion in the New World with the same zeal that they showed for persecution in the Old . . ."[7] But this did not exclude useful toil. A solemn priestly commission on colonial practices concluded, in Prescott's words, ". . . that the Indians would not labor without compulsion, and that, unless they labored, they could not be brought into communication with the whites, nor be converted to Christianity."[8] By this means Christianity became the sanction for slavery. It was not an association, it may be added, that escaped the notice of the inhabitants. Around 1511, an Indian chief named Hatuey was taken into custody in Cuba for developing a small-scale resistance movement and was sentenced to be burned at the stake. As a compassionate gesture he was advised to embrace Christianity so he would, in the end, gain admission to heaven. He inquired if white men would already have arrived. On being assured of this probability, he said, "Then I will not be a Christian; for I would not go again to a place where I must find men so cruel."[9]

The Bureaucracy

The Crusaders were subject to no control by home governments in France, England or Germany, and only the slightest by Rome. The Spanish Empire, in contrast, was a closely administered enterprise or was meant to be so. Wonderful proof of this, and of belief in the higher wisdom of the state, is available to this day in Seville. Until 1717, Seville was the headquarters for colonial administration. The colonial files survive there, row upon row, room after room, in the Archivo General de Indias. Built in 1598, this great square building was the stock exchange until 1875, a place where businessmen of various sorts met to exchange money, property or goods. After that, it was used, as it still is, to house the paper produced by the colonial bureaucracy.

The amount of paper so produced was truly immense. By 1700, some four hundred thousand regulations governing colonial affairs had been issued. An effort in 1681 to consolidate and codify these produced some eleven thousand laws. All these the colonial administrators were presumed to know and follow. The Spanish Empire may well have worked only because its regulations were so numerous that no one imagined they would be enforced. The petty annoyances that caused the English colonies to revolt — the Stamp Acts, for example — would never even have been noticed among the Spanish regulations.

Some of the surviving paper is a delight. There is a letter from Columbus himself, dated February 5, 1505. It is to his son Diego, and it deals with family, financial and business affairs. Another letter, from Cortés in 1526, describes his voyage from Havana to Mexico by way of San Juan, Puerto Rico. He warns of some very rebellious tendencies in the New World. A letter in 1539 from Francisco Pizarro to the Queen of Spain tells her that he is sending some emeralds. He asks thoughtfully for a receipt. Some, I've suggested, believe that Urban II launched the Crusades because he was attracted by the idea of having the Crusaders safely away from Europe in the Holy Land. Anyone who knew the Pizarro brothers, the conquerors of Peru, must certainly have rejoiced at their being in the Americas. Francisco Pizarro's caution in the matter of a receipt may well have come from the tendency to measure

118

The Archivo General de Indias in Seville.
By 1700, Spain had some 400,000 regulations
governing colonial affairs.
The flow of paper became a flood.

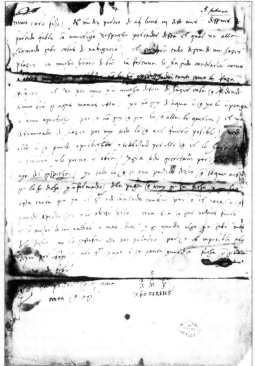

Letters from some notable colonialists:
Columbus to his son.

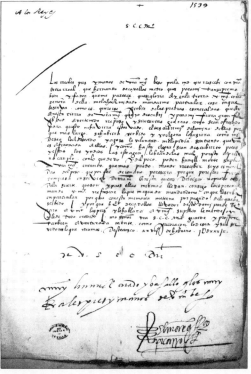

Francisco Pizarro sending jewels
to the Queen, requesting a receipt.

other people's character by one's own. Prescott's assessment of him is blunt: "Pizarro was eminently perfidious."[10] He goes on to his cruelty and that of his brothers.

The documents in the Archivo have also their own tale to tell about the colonial bureaucracy. In 1654, one file advises that the Cathedral Church at Valladolid, Mechoacan, needs repairs and restoration. Permission to proceed is sought. The question was still under discussion twenty years later in 1672; the repairs were finally completed some sixty years on.

Along with much else, the legacy of bureaucracy was real. Long after Spain had left, the government of the erstwhile colonies was highly centralized. It was also casual and rejected the common reaction to what had gone before. British colonialism, in contrast, was informal, decentralized, relaxed, even careless. Until the last century, apart from an Indian office and briefly an American secretaryship, Britain did not have a government department with responsibility for colonial affairs. This tradition, in turn, encouraged Smithian ideas in the colonies and caused the colonists to look to themselves, not to their government, for their own well-being.

Mexico

In the third decade of the last century, Spanish rule on the American mainland came to an end. Again there was the declining interest. Spanish governments were no longer willing to recruit and pay the required military force. Men were no longer eager to fight in the colonies to preserve the glory of Spain and the property of other and richer people. Local military levies, on which there was increasing dependence, were loyal not to Spain but to the lands of their birth. The mass of bureaucratic instruction emanating from Spain was an annoyance even when ignored. The occupation of Spain by the Bonapartes was the *coup de grâce*; it removed all claim by the Spanish Crown to the loyalty of the subjects beyond the ocean sea. The task of the liberators — Bolivar, San Martin — was again the kicking in of the rotten door. It was also something less than liberation.

When the ties with Spain came undone, the great estates which had been the economic reward for colonial adventure were undisturbed. The right of the owners to live on the toil of others was not affected. Indeed, it was partly the effort of Madrid to limit the power, restrict the privileges, control the graft and regulate the predation of the local landowners that encouraged them to think of independence. Nothing was more central to the colonial experience than the tendency for conscience to be a far more troublesome thing in the mother country than among those more immediately involved in the exploitation of the natives. The colonists felt they spoke from experience, felt they knew "their people," how feckless they really were, and knew how necessary it was that they be governed with a firm hand. Also it was the economic interest of the colonists that was directly involved. After independence, power in Spanish America remained with land. There were now constitutions and legislatures but there was less here than met the eye. It was acreage and not votes that continued to count.

The result in Mexico was another longer and much deeper revolt a century after the first. This was the true revolt against colonialism. The first was a changing of the guard; that in 1910 and after involved the land and the people. More being involved, this revolution, not surprisingly, was far bloodier than the first.

So it was also in Cuba. There too, when Spain left, power remained with the handful who owned the land. In the years that followed, the ownership was further concentrated, quite a bit of it in New York. It was not until Fidel Castro that Cuba made its final break with colonialism. In much of the rest of Latin America the break is still incomplete. Dictators, military and otherwise, protect old or more modern privilege. The United States serves a dual role: sometimes it helps the local dictators; sometimes it gets blamed for injustice and exploitation which might better be attributed to local talent.

There are rough empirical grounds for thinking the native despots more powerful. The two countries closest to the United States, Cuba and Mexico, are the two that have had the truly deep revolutions — those that swept away completely the old colonial structures. I used to tell my many Latin American students that the misfortune of the rest of Latin America was in being too distant from the revolutionary tutelage of the United States. This was not believed.

The Louisiana Case

In California, Texas, Florida and the southwestern states, the United States also had experience of Spanish colonialism. But, with Florida as a slight exception, these were distant and sparsely populated lands, and they remained unpopulated and unused. The Spanish colonial legacy was far slighter and less enduring than in Mexico and Central and South America. The much more interesting colonial influence was that of the French, although here there was also a Spanish interlude.

Again economics and religion were joined. The pursuit of precious metals was the economic objective. In 1719, John Law, of whom I later tell,[11] was issuing banknotes by the bale in Paris. They were backed by gold and silver that only remained to be mined in the Mississippi Valley. This gold and silver has not yet been found but the prospect seemed better then. Maps were in circulation in France that showed mines of unimagined wealth, all products of the imagination. The saving of souls was less important than in the Spanish

Empire, partly, no doubt, because the French were less devout and partly because there were fewer souls available in the area for saving. A further problem arose from the very poor quality of the souls of the colonizers themselves. In 1718, a hundred miles up the Mississippi, the first small settlement was established. It was called New Orleans for the Regent — not the best in nomenclature. One thinks of a city named, say, for Edward VIII — New Windsor. Soon after New Orleans was founded, an Ursuline nun, Marie-Madeleine Hachard, surveyed the state of morals not among the heathen but among the newly arrived Christians and concluded: ". . . not only do debauchery, lack of faith and all other vices reign here, but they reign with immeasurable abundance!"[12]

Unlike Spanish colonialism, that of France was casual in the extreme. Once the shortage of precious metals became evident, interest declined. Frenchmen did not hunger for great estates in the wilderness. Natives were not available to work them. The French did not forget that the colony was one of the pillars of Law's fraud. As an indication of how slight was the interest, the Louisiana colony in 1762 was ceded to Spain. The colonists resisted the more systematic Spanish rule until Spain dispatched an officer of Irish origin, Alexander O'Reilly, to be the governor. O'Reilly was a man of affability and much charm. He won the hearts of the dissident, invited their leaders to a reception and had them executed.

In 1800, Louisiana was taken back by Napoleon, and three years later it was sold to Thomas Jefferson. With Alaska, it was one of the few great colonial areas to be acquired not as booty or by right of discovery but in a straightforward real estate transaction. The 530 million acres (embracing some water) cost $27.3 million, including interest, or about five cents an acre.

Now, as in Latin America, land was alienated in large tracts. There it was the hacienda; here it was the plantation. Since no workers came with the land and they were needed to plant and cut the cane, and plant, chop and pick the cotton, they were brought from the older states of the American union or from Africa. The colonial idea took hold here as completely as in Mexico. Only the superficial forms were different. And, as in Mexico, it ordained a later revolt, one rejecting the power of the planters and affirming the rights of the people. This began in 1861 with the Civil War and has continued to our own time. As in Mexico, the Civil War was the true revolt against the colonial society. As in Mexico, it was a very bloody passage.

Here too there was the classical admixture of motives. The plantation owners made much of their moral obligation to their slaves. They provided for their religious instruction and eventual salvation, protected them in a harsh, cruel world for which, being, it was held, happy, feckless children, they were unprepared. Religion entered in another way: men spoke of the sacredness of

American colonial architecture after the fall:
Hacienda in Mexico.

Plantation house in Mississippi.

property rights, and slaves were property. But, as in the other colonial societies, none doubted that the people were very useful for growing crops and making money.

Lahore

In British times Lahore, in what is now the Pakistan Punjab, was called the Queen City. The legend of Shalimar survives even now, as does the Garden. To be a Punjabi in the days of the Raj was to be thought adaptable, progressive, intelligent, martial and, by Indian standards, relatively prosperous. This is still the case.

When British rule first came to Bengal and Madras far to the south and east, it was like that of Spain and France in America, a relatively candid thing. Indeed, no one seriously suggested that the East India Company was a religious or philanthropic foundation. It came to trade and make money. It conquered, pacified and ruled but these were necessary if money was to be made.

Colonialism came late to the Punjab; the Sikh rulers were finally subdued and the territory annexed only in 1849. By then the Honourable Company was dying and British rule was acquiring a different faith. This involved an important revision of the colonial idea, one of much importance also for the French and Dutch in the nineteenth century. The higher purpose of colonialism was no longer religion. The Church of England was for Englishmen; missionaries were tolerated but not much encouraged, and to many colonial administrators they were frankly a nuisance. The new faith was law. The British were in India to trade and make money. There was nothing wrong with that. But the redeeming purpose was to bring government according to law. It was an idea of genuine power.

In 1859, the year after the Honourable Company was interred, a young Englishman, John Beames, aged twenty-one, came to the Punjab as a civil servant. He was posted to Gujrat, a large district north and west of Lahore. Here he was Assistant Commissioner, which is to say judge and general deputy to the man who ruled the region. Later, Beames went on to serve in Bengal, Orissa (between Calcutta and Madras) and Chittagong in what is now Bangladesh. When, in the full course of time, he retired to Britain, he set down the story of his career.[13] Especially as regards his early life, Beames had something very near to total recall.

He was not himself concerned in the slightest with making money; that would have been unthinkable. That other Englishmen found India a profitable possession was something he merely took for granted. This had nothing to do with him; those so concerned, the businessmen and planters, were a thoroughly inferior caste. Beames's concern was with government — with the

John Beames: "Governing men is grand work, the noblest of all occupations . . . though perhaps the most difficult."

British justice under a tree.

British recreation: The hunt breakfast.

people being governed, with his British colleagues and superiors in the government (of whom he was usually critical), and with the tasks of government which he approached and of which he wrote with a craftsman's pride. He confessed his faith. "Governing men," he wrote, "is grand work, the noblest of all occupations . . . though perhaps the most difficult."[14] This functional separation of government from pecuniary concerns and its own categorically superior status was the prime achievement of late British colonialism.

Largely in consequence, in the hundred years following Beames's arrival in the Punjab, India was one of the best-governed countries in the world. Persons and property were safe. Thought and speech were more secure than in recent times. There was effective action to arrest famine and improve communications. The courts functioned impartially and to the very great pleasure of the litigiously-minded Indians. The cost of the government, no detail where so many were so poor, was relatively light, far lower than under the rulers and predators that the British displaced. In other respects — building railroads, putting down communal riots — it was far more efficient than the petty, corrupt, arbitrary and anarchic despotisms which had gone before and which, in later years, the British tolerated. The British rulers were snobbish, race-conscious and often arrogant. But if colonialism could anywhere have been considered a success (the empty lands always apart), it was in India. And it was the case above all that proves the ultimate point: the one certain thing about the efforts of some people to rule other people at a distance is that it will fail, and the departure will reflect the wishes of rulers as well as ruled.

The end in India came on August 15, 1947. The British, too, could have remained. The effort would have been cheaper and easier than defeating the Germans in which they had just been involved. But they had ceased to believe that the colonial purpose justified the modest increase in effort. And while Hindus, Sikhs and Moslems disagreed deeply on the terms of their going, they agreed in wanting them to go.

The British reputation for fair rule survived the withdrawal from India, a testament to the commitment. The law, in the immediate aftermath, did not. In northern India the end of British rule brought what was, perhaps, the most intimate cruelty of modern times. Moslems slaughtered Sikhs; Sikhs slaughtered Moslems. This they did with clubs and knives, by hand. All of the pent-up lawlessness of a century was suddenly released. The rules governing colonialism were affirmed. They are the reaction to previous achievement — and the always messy end.

The American Experience

It wasn't the last such ending. There were also the Congo, Algeria, Angola, Vietnam.

The always messy end:

India, 1946. (Opposite) Vietnam, 1975.

For the current generation of Americans the experience in Vietnam has seemed unprecedented, unique. We sought to guide the political development of a country distant from our own. We failed and were rejected. The end was terrible.

Viewed in the long reach of history, the experience cannot seem remarkable or the end surprising. Oddly enough, we had been warned by the most eloquent of all the voices on the colonial idea. He had warned not because he was against colonialism but because he had been a part of it.

Not one American in a thousand, and even fewer Englishmen, know that Rudyard Kipling once lived (from 1892 to 1896) outside Brattleboro in southeastern Vermont. The house he built is still there, a rather grim Victorian affair; sensitive souls now think it a bit spooky. There is nothing grim about the view; it extends for forty miles across the forest, across the Connecticut River, across southern New Hampshire, all the way to Mount Monadnock. In his study, which is unchanged since he used it, Kipling wrote *The Jungle Books* and *Captains Courageous*, among his most famous works.

Having lived in America, Kipling felt obliged to give advice when, in 1898, with the Spanish-American War and the acquisition of the Philippines, the American colonial experience began. No one then blushed to speak of white men and their responsibility. However, one should know what to expect.

> Take up the White Man's burden —
>   The savage wars of peace —
> Fill full the mouth of Famine
>   And bid the sickness cease;
>
> . . . .
>
> Go make them with your living
>   And mark them with your dead!
>
> Take up the White Man's burden —
>   And reap his old reward:
> The Blame of those ye better,
>   The hate of those ye guard —[15]

The wars of peace began almost immediately with the Philippine insurrection — a long, frustrating struggle. But the truly savage one came sixty years later in Vietnam.

In Vietnam the words were different, the colonial idea was the same. Earlier it had been to rescue people from backwardness, idolatry, indolence, misrule. Now it was to save them from Communism. The British had governed in Western India through the princes, in Malaya through the sultans, in Africa through the chiefs. It was called indirect rule. In Vietnam we governed or sought to govern through Diem, Ky and Thieu; they were not called princes, sultans or chiefs but freely chosen rulers.

For some, saving Vietnam from Communism was a crusade, was so called, and seemed as high-minded as saving Constantinople from the Turks or redeeming Jerusalem from the infidel. For others, it was an opportunity to make a little money. For yet others, the admixture of motives was more subtle; united with free enterprise was freedom. The second was both important and a cover for the first. If Communism succeeded in Vietnam, freedom and therewith free enterprise would be in danger in Thailand, Malaysia, Singapore, Hawaii. This was the domino theory; the economic motive lurked just behind. Better to fight for freedom and free enterprise in Vietnam than on the beaches of Oahu. Or after that maybe Malibu.

The United States could have remained in Vietnam — of that there is not the slightest doubt. But, as with the Portuguese, the British, the French, the Spaniards and among the Crusading knights and kings, there came a decline in the colonial *esprit*. What had been a slow decline in other countries went rapidly in the United States. People would no longer suspend disbelief, accept the higher motives, ignore the lower economic ones. Again there was the messy end.

As at Acre, they came with cash in Saigon. Then, as noted, it was for space in the galleys. Now it was for space on the helicopters. These were faster than the galleys, and the trip out was more quickly over. Also it could all be watched on television. By this much only had the experience of colonialism changed over seven hundred years.

Requiem

Does the colonial experience belong forever to history? The United States has badly burned fingers; the effort to govern indirectly and shape political development in distant lands will henceforth surely be viewed with caution. And it is not only the United States that has had this pain. The Soviet Union, in the years following World War II, sought to extend its influence in Yugoslavia, China, Egypt, Indonesia and Ghana. Contemplating the results, it can hardly feel pleased. When Ben Bella, a Soviet acolyte, was deposed in Algeria, a Russian newspaper correspondent said to me rather sadly, "They used our tanks. Well, at least they didn't use our advisers." The Chinese, in their turn, became the bitter enemies of the Russians. Once again "The Blame of those ye better." One hopes that there is now a volume of Kipling in the Kremlin.

But, though colonialism is dead, the scars remain. The old colonial powers are now the rich industrial lands. Their former colonies are the poor countries of the world. Colonialism is blamed for this poverty. As earlier noted, it gets the blame when local failure — that of local governments, politicians, businessmen or economic policy — would be a more salutary explanation.

The colonial experience also makes deeply sensitive the relationships between the rich countries and the poor. That the rich lands have an obligation to help the poor is widely accepted. It's one I strongly avow. But even if the money and the will to help are available, the difficulties do not end. If the assisting country remains remote, waits to be asked, does not interfere, it will be thought indifferent. And, very often, the help will be badly used.

The alternative is to be interested, forthcoming, watchful, anxious to urge what seems wise and right. Then you risk being called a neocolonialist, one who is seeking to re-establish imperial pre-eminence or rule.

To the delicacy of this line I can testify as a onetime ambassador in India, although India was never the most difficult case. My instinct was to get involved. Economic development is a great and fascinating enterprise. There is none like it. How does one ease the escape from the age-old tradition of hunger and deprivation? I had no shortage of thoughts. Also the United States was supplying much food and much money. For their use I had in some degree to answer. The late Krishna Menon, in a memoir, concluded that it was my far-from-secret purpose to be the new viceroy. By most others I was forgiven. But, unlike numerous other Americans, it was my good fortune to have been warned. I had lived much of my life in southeastern Vermont and knew all about Kipling.

I said earlier that to bring the colonial idea and experience into our discussion is to digress from the main development of capitalism and socialism in what we choose to call the advanced countries. It is now time to return.

5.
Lenin
and the Great Ungluing

People of the World War II generation, my generation, will always think of their conflict as the great modern watershed of change. Hitler was defeated, fascism destroyed. For the great colonial empires just discussed, it was either the end or the beginning of the end. The nuclear age arrived. The two superpowers emerged. Soviet influence and power advanced into Eastern Europe, American into Western Europe. The Chinese Revolution came. What greater change could there be than this?

We should be allowed our vanity, our personal rendezvous with history. But we should know that, in social terms, a far more decisive change came with World War I. It was then that political and social systems, centuries in the building, came apart — sometimes in a matter of weeks. And others were permanently transformed. It was in World War I that the age-old certainties were lost. Until then aristocrats and capitalists felt secure in their position, and even socialists felt certain in their faith. It was never to be so again. The Age of Uncertainty began. World War II continued, enlarged and affirmed this change. In social terms World War II was the last battle of World War I.

What came unglued in the First World War was a class structure and the associated exercise of power. This had everywhere involved a coalition, one partner of which was an aristocratic class whose power had originated in the possession of land and the allegiance of the people who tilled it. Their eminence now depended partly still on land ownership, partly on education and social position, partly on an accepted right to public and military office, most of all, perhaps, on tradition. The other partner in the coalition was the increasingly influential businessmen who, ever since 1848, had been asserting their claim both to social position and public influence.

The relative strength of the partners varied. In Eastern Europe the principal power was still with the landed aristocracy, the family elites, the officers and officials they spawned. The monarchies still ruled; capitalism and capitalists were as yet a secondary force. In Western Europe and in the United States, however it might be denied, there was also a traditional ruling class. But here the capitalists asserted a primary claim to influence, even though they left the tasks of government to old families, graduates of Oxford and Cambridge, Princeton, Yale and Harvard.

In Western Europe and the United States there was a large industrial proletariat. In Britain, France and Germany trade unions were commonplace, and in France and Germany they were represented in parliaments by large working-class parties. The trade unions and their parties annoyed the ruling coalition and were greatly disliked by it. They did not threaten it. In the United States, by now the greatest of the industrial powers, there was no labor party at all and not much in the way of trade unions.

In 1914, in all the industrial countries except Britain, farmers and peasants still rivaled or exceeded in number the industrial workers. They, not the industrial workers, were also the hard substance of military power. Especially in Eastern Europe the peasants, led in war as they were dominated in peace by those who owned the land, were to prove the decisive class. It was not necessary that they should revolt; it was only necessary that they should cease to obey.

The Eastern European scene is especially important for us. It was here, not in Western Europe, that the cracks in the old order first appeared. It was here that it dissolved, first in disorder, then in revolution. The Western coalition, where the capitalists were more powerful, was meant to be much more vulnerable to revolution. That was the lesson, at least, from an offhand reading of Marx. It showed itself, instead, to be far stronger.

The View from Cracow

If one had to select a city from which to watch the change, it would be Cracow, in what is now Poland. There is the greatest precedent possible for the choice. Cracow was the city that was selected for this purpose by the man who, more than any other, led and catalyzed the breakup of the old order — Vladimir Ilyich Ulyanov, known, except to his intimates, as Lenin. He came to Cracow in 1912.

He selected Cracow because it was on the border between the two great empires of Eastern Europe. It was then part of the Austro-Hungarian Empire but the Russian Empire began only a few miles away.

The imperial and colonial idea discussed in the last chapter was the rule by white men in Asia, Africa and Latin America. It is what the British had in India, the Americans in the Philippines, the Portuguese in Angola and Mozambique. There was also another kind. Its primary manifestation was here in Eastern Europe. This was the rule of Europeans by other Europeans.

Here Austrians ruled Bohemians, Slovaks, Ruthenians, Croats, Slovenes, Italians and, in a more tactful way, the Hungarians. Here likewise Russians ruled Latvians, Lithuanians, Estonians, Finns. And in Poland, specifically, almost everyone — Austrians, Germans, Russians — ruled the Poles. Cracow was ruled from Vienna. (So, a couple of hundred miles west, was the much larger city of Prague.) Warsaw, to the north, was ruled from St. Petersburg.

Lenin.

The Castle over Cracow.

Poznan, north and west, the cradle of Polish civilization, was ruled with considerable difficulty from Berlin. There were examples of this kind of imperialism in Western Europe — the rule of the English in Ireland and of the Germans in Alsace-Lorraine — and they were famous for the resentments they nurtured. In the East it produced the same resentments and cultivated the same exquisite hatreds but on a much larger scale.

The tensions were far greater than in the outlying empires of the Western Europeans because the subject peoples in this colonialism could not be persuaded that they were inferior to their rulers. Rulers and ruled alike, when washed, were white. Many of the ruled were the equal of their colonial masters in education, cultural achievement, economic well-being. Some regarded themselves as superior; this was almost always true of those who were ruled by the Russians. To be governed by one's inferiors or, more exactly, those so regarded is an especially bitter thing.

As just observed, we think of the years following World War II as the time when the colonial empires came to an end. This is another vanity of our day. It was in Eastern Europe after World War I that the great retreat from imperialism began.

In 1914, however, the hold on the subject peoples seemed secure. Independence was not a threat; rulers worried mostly about rival rulers who could claim closer ethnic affiliation with those ruled. It was this and the general territorial ambitions of the other rulers that were feared.

Out of these fears had come the alliances. Austria had turned to Germany for the industrial support and the disciplined, reliable military force that Germany could provide. On her side, she offered her large, though excessively diversified, supply of military manpower. Russia reached out to France for financial and engineering help in building her railroads and industry. France and Britain saw in Russia a vast reserve of armed manpower. This manpower, in the early days of World War I, led to the innumerable references to the Russian steamroller. It was meant to roll inexorably over Germany. Instead it rolled back on Russia herself.

The Territorial Imperative

No subject known to history, not even the reasons for the long decline of Rome (the more interesting question is how it lasted so long), has been so much debated as the causes of World War I. Perhaps great events can have simple explanations; Lloyd George once suggested that the powers simply stumbled into the war. A. J. P. Taylor has put almost the same case in fuller and more persuasive form. Marxists and many others saw, and still see, the war as the inevitable outcome of the capitalist and imperial rivalry between Britain and France on the one hand and Germany on the other. German capitalism was challenging that of Britain and France for the markets that were indispensable for capitalist survival. Any explanation derived from Marx has, even for non-Marxists, the appeal of forthright truth. This one leaves us with the problem that the war began in Eastern Europe, and also that, in these last thirty years, the same capitalist countries have found it possible to shed their colonies and live with each other in remarkable harmony.

The better explanation lies in the traditional territorial attitudes of predominantly rural societies. Their governments, at least in that time, were dangerously belligerent — more so, Marx notwithstanding, than those of the capitalist world.

Ever since the beginning of historical experience, land and men had been the basis of both wealth and military power; the two went together. The wealth of a prince had always been in proportion to the extent and quality of the land he controlled. For varying with the extent and quality of the land were the number, and perhaps also the quality, of the peasantry it supported and therewith of the soldiers he could muster. Thus his military power. Thus the territorial imperative, the belief that nothing should stand in the way of acquisition or defense of territory.

In 1914, the belief in land and men — this territorial imperative — was part of the deepest instinct of the old ruling houses. It was a factor as between France and Germany. Had Germany won, something more of France would have been added to Alsace and Lorraine. Between the Habsburgs and the Romanovs, and in the Balkans, it was mortal. It was for this reason that the rulers eyed each other with suspicion; each believed that his neighbor wanted the territory that was decisive for wealth and power.

In 1914, all the continental powers had immensely detailed mobilization plans — plans for getting troops into uniform and to the frontier. Once started, this mobilization had a further momentum of its own; the act of mobilization signified an intention to fight. And, given the importance of territory, it naturally signaled a preference (and thus an intention) for fighting on someone else's land. Better, if you were the other party, to mobilize, strike first and fight beyond your frontiers. Mobilization in 1914 did not, as is sometimes suggested, make war inevitable. It did provoke the atmosphere of fear and crisis in which rational decision was even less probable.

The Stupidity Problem

There was a final consideration, one that it is always thought a trifle pretentious to stress. Rulers in Germany and Eastern Europe, generals in all countries, held their jobs by right of family and tradition. If inheritance qualifies one for office, intelligence cannot be a requirement. Nor is its absence likely to be a disqualification. On the contrary, intelligence is a threat to those who do not possess it, and there is a strong case, therefore, for excluding those who do possess it. This was the tendency in 1914. In consequence, both the rulers and the generals in World War I were singularly brainless men.

None was capable of thought on what war would mean for his class — for the social order that was so greatly in his favor. There had always been wars Rulers had been obliterated. The ruling classes had always survived. To the extent that there was thought on the social consequences of war, this was what was believed.

The Rogue Reaction

In August 1914, the territorial imperative, the fears it engendered, the threat inherent in mobilization and the stupidity of rulers and generals combined to put the war process out of control. The alliances then made the conflict general. Historians have always spoken of a chain reaction. A chain reaction is predictable, has a known result. One needs a better metaphor. This was a rogue reaction — one with a course no one could foresee, a result no one could foretell.

The Workers

Though the rulers had not given consideration to the social consequences of war and were largely incapable of doing so, the workers had given it great attention. Their leaders were much more capable of thought. Also there was no doubt as to who suffered on the battlefield, who got killed. So for a generation or more before 1914, in trade-union meetings, political meetings and the conferences of the Second International, policy in case of war had been exhaustively discussed. Workers, it was agreed, must unite across national frontiers for their common protection. So united, they could use their parliamentary power to oppose credits — money — for war. And strikes would make mobilization impossible.

If necessary, the final weapon would be employed — the general strike. This was thought to be a truly awesome thing, the ultimate social weapon. All movement of people and things would end, all production would stop, all economic life would come to a halt. War would then be impossible. The warmakers would be defeated by the massed power of their own workers. No one thereafter would doubt the power of the working class.

It didn't happen. When the call to arms came in 1914, the German Social Democrats, the most numerous and best organized of the working-class parties, voted in the Reichstag under what, in the United States, is called the unit rule. The vote was for the war credits. Hugo Haase, their parliamentary leader, opposed the vote in the party caucus. But then, with an admirable sense of party responsibility, he spoke for the majority position in the

Reichstag. "In the hour of danger we will not desert our own Fatherland."[1] The vote was symbolic and not financially decisive, as some historians have supposed. The Imperial German government would not have been stopped by the defeat of an appropriations bill. By September nearly a third of the membership of the Social Democratic Party was in the army.

It was the same in France. The Germans, as any good Frenchman could see, were coming across Belgium. So, *La Patrie*. Prior to 1914, the French government had prepared a comprehensive plan to deal with working-class opposition in the event of war. This provided for the arrest of strike leaders, the mobilization of strikers into the army, a crackdown on public protest. To the undoubted regret of some of its authors, the plan had to be shelved. There was no need.

In Britain, there was no conscription, no plans as on the Continent for mass mobilization. Being on an island, the British had been generally exempt from the anxiety about their frontiers, although in the years before 1914, with the rise of German naval power, alarm had increased. A verse at the time had even celebrated (or undercelebrated) the concern:

> I was playing golf that day
> > When the Germans landed.
> All our soldiers ran away,
> > All our ships were stranded.
> Such were my surprise and shame
> They almost put me off my game.[2]

With war the British workers flocked as volunteers to the recruiting offices, and their leaders affirmed support of the government. The only political opposition was from a handful of socialists and pacifists, the most prominent of whom was Ramsay MacDonald. It was a stalwart act; many think that it cured him of all further such tendency for life.

In St. Petersburg, now suddenly become Petrograd, the Social Democrats in the Duma did abstain from voting and, instead, walked out. But they were few in number, and very soon the militants among them — the Bolsheviks — were arrested and evicted from the chamber. In Russia, unlike Germany, no one supposed that the workers really counted. It was the peasants who mattered, and those who were called marched as a matter of course.

Lenin in Poland

All these events were watched with the most profound interest by Lenin in Cracow. Following jail and a three-year sentence in Siberia, he had been out of Russia (except for short periods during and after 1905) since the beginning of the century. But the Polish police were tolerant, even friendly — Krup-

The war aims were not disguised: It was
for King and country, roughly speaking, the
traditional ruling class and the system.

And they rushed to join.

skaya, Lenin's wife, speaks of them with appreciation. And access to Russia was easy. Revolutionaries came and went across the border, many coming to visit Lenin whose stature as a revolutionary leader was now widely accepted. Though easy, it remained a wonderfully conspiratorial traffic. Once one Muranov, a leading Bolshevik member of the Duma, came to visit Lenin. He had parliamentary immunity so no one could question his right to travel. Nonetheless he made a clandestine crossing. When Lenin rebuked him for doing so, he apologized and explained that it had never occurred to him that one could cross a border legally.

Like Marx, Lenin combined revolutionary action with journalism. *Pravda*, as many will be surprised to know, was then being published in Russia. Lenin was a regular contributor, and Cracow was an excellent place from which to smuggle copy to the paper. Lenin's articles had mostly to do with Russia but he reached out to the literacy rate among American Negroes which, he noted with much indignation, was twice as high as that among Russian peasants. Edward A. Filene, the Boston philanthropist and merchant ("I got it in Filene's basement"), attracted his attention. Filene held that American employers were coming to understand their workers better and that the workers were coming to see the problems of their employers. Both would eventually realize that their interests were in common. "Most esteemed Mr. Filene!," Lenin wrote, "Are you quite sure that the workers of the world are the simpletons you take them for?"[3]

The revolutionaries seeking Lenin in Cracow could often find him at Jama Michalikowa. This, a deep, darkly pleasant café, still exists. It was then a great center of political discussion, and, Poland being Poland, the discussion continues. But in August of 1914, Lenin was not there. He had long believed that capitalist rivalry made war inevitable. But no more than anyone else in those summer months did he think it imminent. So, like any good bourgeois, he was vacationing in the country. He was in the tiny village of Poronin in the Tatra Mountains, not far from the modern Polish ski resort of Zakopane. The house in which he was staying, a singularly beautiful and roomy structure with clean, amber log walls and gleaming wood floors, is now another minor place of socialist pilgrimage.

The True Revolutionary

Lenin was forty-four that summer. Like the other revolutionaries, he was of middle-class origin; his father was a schoolteacher and school superintendent. But revolution ran in the family: Lenin's older brother was hanged while a young student for participating in an amateurish plot to assassinate Alexander III. His mother had gone to St. Petersburg to urge her son to ask for a pardon. This he had refused to do. He was not sorry. An appeal was carried to the Czar, who spoke admiringly of the boy's staunch character. Then, with a thoughtful view of the lesson involved, he allowed the hanging to proceed.

Marx, no one could doubt, was a revolutionary; the free-flowing beard, piercing eye, exceptionally untidy appearance were all in keeping. It may, indeed, be Marx who has given us our mental image of how a revolutionary should look. Far more than Marx, Lenin *was* a revolutionary. Marx wrote; Lenin led. He remains the revolutionary colossus who stands astride a whole age, the point of reference still for the long, slowly moving lines beside the Kremlin Wall. With his high forehead greatly accented by the bald dome above, his neat mustache, dark, quiet suit and something very near a Van Dyck beard, he looked like the head of a firm of chartered accountants. Leon Trotsky, with his fierce and glittering eye and much less disciplined beard, was a man of far more satisfactory aspect.

Once quite a few years ago a Soviet historian visited Harvard. He was an old man and had served in Budenny's cavalry during the Revolution. He had known Lenin well and told with amused pride that Lenin had once paid him a high compliment; he was, Lenin had said, the world's only known case of a cavalryman with brains. I asked him the source of Lenin's leadership — a man so tidy, looking so much like a clerk. He replied: "When Lenin spoke, we marched."

Lenin and Marx

Lenin was the disciple of Marx but not his slave. On several matters he went beyond the master, and two were vital. He believed that the first essential for successful revolutionary action — a point Marx did not emphasize — was a closely knit, intellectually disciplined, utterly committed group of men. Far better such a body than a larger, less reliable, more contentious mass. The aim was ". . . not indiscriminate unity, but unity . . . for the merciless revolutionary struggle of the proletariat against the ruling class."

This belief was further affirmed when the working-class parties of Germany and France voted for the war. They were large, lacking in strong, coherent purpose. Their action led also to a new terminology on which Lenin was insistent. Until then a reference to Social Democrats was a reference to the revolutionary workers' party. Thereafter the truly disciplined cadres, those who were wholly committed to revolution, would be called the Communists.

And, though it is thought reluctantly, Lenin departed from Marx on the role of the peasantry in the revolution. This was an intensely practical matter. Lenin was a Russian; the industrial proletariat in Russia was still small. To wait for a bourgeois revolution in Russia, then for the growth of Russian capitalism and therewith the growth of a large industrial working class, would be to wait forever. Why not enlist the peasants? They were infinitely more numerous. They were also poor, abused, ridiculed, ignored and often, though by no means always, landless. Those who were, believed that, as a matter of ancient right, they owned the land that they tilled for the landlords. They had given up their title only for military protection that was no longer needed. Marx saw capitalism bringing the peasants, many of them, into industry and rescuing them from the "idiocy of rural life." Lenin believed it a far more practical course to win their support by promising them land, and this he did. Once the peasants had their land, they would, no doubt, become conservative property-owners. Another (or continuing) revolution would be necessary to redeem the land for the truly socialist society. That problem could be faced when the time came, as by Stalin it was.

In the end, things went in accordance with Lenin's design. His slogan — peace, bread and land — appealed wonderfully to the peasants in the armies of the Czar. When the revolution came, they were not socialists but they were not hostile. The armies comprising them were not a threat, and soon many were no longer enrolled. The peasant soldiers were voting with their feet, against the war and for the land that, by then, was being taken from the landlords back home.

The Guns of August and the Police

All this was still in the future. For Lenin the guns of August brought more practical problems in the form of the police. Previously, to the Austrians, he had been a useful thorn in the side of the Czar. Now, conceivably, he was a Russian patriot and a spy. So the police came to the house in Poronin, and he was arrested. The arresting officer seized several notebooks containing statistics on the agrarian problem. He thought these might be codes. There was a suggestion, perhaps ironic, that a jar of paste in Lenin's room was probably a bomb. Austro-Hungarian despotism was, as ever, being tempered by casualness, if not incompetence. After a short stay in jail, Lenin and his family were allowed to go to Switzerland, a country where, from earlier years of exile, they were very much at home.

Machine Guns and the Officer Class

Meanwhile the great armies came together, fought, slaughtered each other and then settled into trenches, to come out at intervals to be mowed down again.

The stupidity was showing itself a force of real power in human affairs. In the old social structure, we have seen, it was predictable among rulers and generals and was, in some degree, congenital. So it explained much that happened in World War I. Part of the explanation was the result of a military and technical accident.

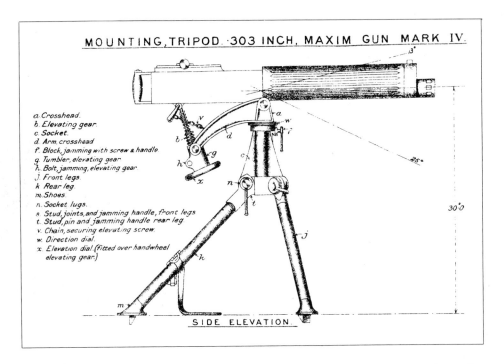

In the years before 1914, military technology had advanced greatly in the matter of small arms ordnance. This was a cheap and easy field for technical innovation; the product was one that the generals could, though with difficulty, understand. The most important result was the machine gun. Two men so equipped were the equal of a hundred, sometimes even a thousand, armed with rifles. At Hyde Park Corner in London there is a memorial to the British machine gunners of the First World War. It has a simple, terrible inscription: "Saul hath slain his thousands; and David his ten thousands."

Supporting this unlimited capacity to kill was the limited capacity for thought. Adaptation of tactics was far beyond the capacity of the contemporary military mind. The hereditary generals and their staffs could think of nothing better than to send increasing numbers of men, erect, under heavy burden, at a slow pace, in broad daylight, against the machine guns after increasingly heavy artillery bombardment. This bombardment the machine guns, enough of them, invariably survived. It did, however, eliminate all element of surprise. So the men who were sent were mowed down, and the mowing, it must be stressed, is no figure of speech. The political leaders, for their part, could think of nothing better than to trust the generals. Thus the continuing, unimaginable slaughter. Those who went to fight in World War I could not expect to come back. If, as Churchill once said, they survived the first hurricane or the second, they would surely be swept away in the third or the fourth.

Switzerland

The Switzerland to which Lenin came was the revolutionary capital of the world. By modern standards it was an almost unbelievably tolerant community. Highly subversive citizens were in residence from every part of the Continent. People whom their own governments wanted elsewhere had unlimited freedom for agitation, and the Russians were an exceptionally large and notoriously articulate band. Geneva landladies had two rates: one for ordinary people who went to bed; another, and higher, rate for Russians who remained up all night arguing.

In Switzerland Lenin lived first in Bern. With him were his wife and mother-in-law. Money was scarce, though small sums came from Russia to help support him, something now hard to believe possible in wartime. His place of work was the library, where his hours were as regular as those of the chartered accountant he resembled. However, he still found it possible to get away to the mountains, and he was greatly pleased to discover that the librarians would mail him the books he needed. Previously in London he had been astonished that the library at the British Museum was run for the public and that the librarians actually regarded themselves as the servants of the readers. (Years later, according to legend, it occurred to someone to ask one of the library attendants if he remembered Lenin. He did, a most diligent little man. The librarian wondered whatever had become of him.) Now the Swiss impressed Lenin as favorably; Krupskaya later recalled that her husband was "lavish of praise for Swiss culture."[4]

The library was the source of the first of the weapons of revolution; this was the tract or pamphlet. Every revolutionary task required one. When Lenin left the library, it was to involve himself with the second instrument of revolution. This was the conference.

The Conferences

Conferences were a very serious business for the revolutionaries. Nothing could be accomplished without one. After a conference everything would be possible. Any new development demanded one. Not even the modern sales executive is more committed to the conference as a way of life than were Lenin and his revolutionary friends.

Conferences need to be understood. Some, of course, are purely recreational. Men and sometimes women gather at the expense of a corporation or a foundation. The purpose is free or tax-paid enjoyment. The justification is the exchange of ideas, and the value of this is fiercely proclaimed. It is very difficult to say in criticism of such a conference that no ideas were exchanged.

Of serious conferences, very few are to exchange information and fewer still are to reach decisions. Most are to proclaim shared purposes, to reveal to the

Trotsky. At the wartime conference at Zimmerwald the revolutionaries were rumored to be bird watchers. The birds looked back at these nature lovers and were amazed.

participants that they are not alone and thus to reinforce confidence. Or they are to simulate action where action is impossible. By occurring, they persuade the participants, and often others, that something is happening when nothing is happening or can happen.

The most ambitious of the wartime conferences was held at Zimmerwald in September 1915, now a few minutes out in the country by car from Bern. Attending were the Left or militant Social Democrats; the avowed purpose, of course, was to settle on a strategy toward the war. This conference was both to simulate action and to prove to the participants that, in a hopeless situation, there might still be hope. Thirty-eight delegates were present from eleven countries. Conspiratorially, they were in top form. They allowed it to be believed that they came as ornithologists, bird watchers. The birds looked back at these nature lovers — Lenin, Trotsky, Zinoviev, Radek — and were amazed.

Lenin's position was as before: workers of different countries were not enemies. All had enemies in common — the Czar, the other rulers, the capitalists. Let the workers turn the guns on these enemies, not on each other. He argued his case for a manifesto along these lines with force and eloquence but without success. Only a handful supported him. National feeling was strong even among the militants. There was also some simple pacifism. And, most of all, the delegates had to be cautious. Ornithologists or not, they had to go home again. As in 1914, Lenin found himself isolated, marching almost alone. The conference did little for his morale. He returned to Bern and the library, by his wife's account much irritated.

Imperialism and Capitalism

He turned back to the first revolutionary weapon. If the conference had been a failure, the tract on which he now worked was destined to be a thing of power. It set forth his theory of imperialism — *Imperialism: the Highest Stage of Capitalism*. It was published only after his return to Russia in 1917.

Not even a committed disciple could think it an impressive document, although many have risen to the challenge. It is assertive and contentious, and, though short, it is very tedious. Nor is it original. As Lenin fully concedes, it draws heavily on the ideas of J. A. Hobson, the most original of English socialists and social reformers.

But *Imperialism* filled an enormous gap in revolutionary thought and policy. More than half a century earlier, Marx had predicted the progressive immiseration of the workers — his phrase. From their desperation and the internal contradictions and consequent weakening of the system would come the overthrow of capitalism. This was not a remote contingency as Marx saw it. It was imminent. In the fifty years following, capitalism had grown stronger; workers, as Lenin was far too realistic to deny, were less revolutionary than fifty years before. This he now explained. Capitalism had gone on to a new stage. In this stage colonies were important not as markets, as Marxian orthodoxy held, but as an outlet for investment and for the resulting development. This colonial investment and development had given European and American capitalism new strength, new staying power. It had also rewarded the workers in the capitalist countries and made it possible, in Lenin's words, for the capitalists "to bribe the labour leaders and the upper stratum of the labour aristocracy."[5] So bribed, workers were then no longer militant. Instead they rode comfortably on the backs of their Asian, African and Latin American comrades.

However, it would not last. This investment had given capitalism only a brief parole. The world was running out of new colonial territory. The war now going on reflected the desperate need of each capitalist country for more such land. Thus would Marx be redeemed. Meanwhile the wartime behavior of the working-class leaders — opportunists Lenin called them — was explained. There was another, even greater consequence.

Marx had thought revolution only an issue for the advanced industrial countries of the West. Others had first to industrialize and develop a proletariat. Then and then only would the idea of revolution become relevant. Imperialism and associated industrial development helped bring the day of revolution nearer in the colonial world. This was why, for Marx, the British in India were a progressive force.

Lenin, in contrast, made revolution as urgent for industrially backward countries as for the advanced — as necessary for the Chinese, Indians, Africans and the other people of what is now the Third World as for Europeans and Americans. The blame for the poverty of the poor countries lay with the rich. Only by revolution could the poor countries get both the capitalists and the workers of the advanced countries off their backs. Lenin took the revolution to Russia. But he also sent it on to China.

The Supreme Test

I've run ahead of the story. Back in Switzerland, the socialists once again convened one of their conferences. This one was in the spring of 1916 at Kienthal. The slaughter, West and East, was by now having some effect — twelve instead of eight delegates now went with Lenin. The resulting manifesto, though still careful, held that it would be "impossible to establish lasting peace on the basis of capitalist society . . . the struggle for a lasting peace can only be a struggle for the realisation of socialism."[6] To prove that the caution had been in order at these conferences, three German officers and thirty-two privates were shot in the following month for distributing copies of these sentiments in the trenches.

This was brutal but hardly essential. For the war in the West was showing not the weakness of the coalition of capitalists and the old ruling classes in its power to command the masses; it was showing its almost incredible strength. It was showing that it could command millions to their death with scarcely a murmur, more often than not with enthusiasm.

On D-day in 1944, the great decisive day of that war in the West, 2491 American, British and Canadian soldiers were killed. On July 1, 1916, on the first day of the Battle of the Somme — but one day in one battle — 19,240 British soldiers were killed or died of wounds. To liberate France in 1944 cost all of the Allied armies around 40,000 dead. For a gain of under six miles on the Somme in 1916, British and French deaths were an estimated 145,000. The Battle of the Somme was partly to relieve pressure on Verdun — a disputed point. At Verdun, within that same year, 270,000 French and German soldiers were killed.

No battlefield of World War II, unless it be in Russia, much recalls the horrors of that war. There are dozens a few hours from Paris that overwhelm one with the tragedy of World War I. One of the most compelling is a three-quarter-hour drive south from Arras, a similar distance west from Amiens. It is only a few hundred acres; sheep move across it as over any pasture. It is called Newfoundland Park. It was the scene of one of the most luminous acts of cruelty of the entire struggle.

On the first day of the Somme, from trenches and over shell holes that you still can see, the First Newfoundland Regiment attacked, against the German machine guns and artillery and against barbed wire that was largely intact. The Germans beyond were admirably sheltered in a deep natural ravine served by a railroad. They had been amply warned by the preparations and the premature explosion of a large mine near their lines. (They promptly occupied the crater.) Because the attack had been programmed to succeed quickly, there was not only no surprise but this time no artillery support. Within forty minutes, 658 men and 26 officers were dead, wounded or missing. That was 91 percent of the entire attacking force. All the officers were casualties. The survivors were then calmly ordered to regroup and attack again. The order was rescinded only when the higher command discovered there were almost none. The signs on the battlefield say "Newfoundland Lines," "German Lines." The result was much as though the Crown Colony of Newfoundland had made war on the whole German Empire.

In such fashion was the system tested. Nor was there any effort, initially at least, to disguise the nature of the war. It was for King and country, roughly speaking for the rulers and the system. The men were not told that they were fighting for their livelihood or their liberty; they were responding, in a personal way, to the bad character and outrageous ambition of the Kaiser. Not

Further to remind the men for whom they were fighting, the traditional rulers showed up on a quiet day: George V.

The Kaiser.

until the United States entered the war did our superior capacity for finding moral justification assert itself. It then became a war to make the world safe for democracy.

Further to remind the men for whom they were fighting, the traditional rulers or their offspring showed up in the trenches from time to time on a quiet day. They were always elegantly caparisoned and suitably attended. On occasion, on the German side, duckboards were put down so that boots would not be soiled by old blood. It was accepted that men would be led or sent to their death by officers who held that rank because of superior birth and social position.

The men accepted without seeming complaint the current concept of heroism. This was a matter not of courage but of rank. The greatest heroes were Hindenburg, Haig, Foch, Pétain and King Albert of the Belgians. The ruling classes, above a certain level, could be both very brave and very safe.

Most important, the system best withstood this awful test where the capitalist power was strongest. The British Dominions were the leading example of the bourgeois as opposed to the traditional power. The relatively well-educated and literate soldiers of these countries most willingly accepted their own death. As fighters, the Canadians, Australians and New Zealanders had an especially high reputation. But the soldiers of the older capitalist countries also fought well. The industrial proletariat of Germany and England was highly reliable, a hard fact for Lenin.

In contrast, the peasants were, on the whole, much less amenable. In 1917, following the Nivelle offensive, the predominantly peasant French soldiers showed signs of objecting to their mass immolation and associated mistreatment. It was touch and go for a time before the mutiny was contained. The backward peasants of Austria-Hungary showed even less enthusiasm for being killed. As might be expected, the national minorities were also unenthusiastic, and the Ruthenians and later the Czechs showed their excellent discipline by marching over to the enemy not as individuals but in units. And the most illiterate and backward of all the armies, the one from the country where capitalism was least advanced, was the one that quit. That was the army of the Czar.

Revolution

On January 22, 1917, Lenin spoke to a gathering of youthful revolutionaries at the Volkhaus in Zurich. This venerable gathering place still serves its old purpose. When I visited it one Sunday morning in 1975, Italian Communist workers employed in Switzerland were having a meeting. It seemed a rather subdued convocation. At his meeting Lenin assessed the prospect. Of the eventual triumph of the proletariat he had no doubt. But he had been in exile now for more than a decade; it was two and half years since he had been expelled from Poland. Years of waiting. Wasted years? He concluded his speech — his wife said sadly — with the thought: "We of the older generation may not live to see the decisive battles of this coming revolution."[7]

He was wrong. One day only a few weeks later, Lenin and Krupskaya had just finished lunch at 14 Spiegelgasse in Zurich, a house that still survives. A comrade called in with what seemed rather important news. Special editions were on the streets; apparently there was some kind of revolution in Russia. Lenin and Krupskaya hurried out and down to the lake where the papers were posted on the wall and could be read free. It was true.

The moment of all moments had come, and he was in Switzerland — Switzerland of all places. And with him were his most reliable collaborators, the very best of the revolutionaries. Who could lead a revolution from Spiegelgasse, a thoroughfare later more celebrated as the home of Dadaism?

In the next days Lenin was desperate. How could he, and they, get to Russia? An airplane? That was mentioned, though in those days only as an idle dream. Out through France? The French would not think Lenin a helpful influence in Petrograd. They would arrest him forthwith. He could not lead a revolution from a French jail. To go through Germany would be to risk the suspicion, when he arrived in Russia, that he was a German agent. Still, that was the only chance. The German view of Lenin's contribution to the Russian war effort, which was surprisingly sophisticated, was the same as that of the French but it led to the opposite conclusion. How good to have Lenin in Russia.

With, one must believe, a good deal of initiative and skill, a Swiss socialist, Fritz Platten, made an arrangement: Lenin would go through Germany. But it would be on an extraterritorial or non-German train. The concept of an extraterritorial train passing over the German railroads proved too difficult for the average later historian, and from this came the reference to a *sealed* train. And eventually it came to be imagined that the Germans had sealed Lenin up because they wanted protection from the Bolshevik infection. They weren't that troubled. It was Lenin who wanted to minimize his exposure to the Germans.

About twenty of Lenin's fellow Bolsheviks were on the train. There was a child or two, and also Inessa Armand, a sharply beautiful, French-born revolutionary and a close friend, brilliant collaborator and possibly — it does not seem important — a mistress of Lenin's. The journey was not a very festive excursion. Lenin was deeply worried about his reception in Russia. After all, Germany and Russia were still at war. He might not even be allowed in. He was, although Fritz Platten was excluded as a foreigner. On April 3, 1917 (according to the Russian calendar), he arrived at the Finland Station in Petrograd. In October he took power.

Lenin, Krupskaya and party in Stockholm on the way home.

Moscow, May 1919. Lenin's great achievement was not the Revolution but in conquering the resulting anarchy.

Again the Rotten Door

Not everything had gone smoothly. A few weeks after arriving in Petrograd, Lenin was back in Finland, in hiding. But in the end his disciplined political followers, the tiny Russian proletariat in Petrograd, their allies among the soldiers and sailors, together with the Anarchists and the Left Social Revolutionaries, served him well. There was much motion, much oratory but little bloodshed. Again revolution was the kicking in of a rotten door.

The Czarist regime had been more incompetent than even the selection of talent by class and caste would have led one to expect. Its generals, with notable exceptions, were the supreme example of promotion by family, social position and personal style — men who made Haig and Pétain seem cerebral. So the regime had sunk under its own inadequacy. And so did the government, if such it could be called, that succeeded it. One of the notable historians of the period is Adam Ulam, my Harvard friend and colleague. Soviet scholars concede the worth of his work on Lenin, although communism is a faith the author does not much admire. Ulam holds that Lenin's achievement was not in taking power; power was there for the taking. As early as July, workers and soldiers had demonstrated to urge the Petrograd Soviet to seize the government. One worker with a gift for a phrase had — it is said — shouted to a leader: "Take power, you son of a bitch, when it's given to you."[8] Lenin's great achievement was in keeping and in consolidating power, in proceeding from anarchy and civil war to unresisted authority in the next five years.

The View from Turin

Lenin's failure was in not seeing how great would be the further task of building a socialist economy, how complex would be the problems of socialist planning and management. "Accounting and control — that is *mainly* what is needed for the 'smooth working', for the proper functioning, of the *first phase* of communist society," he had written.[9] End capitalism and what remained would be a job for clerks. Among socialists to this day there remains the view that, after capitalism goes, faith will do all. The awakening is always unpleasant.

Lenin lived to reflect on his miscalculation. "Maybe our apparatus is pretty bad . . . the first steam engine invented was bad too."[10] He was astonished and depressed at how bureaucratic socialist management quickly became. The problem ". . . absorbed more and more of his energy and filled him with increasing anguish."[11] It continued to oppress him until his stroke in 1922 and his death a year later. Eventually, in industry, there would be no small success.

The peasants, whom Lenin had made part of the revolution, were its greater nemesis. After 1929, as the script required, farms were collectivized, private property in land effectively abolished. That was half a century ago. To have responsibility for agriculture is still to have the most perilous post in the Soviet administration. It was the failure here that cost Khrushchev his job. In more recent times the shortcomings of Soviet agriculture have been one of the most important factors in capitalist living costs. When the Russian grain buyers arrive, prices go up and up.

It could be that land is tilled well only by men and women who are encouraged by high prices and dissuaded by low prices, who reap the rewards of their toil, suffer the penalties of their own sloth, who exploit themselves with long hours and little sleep. The other socialist countries — Poland, Yugoslavia, Hungary — have made concessions to this necessity. So, in smaller measure, has the Soviet Union, where a surprising proportion of marketable production comes from privately owned plots of land. Where agriculture (and other small-scale enterprise) is concerned, there is a perceptible convergence, East or West, that accepts the rule of the market.

From Turin, Italy, home of the vast Fiat works, one perceives another convergent tendency. Large-scale production under socialism, no less than under capitalism, requires large business enterprises, and these must have intelligent, careful, disciplined management. Peter Kapitza, the great Soviet scientist, once said, on a visit to Harvard, that automobiles were not part of the "instinct" of the Russian people. However that may be, the Soviet authorities some years ago sought the assistance of Fiat in developing and improving their automobile industry. In consequence, broadly similar equipment and assembly lines are now used to make a similar car in Turin and Togliattigrad. The two plants are among the five largest in the world. The organization is similar. So are the tests of performance — the cost of production and the profit made. We see from this case how universal is the modern business firm. If in agriculture there is convergence on the market, for large-scale production modern capitalism and modern Communism converge on the business corporation.

There is another similarity between the Turin plant and its Soviet counterpart. In Turin a good many of the workers are Communists. So, it must be assumed, are those in Russia. But here the parallel ends. The Italian Communists no longer look forward to the day when, as triumphant revolutionaries, they will take over the government and have a monopoly of power in Rome. The growth of the modern corporation is a prime cause. It develops a huge administrative, technical, scientific apparatus. It has a penumbra of smaller firms that supply it with materials, parts, legal and advertising services, and that sell, and sometimes repair, its products. It is regulated and assisted by a huge state bureaucracy. Its talent is provided by a big educational establishment. Not only are the people so required numerous,

Fiat in Turin.

Its counterpart in Togliattigrad.

they are not disposed to surrender power to the proletariat. And the proletariat, now submerged in this huge army of technical, administrative, white-collar personnel, acknowledges the reality. The Italian Communists were, in fact, the first to do so.

This, of course, Lenin did not foresee. His first reaction, if he came now to Italy, would surely be adverse — another cop–out, as by the German workers when they voted with the bourgeois parties for the war credits in 1914. But Lenin was also a very practical politician, as we have seen. He would have perceived how power, since his time, has been diffused to new groups and the impossibility of its being seized and monopolized by one. There might well have been another pamphlet. The dictatorship of the proletariat, he would have conceded, had surrendered like so much else to the tyranny of circumstance.

The Western Contrast

In the West the war ended, Germany was defeated but the glue seemed to hold. In Germany Friedrich Ebert, a Social Democrat, became President. Rosa Luxembourg and Karl Liebknecht led a militant minority whose view of revolution was as Lenin's. But the moderate opposition in Germany, the counterpart of the Mensheviks, was far stronger than in Russia. Gustav Noske, a Social Democrat, became Minister of Defense and put down their revolt. Luxembourg and Liebknecht were both killed by anti-Communists. But in the Western countries too, the United States partly excepted, there was a quiet revolution, one that deserves the name.

In all European countries the old coalition of capitalists and traditional rulers was at an end. There would still be a ruling coalition; it would be of business interests, large and small, and the trade unions and their parties. Sometimes these joined in power. More often they traded it back and forth, increasingly sharing it with yet other groups. So it was in Britain, France and the British Dominions. And so, with the passage of time, it would be in the United States. It was a prospect that Marx did not foresee.

The new ruling coalition of capitalists and workers (and others) lacked the certainties of the old; it had none of the old sense of a natural right to rule. The partners eyed each other with dislike, sometimes with suspicion. They didn't follow Marx but they remembered that he had said they were meant to be enemies. And eventually Italy and Germany would seem to bear out Marx's warning. Blackshirts and Brownshirts, with the active or tacit backing of industrialists, would seize power. One saw thereafter what happened to workers, unions and their political parties. But then in Britain, the United States and the British Dominions capitalists and workers would come together in unparalleled harmony with enormous power to put down fascism. And they

The two who failed:
Rosa Luxembourg.

Karl Liebknecht.

would fight side by side with the Soviet Union to do so. Another problem for Marx and Lenin. More things unglued.

A Recollection

The change brought by World War I went far afield. In the years following, I was a youngster in southwestern Ontario. My father was actively concerned in politics. He had been opposed to the war, although his opposition by modern standards took a distinctly nonviolent form. He was the dominant influence on the local draft board, as it would now be called. The board then granted exemptions on the basis of one grave necessity or another to nearly all who did not wish to die. The Scotch who made up the farm community of the area were not strongly so inclined. My father's position and action were open to some patriotic rebuke. But after 1918, his position quickly became the approved one. Decades later, in the early sixties, I found myself in opposition to the Vietnam intervention at a time when the conflict was generally considered wise and essential. I have no natural preference for unpopular, highly criticized positions. I disliked being excluded from foreign policy discussion — I was then in the government — because I took an unrealistic line. I comforted myself, though not much, by recalling the speed with which the reaction to my father's position had changed.

It changed because even in rural Ontario the revolution had echoes. Canada too, in a primitive way, had had a traditional ruling class. It was conservative, English, with a prestige and influence that came from its Englishness, its identification with the King, Empire and the Church of England, and its feeling that it had a natural claim on positions of power and reward under the Crown. In the nineteenth century people had spoken freely of the monopoly of high position so enjoyed. It was called the Family Compact.

The Canadian ruling class had also invested its prestige heavily in the war. And as Canadians now reflected on what had been gained and at what price, and especially on the mindless emotion and propaganda that had sustained the slaughter, that prestige evaporated like the morning mist. What had been an influential if amorphous aristocracy became an anachronism. The leader of the Canadian forces in Europe, General Sir Arthur W. Currie, had returned home to great acclaim. Soon he was in a courtroom in a libel case to defend himself against the accusation that he had caused unnecessary casualties among the troops he led. He was held to have kept them advancing when it was known the war was over. Canadian farmers now asserted their political power. So, though less visibly, did workers. So did French Canada, which made it clear that its sons would never again be conscripted for a European war. My elders did not doubt, even in those distant precincts, that something very important had happened to power.

Thus the beginning of the Age of Uncertainty. Its character derived ultimately from the new social alignments, the new governing coalition that now emerged. But there was an effect on the narrower questions of economics. A notable case was money. In the years before 1914, that had been one of the great certainties of life. It was good and eternal. After 1914, it was never the same again. It is worth a special look.

6.
The Rise
and Fall of Money

Money is a singular thing.° It ranks with love as man's greatest source of joy.
And it ranks with death as his greatest source of anxiety. Over all history it has
oppressed nearly all people in one of two ways: either it has been abundant
and very unreliable, or reliable and very scarce. However, for many there has
been a third affliction: for them money has been both unreliable and scarce.

For studying the full range of human emotion, the next best thing to the
psychiatrist's couch is, perhaps, the modern supermarket. It could be why the
modern politician goes there to solicit votes. People entering or emerging from
a supermarket are in the grip of their most common fears, are deeply sensitive,
accordingly, to the political issues that bear upon this anxiety. In times of
depression or recession they are wondering if their money will continue, if
they will have any to spend the next time they push a cart. In times of boom
and inflation they are asking themselves if next time there will be anything to
buy that they can still afford.

In recent years this last worry has been the worst. It is the special terror of
the person whose days of work are over, whose income for the rest of life is
given and will never, by any magic, increase. What if that money ceases to buy
enough to sustain life or, what may be equally important, to maintain accustomed respectability? But there is equally the anxiety of the person who does
not know whether next week's purchases will be supported by a job. Is a layoff
in prospect? How long will the unemployment last? How will I, or we, get by?

The anxiety in the supermarket has its focus on money. It is one of the great
uncertainties of life. It has been so for a long time. More than most things, an
understanding of money requires an appreciation of its history. What was
once simple has become complex. But if we see how money has evolved — if
we take the complexities one by one as they were added by its history — an

° In 1973, when the BBC series on *The Age of Uncertainty* was being planned, I prepared a
memorandum on the subject of money for the guidance of my colleagues in the enterprise. In
the process of amplification and revision it became a rather lengthy book and was published as
such in 1975. (*Money: Whence It Came, Where It Went.* Boston: Houghton Mifflin, and
London: André Deutsch.) There are echoes of the book in the pages following. Anyone who has
read it can, with the very best conscience, omit this chapter and, though less conscientiously, the
next.

"In the supermarket people are in the grip of their greatest fear. Will my money last?"
Politicians come to exploit or reassure.

understanding of the final result is not so difficult. We see with fair ease the uncertainties of which it is the focus.

The Origins

Money has been an everyday fact of life for at least 2500 years. Herodotus, more or less as an afterthought and with a nice juxtaposition of concepts, tells of the invention of coined money in Asia Minor:

All of the young women of Lydia prostitute themselves, by which they procure their marriage portion . . . The manners and customs of the Lydians do not essentially vary from those of Greece, except in this prostitution of the young women. They are the first people on record who coined gold and silver into money, and traded in retail.[1]

It seems certain that there were much earlier experiences with coinage in the Indus Valley and China of which Herodotus was unaware.

For the next many centuries, a few brief episodes apart, no one receiving coined money could be quite sure what he or she was getting; few inventions ever lent themselves more profitably to abuse. The coin might be of its proclaimed weight of gold and silver. It might be less. It might have a lesser metal melted in. Banks and governments made promises to pay such coin as a substitute for money, and the promises then became money. Abuse of these promises was one of the few inventions more profitable than mistreating coins. The measure of the abuse was the grave uncertainty on the part of the recipient as to what he was getting and the counterpart uncertainty as to what that money would buy.

Then, in the last century, money became reliable. The major problems of its mismanagement seemed solved. What now became uncertain was the opportunity for earning it; jobs, farm prices, the earnings of the small businessman were anything but secure.

It was World War I that showed that the new reliability of money was an illusion. Along with the old political systems monetary stability also came unglued. There would be greater uncertainty than ever about getting money. And there would again be uncertainty as to what it would buy.

Most of us, whether we admit it or not, live with a linear view of history. We think that, over a long enough span of time, men learn, things improve. The history of money gives no support for this optimism.

The Function

Though one begins the history of money with the invention of coinage — the stamping or minting of pieces of metal of a specific (claimed) weight and quality — this is quite arbitrary. Cattle, shells, chunks of metal, whiskey, tobacco have also been used. They perform the essential function of money,

Every monetary innovation contains the seeds of its own abuse: Coinage eliminated weighing . . .

which is to avoid the awkwardness of barter — the natural difficulty of finding someone who wishes to trade cattle or whiskey directly for a house. What serves as money need only be durable, reasonably uniform and evident as to quality. It can then be held for a time and will be generally acceptable to buyers and sellers. Given these qualities, almost anything will serve as an intermediate stage in transactions. In nonpastoral societies it is also helpful if it can be carried or kept around the house. Coins came into use because they were durable, improved on chunks or sacks of gold and silver by being in predetermined amounts, and could be carried in a purse. Scales for weighing the metal were no longer needed, at least in the comparatively rare instances where the weight of the coins could be trusted.

Coins, although not many have noticed it, are now obsolescent. They no longer figure in major transactions. They survive only as minor change, for occasional nervous hoarding, as collectors' items and as an adjunct to slot machines. They are only an attenuated reminder, a souvenir, of what was once all money.

Banks and Money

After coins came banks. They flourished in Roman times, reached a high level of development in Venice, Florence and Genoa. With banks came the power,

164

. . . Coins were then debased, so back to weighing.

given to few private citizens, to create money. It may be why bankers are so solemn. A certain responsibility is involved. For a full view of banks and money the city to visit is Amsterdam. It is associated with not one but two of the great developments in their history.

In 1609, money — hard, coined money — was, as money goes, abundant in Amsterdam. Mostly it was silver, an important point. Through most of history silver, not gold, was the primary metal for coinage. That Judas got silver for Jesus does not mean there was anything derogatory about the payment; only that it was, for the time, a normal commercial transaction. Following the voyages of Columbus, silver mines of unparalleled richness had been discovered in the New World, principally in Mexico. In the sixteenth century this metal flooded into Europe to demonstrate one of the fundamental propositions regarding money: the more abundant the money, *everything else equal*, the less it will buy. As silver became abundant, prices are believed to have risen almost everywhere in Europe. A good many people who hadn't heard about the discovery of America saw its effects in the price of whatever trifle they had to buy.

Though silver and silver coins were abundant, another firm proposition concerning money was also demonstrated in these years. However much they have, people feel they can do with more of it. So everywhere in Europe men were taking the coins and sweating and clipping them, thereby getting metal to make more of them. In 1606, the Dutch Parliament had issued a manual for money changers. It listed 846 silver and gold coins, many of them appallingly deficient in weight and purity. Such was the state of abuse that no one, when he sold goods for money, could be sure what he was getting. It was to this problem of quality that the merchants of Amsterdam now addressed themselves. They created a bank owned by the city; the bank solved the problem of the quality of the coins by going back to the system that antedated the invention of coinage. That was weighing.

In this action the town fathers pioneered the idea of public regulation of the money supply by a public bank. A merchant brought his good and wretched coins to the bank, the bank weighed them, and the weight of the pure metal was then credited to his account. This deposit was a highly reliable form of money. A merchant could transfer it to the account of another merchant. The recipient knew that he was getting honest weight, nothing funny. Payments through the bank commanded a premium.

Then came the second Amsterdam discovery, although the principle was known elsewhere. The deposits so created did not need to be left idly in the bank. They could be lent. The bank then got interest. The borrower then had a deposit that *he* could spend. But the original deposit still stood to the credit of the original depositor. That too could be spent. Money, spendable money, had been created. Let no one rub his or her eyes. It's still being done — every day. The creation of money by a bank is as simple as this, so simple, I've often said, that the mind is slightly repelled.

The important thing, obviously, is that the original depositor and the borrower must never come at the same time for their deposits — their money. They must trust their bank. They must trust it to the extent of believing it isn't doing what it does as a matter of course. That is the thin edge on which creation of money by a bank always rests.

The Amsterdam Scene

In the first hundred years after the founding of the bank, the city of Amsterdam grew wonderfully; the population and area greatly expanded. The arts — painting and music — flourished. After 1631, the city had a fair claim to being considered the center of the whole art world, for it was in that year that Rembrandt moved there from Leyden. The Merchant City, as we shall later see, was a place of great good taste. Amsterdam, the most eminent merchant city of its age, is very good evidence for the case. Many houses from this time survive. Some are still in the possession of the same families. One, that of the merchant Jan Six, is as lovely as any in Europe. Among the forty-odd paintings by Dutch masters still in the possession of the family are no fewer than three by Rembrandt. Rembrandt was a friend, and his name is prominent in the guest book of the time.

It is tempting to attribute the prosperity of Amsterdam and the consequent flowering of the artistic spirit to the excellence and stability of its financial institutions and particularly to the Bank of Amsterdam. Bankers would applaud; David Rockefeller would be especially pleased. There were other factors.

Amsterdam was admirably situated on what, with some canal-digging, became one of the outlets of the Rhine. It was, like all successful merchant cities, a tolerant place; men who wanted to make money could do business here regardless of race, creed or national origin. Much of Amsterdam's prosperity was the achievement of its large settlement of Huguenots and Portuguese and Spanish Jews. The city had a reputation for doing business with anyone who wished to do business, including, on occasion, those who might be fighting the Dutch. But, unquestionably, the Bank helped.

I should complete its story. As will now be evident, every monetary innovation or reform carries the seeds of some new abuse. So it was here. One of the important borrowers from the Bank was the Dutch East India Company. The members of the Company were often the same men who ran the Bank. With the passage of time, lending and borrowing became incestuous, even narcissistic. Nothing is new; the failure of the Franklin National Bank in New

Amsterdam.

Jan Six by Rembrandt. Triumphant meeting of economics with art.

York in the nineteen-seventies, the London and County in the same years in England, was partly the result of bankers lending to business firms which they greatly admired and trusted because they were their own. In the eighteenth century the East India Company fell on hard times; there was war with England, ships did not come back. It was slow pay at first, and then its loans went into default. The making of loans and the creation of money by a bank, to repeat, is only possible if depositors do not come all at once for their money. If they suspect that they can't get their money, they will surely come. Suspected weakness ensures weakness.

Early in the last century suspicion spread, the weakness was affirmed. The depositors started coming, and they couldn't be paid. In 1819, after two centuries of service, the Bank of Amsterdam was wound up. By then, however, there had been a far more spectacular demonstration of how a bank can create money and how this ability can be abused.

Paris, 1719

Louis XIV died in 1715. His legacy to France was great and varied, and it included two major misfortunes. One was the French Treasury which was bankrupt; the other was the Regent, the Duc d'Orléans, who was intellectually and morally bankrupt. The result was the seemingly hopeless situation that gives opportunity to a rascal, someone who promises by magic or legerdemain to put everything right. Men who are desperate for a solution are easy to persuade because they wish desperately to be persuaded. The Duc d'Orléans was an especially easy case.

The available rascal we have already encountered. He was John Law, and to this day some historians regret the word rascal. Perhaps he was a genius who got carried away by his own achievements.

He had a background in financial matters. His father was a well-to-do Edinburgh goldsmith. In that time goldsmiths, since they had to have good strongboxes, stored valuables and coins for other people, and by this service had become bankers. On the Continent Law was engaged in selling an idea for a new kind of bank, the deposits of which would be secured by land rather than by silver or gold. He was also avoiding English justice; he had been unduly successful in a duel.

In Paris in 1716, he got permission from the Regent to establish a bank, the Banque Royale. As part of the bargain the bank took over the debts of the Regent and of the realm. These debts were then paid off with notes of the bank, promises by the bank to pay off the face value to the holders in silver or gold. It is not hard to see how the Regent was persuaded.

Then in 1717, Law organized the Company of the West, later the Company of the Indies but known ever afterward as the Mississippi Company. There

John Law at High Noon. Dictator of French finance and Duc d'Arkansas.

was no doubt as to its assets; potentially they were greater than those of any company before or since. It held absolute title to all land north from the Gulf of Mexico to Minnesota and east from the Rockies to the Alleghenies.

This spacious endowment served Law's purposes in two ways. The notes that his bank was issuing were backed, as noted, by gold and silver. The needs of the Regent being large, so was the issue of notes. By no stretch of the imagination was there enough gold and silver in France to redeem the notes, so the imagination of the note-holders was stretched to include Louisiana. There, it was said, gold and silver were in unlimited supply. As I've told in an earlier chapter, maps of the period showed the mines, although no one has seen them since. The nonexistent metal in the imaginary mines was the backing for the notes.

But Parisians were by now in a trusting mood. Hearing of these conceptual riches and that colonization was under way to get them, they rushed to buy the stock of the Company of the West. The stock boomed. Law helped the price along by sundry forms of thimblerigging and fiduciary levitation. In a strong market some well-timed purchases of stock, in combination with some suitably reckless promises, will send up prices and attract the buyers who will send them up much more. By 1719, the boom had become a wild speculation. The price of the stock went up, sometimes by the hour. The old Paris Bourse was outdoors in the Rue Quincampoix. The excitement was intense and even violent, and the noise was hideous. Crowds swarmed also to the Place Vendôme, to Law's headquarters. Some hoped only to catch a glimpse of him; some, on one pretext or another, tried to get inside. Those who got inside asked Law to sell them stock. Women investors, the histories tell, offered themselves as an added inducement. This must have been an unprecedented experience for someone from Scotland.

The year 1719 in Paris was truly a wonderful time. Law's notes went out by the hundreds of millions. Government creditors who were paid off in the notes then rushed to buy stock in the Banque Royale or in the Mississippi Company. From the money so invested more could be lent to the government, yet more notes could go out and yet more stock could be sold. It was a complete closed-circle system for recycling worthless paper. In consequence, all involved were getting rich — on or in paper. It is to that year that we owe the useful French word "millionaire."

In 1719, John Law was the most famous man in all France. He was ennobled as the Duc d'Arkansas, a title not revived in later years even by Congressman Wilbur Mills. On January 5, 1720, he was made Comptroller General of France, the supreme arbiter of all French finances.

There was no way to go but down, and presently this became evident. Doubts began to develop about the notes. So people started bringing them to

The collapse of Law: Dragoons regulate the frenzy.

A London comment after Law's fall. The English, as always, found pleasure in the foolishness and caprice of the French.

the Banque Royale for the silver and gold that were still in Louisiana, and also not there. The Prince de Conti sent three wagons to carry back the gold to which his notes entitled him. Paying off the notes in gold and silver was suspended; in modern terms, the Banque Royale went off the gold (and silver) standard. And, in a further, rather severe step, ownership of precious metals except in small quantities was made a crime. But nothing could disguise the elementary fact that the Banque Royale could not pay, that the notes were now worthless. Law only narrowly escaped from Paris with his life. Parisians got what pleasure they could from a song that recommended that the paper be put to the most vulgar possible use.

Law's colonization and gold mining had not been attractive to the average Parisian. Press gangs, accordingly, had been sent out to round up sundry vagabonds and even reputable citizens who were not sufficiently aware of their opportunities abroad. There was a special need for wives and a special effort to recruit what were then called women of medium virtue. Paris, in my youth, was considered a place of imaginative wickedness, a reputation long ago lost to Amsterdam, Copenhagen and Times Square. But there are still links with the past. The Rue Quincampoix is today a minor resort of women of medium virtue.

Though the end was unhappy, something was accomplished. Like the deposits in Amsterdam, Law's notes were money created by a bank. This money got the Regent out of a tight spot, encouraged colonization and made France prosperous, at least for a while. Law — a somewhat neglected point — had directed a substantial amount into canal building and other useful public works. Issued in excess, the notes clearly were a disaster. Used in moderation, might they not do good? That, now, the British were to prove.

The Bank of England

Some of the most interesting observations on John Law we owe to the Duc de Saint-Simon, the relentless chronicler of life at Versailles and in Paris during the reign of Louis XIV and after. He thought Law's bank was a good idea for any country but France. The French, he said, lacked restraint.

There is much to his case. Twenty years earlier, a fellow countryman of Law's, one William Paterson — on money, as on political economy, the early pre-eminence of the Scotch is unchallenged — had sold essentially the same idea as the Banque Royale to William of Orange. William too needed money; his debts came not from succeeding Louis but from fighting him. In 1694, the Bank of England was formed; its founders subscribed the money the King needed. In return, they were given the right to make loans to others with newly issued notes backed by the King's promise to pay. Paterson soon left, most likely, it now seems, over a conflict of interest. He was promoting a rival

Bic vos. non vobis.

William Paterson, 1658–1719. Founder of the Bank of England.

bank. A few years later Scotchmen were seized with the notion that vast fortunes could be made by founding a colony (Darien) near what is now the Isthmus of Panama. It was thought, rightly, to be a strategic location. Few survived the climate and the fever. Paterson was the leading promoter of the Darien adventure. He lost his wife and children there and barely escaped with his own life.

But Paterson's bank survived and flourished, and no financial institution before or since has had such prestige. To be a member of its Court of Directors still suggests grave financial wisdom and ominous economic power. The power can be questioned. Outside directors are not told of important decisions until after they are taken. This ensures against conflict of interest, a matter on which the Bank is still vigilant. It does reduce appreciably a man's impact on the decision.

The glow extends across the seas, continues down through the generations. In the United States in past years, the Federal Reserve Board has regularly been used by American presidents as a place of deposit for men who could not reliably be trusted to balance their own checkbooks. Once in office, they are addressed with reverence as Governor and dispense deeply ambiguous judgments on the economic and financial prospect, which susceptible journalists, bankers and economists treat with the utmost respect. However illiterate, economically or otherwise, they are sustained by the reputation of the Bank of England.

In the early years of the eighteenth century the Bank was saved from a principal role in the South Sea Bubble because the South Sea Company outbid it in recklessness. Later it was thought far too generous in its loans to Pitt for the wars against Napoleon. David Ricardo held this view, although neither Ricardo nor his fellow critics offered any better ideas about where to raise the money. But, in time, the Bank became an accomplished instrument for regulating the creation of money by lesser banks — in placing limits on lending and consequent deposit expansion and note issue. In doing so, it provided the restraint that, in its absence, had brought misfortune in Amsterdam, disaster in Paris.

As the creation of money — deposits and bank notes — by banks is a simple thing, so is the mechanism for its control. In London in the eighteenth century the goldsmiths, now become the banks, made loans in notes against their holdings of gold and silver coin. The Bank of England, when it received these notes, returned them for collection in gold or silver. This required the banks to maintain reasonable reserves of cash against their note issues. They could not be reckless in the issue of notes as was Law. Later the Bank acquired for itself a monopoly of note issue, first in London, then throughout the country. It had then only to discipline itself.

MIDAS, *Transmuting all into* GOLD PAPER.

History of Midas.— The great Midas having dedicated himself to Bacchus, obtained from that Deity, the Power of changing all he Touched. Apollo fixed Asses Ears upon his head, for his Ignorance — & although he tried to hide his disgrace with a Regal Cap, yet the very Sedges which grew from the Mud of the Pactolus, whisperd out his Infamy, whenever they were agitated by the Wind from the opposite Shore. — Vide Ovids Metamorphoses.

The Bank condemned. The paper so criticized helped finance the defeat of Napoleon.

The subordinate or commercial banks could still lend the funds of their depositors. This would mean deposits — money — for those who borrowed. And this money-creation could be carried to excess. The Bank of England developed a method for preventing this. When the ordinary or commercial banks seemed too generous with their loans, the Bank allowed some of its own loans to run out or it sold some of the securities it held. In repaying these loans or paying for their securities, customers of the commercial banks would transfer gold and silver from the vaults of the ordinary banks to the Bank of England. The reserves in gold and silver of the commercial banks, their protection in case depositors came for their money, would thus be depleted. Their lending and associated deposit- and money-creation would then have to be curtailed. This is the procedure now celebrated as open market operations. Another simple thing. The clearing banks, as the commercial banks are called in Britain, could replace their depleted reserves by borrowing from the Bank of England. But that could be restrained by raising the rate of interest. This charge by the Bank of England came to be called the Bank Rate, in the last century a mysterious and wonderful thing. In the United States the Bank Rate is the rediscount rate or, latterly, the discount rate.

Such were the regulatory functions as developed by the Bank of England. It found for itself one other major purpose. Recurrently there were the moments of fear and suspicion when depositors came to the clearing banks for their money, for the cash that by the nature of banking was not sufficiently there. The Bank of England would then come to the rescue and lend to the clearing banks, though at a rather stiff rate. The central bank, as banks for other bankers came to be called, served these other banks as the lender of last resort.

It wasn't always easy to rise above the panic that sent people to the clearing banks for their money and these in turn to the Bank of England. Pessimism had a way of infecting everyone, including the great men at the Bank. But it was even harder for them to fall below euphoria when, as recurrently happened, that swept the City and England. In 1720, there was a vast outbreak of company promotions with much speculation in their shares. Trade with Spanish America was the focus of excitement but there was also a notable company "for carrying on an undertaking of great advantage, but nobody to know what it is."[2] All these promotions were the South Sea Bubble, and, as noted, the Bank of England narrowly escaped involvement. A century later, in 1824, there was another wave of speculative enthusiasm, again over investment prospects in South America. Again, there was diversification. Englishmen could invest in a company "to drain the Red Sea with a view to recovering the treasure abandoned by the Egyptians after the crossing of the Jews."[3] Again the Bank was captured by the spirit of the times and did not curb the more

In banking, confidence proceeds from an assured manner and good tailoring. The Court of Directors of the Bank of England in 1903 (top, elegant) and 1974 (bottom, prosaic).

insane lending by the banks. It's the old question: who regulates the regulators? Who is king in the world of the blind when there isn't even a one-eyed man? The problem will recur.

Still, in the last century the Bank of England showed a remarkable capacity for economic innovation. All of the functions of a modern central bank were identified and developed. Not surprisingly, then, its operations were viewed with admiration, even as high art. Victorians heard with grave attention that the Bank Rate had been raised. They did not know what it meant. But they knew that it was an act of extreme wisdom.

Paper Money

Coinage was the invention of the Greeks. The Italians, Dutch, French and English, including always the Scotch, were the developers of banks and central banking. We come now to paper money. This, in singular measure, was the gift of Americans and Canadians to the Western world.

The American colonies, all know, were greatly opposed to taxation without representation. They were also, a less celebrated quality, equally opposed to taxation with representation. It was out of this opposition to taxation that government paper money was born. The birthplace was Massachusetts; the year was 1690. Massachusetts soldiers had just returned from an unsuccessful expedition against Quebec. The loot from the fortress was to have been their pay but there was a miscalculation; Quebec did not fall. Angry soldiers can be a source of unease. So, in the absence of real money — gold or silver — they were given promises of such money instead. These promissory notes then passed from hand to hand as money.

It seemed a most painless way to pay bills. The other colonies followed suit; some, notably Rhode Island and South Carolina, issued notes in huge volume. Any thought of eventual redemption was a mirage. But the restraint that the Duc de Saint-Simon thought lacking in the French was not entirely absent in America. In the Middle Colonies — Pennsylvania, Maryland, New York — in the century before the Revolution, paper money was issued and used with good sense. It was kept reasonably scarce, its redemption in gold or silver continued to seem plausible and thus it was kept acceptable. In the view of modern historians, it was not only convenient for trade but saved these colonists from falling prices with the consequent adverse effect on business.

The prime exponent of paper money in these years was Benjamin Franklin. He thought it a good and useful thing, and his advocacy had an intensely practical touch. He printed money for the colonial governments on his own printing press.

In London this colonial invention of paper money seemed, in contrast, a most foolish contrivance. So, toward the middle of the eighteenth century,

Parliament forbade further issues of it in peacetime. Franklin journeyed to London to oppose the prohibition but was unsuccessful. The action caused much resentment in the colonies, almost as much as the taxes. This grievance has never had much standing in American history. The sound men of the colonies thought that Parliament was absolutely right. So, for a long time, did the reputable historians.

The Canadian Variant

In all countries of the world — Communist, capitalist and those which only dream of such distinction — the convention as regards paper money is now the same. It requires a rectangular slip of paper covered with suitable swirls of ink and featuring a dead hero, a Rubens figure, a cornucopia of vegetables or an heroic monument. This is partly an accident. In the development of paper money, governments followed the dull puritanical model of Massachusetts, not the irreverent and sparkling example of New France.

The Quebec model was the playing card. The French, as all know, were casual about their North American colonies. Ships and money often failed to arrive. When this happened and in roughly the same year as the Massachusetts attack, the intendants at Quebec also paid the garrison and for their supplies with promises. The most readily available and durable paper stock was playing cards. These became the promises by virtue of having the official government signature attached. Then when the ships came in, the cards were redeemed in gold or silver. The innovation shocked Versailles but, eventually, there being no better alternative, it was accepted. In a 1711 issue, spades and clubs were the currency of highest denomination; hearts and diamonds had only half their value.

As with all currencies, if too many cards were dealt, inflation resulted. In the last days of New France this happened. The pressure of need was great, the means for redemption small. At the end, the purchasing power of the cards was greatly diminished.

All must weep that, after Wolfe met Montcalm on the Plains of Abraham, this currency came to an end. Its survival would everywhere have lightened and informed financial life. At Las Vegas men and women would now play for and with the same currency. Anyone making a killing on the stock market would be rewarded in clubs and spades. A reference to gambling in Wall Street would not be a metaphor. The innocent, looking at the money they would get, would be duly warned. Had the playing cards survived, the balance sheet of the Chase Manhattan Bank would set out assets and liabilities in hearts and diamonds as well as clubs and spades. The bank's recent venture into the world of real estate trusts would have been recognized immediately for the gamble it really was.

Paper and Revolution

If one is planning a revolution, he should first, no doubt, get a cause and an army. Then, based on all experience, he — or she — should get a printing press. Revolutionary governments cannot easily levy taxes, especially if the revolt is against bad taxes. Their credit is not likely to be good so they cannot borrow. There remains only the printing of money.

Money so printed paid for the Russian Revolution. Likewise for the revolt of the Confederate States. Likewise for the French Revolution — the famous assignats were issued against the security of the church land and that of the nobility. And paper money, the invention of the colonies, paid for the American Revolution.

Some was issued by the states. The rest, the Continental notes, were authorized by the Continental Congress. A half billion dollars worth altogether was put in circulation. The predictable result, as at Quebec, was inflation: by the end of the war a pair of shoes cost about five thousand dollars in Virginia, a full outfit around a million. But there was no alternative. Taxes could not have paid for the war. Even had the erstwhile colonists been willing, collection would have been difficult. No one thought the new republic even a passable credit risk. Paper money saved the day.

This too has never been recognized. When the war was won, the sound-money men wrote the history. They could not have it said that the United States was conceived in financial sin. So they held that the financing of the Revolution was a terrible mistake, without ever explaining what would have been both practical and right. Their view persists. The Continental note has come down to us only as a symbol of opprobrium. "Not worth a Continental!" If properly treated, it would have a place beside the Liberty Bell. The historians even edited Benjamin Franklin. His position on paper money is rarely mentioned. Children are told only that he was a good man in diplomacy, thrift and electricity.

Banks and the Central Banks

Though paper money financed the Revolution, the resulting inflation bred remorse; this has been, through history, a highly reliable result of runaway prices. There were vows that it would not happen again. In consequence, the Constitution of the United States prohibited the states from issuing paper money, even as the Westminster Parliament had done. It also, more remarkably, forbade the Federal Government to do so too. Only by a very strained interpretation of the Constitution, and after paper money — the Greenbacks — had been issued in volume during the Civil War, was such money made legal in the United States.

Banks had also been prohibited in the colonies by the British. With independence these were now legal, and, as we have sufficiently seen, they too manufactured money. And while the issue of paper money by a government had to await action by a legislature, the issue of money by a bank did not. Almost anyone could do it on very short notice and even smaller capital, and the results were wonderful. The proprietor could print notes and make loans in these notes to his friends, neighbors or himself. The notes, with luck, would be accepted in payment for horses, cattle, machinery, an anvil and forge or the initial small stock of a grocery or hardware store. The borrower would then be in business. Perhaps, with more luck, he would be able to pay off his loan. A wonderful thing, a bank. The citizens of the new republic discovered banking as an adolescent discovers sex.

There were objections, however, from the people who got the notes — from the Eastern merchants to whom they came for payment of accounts, from the more conservative Eastern bankers to whom they came for deposit. When the notes were returned for collection of the gold or silver they promised, the issuing banks were often indifferent and frequently not to be found. The Easterners wanted money that could be sent to England to buy goods and that did not lose its value from one day to the next. The obvious solution was to have a central bank on the model of the Bank of England to keep these new banks in line. No one doubted the pre-eminence of the British in financial matters. George Washington might have fought the Redcoats. But he left Barings, the great London bank, in charge of his personal finances throughout the war, and Barings did not let him down.

The Bank of England, we have seen, disciplined its subordinate banks by presenting their notes systematically for collection in silver or gold. Thus it required them to keep their loans and resulting deposits in some reasonably safe relationship to their hard cash. This would be the basic function of an American central bank. It could impose discipline and restraint on the local banks by similarly presenting their notes for collection. It was a function that the banks on the frontier thought less than necessary. They would have to make good on their bad money. And their purpose, however it might be denied, was to issue bad money for whatever it might buy.

Here were the seeds of the most persistent political conflict in American history and, after slavery, the most bitter. It was between the men who wanted good money and those who wanted the bad money that put them in business. It began with Alexander Hamilton when he redeemed the Continental notes at the distinctly extravagant rate of one cent on the dollar, the act of a sound-money man. It was continued when the First Bank of the United States was established in accordance with Hamilton's recommendations and incurred so much displeasure for its discipline that its charter in 1810 was allowed to lapse. The struggle did not end until the defeat of William Jennings Bryan in the presidential election of 1896, and there were many echoes as late as the administration of Franklin D. Roosevelt. Its high point was in the eighteen-thirties — the titanic struggle between Andrew Jackson, President of the United States, and Nicholas Biddle, President of the Second Bank of the United States.

Jackson versus Biddle

The President of the United States, Andrew Jackson, was from the frontier — Tennessee. His rough appearance and manner are part of the legend and were, for a long time, a damaging model for politicians from the West. Nicholas Biddle, polished, well-dressed, well-bathed, slightly bejeweled, was pre-eminently a member of the Establishment, as the Biddles of Philadelphia have been ever since. Writing home to his mother of his American travels, the eventual Edward VII told, after his visit to Philadelphia, of a most distinguished family called Scrapple, a most appetizing breakfast dish called biddle.

Biddle lacked the tact that the rich and successful have since developed greatly and which has perhaps become second nature. On public occasions he compared his power as President of the Second Bank of the United States with that of the President of the United States. When asked by a Senate committee if he had ever abused his financial power, he praised his own restraint. Although very few of the small banks "might not have been destroyed" by his discipline, "none has ever been injured."[4] This allowed Jackson to thunder back: "The President of the Bank has told us that most of the State banks exist by its forbearance."[5]

The historic showdown came in 1832. Early that year the friends of the Bank in Congress led by Henry Clay — Clay was also from the frontier but the forces of civilization had worked their way — renewed the charter of the Bank. Jackson responded with a stinging veto. The presidential election was then fought on the issue. Biddle had the money, and he had been generous with loans to congressmen, senators and the press. (One of the journalists in his pay was James Gordon Bennett, whose son we encountered in Newport and on the Riviera.) Andrew Jackson had the votes. He won, and the Second Bank of the United States was defeated. Biddle then got it a Pennsylvania charter but power is often a onetime thing. Very soon he went broke. The smaller local banks were to remain free from serious restraint in many of the states for a century.

Once Biddle's hand had been lifted, these state banks exploded in number. To have a bank in the eighteen-thirties became, almost literally, a human

Andrew Jackson. He made Biddle's power an issue and destroyed him. Bankers ever since have been more reticent.

Nicholas Biddle. His power, he said, rivaled that of the President.

One of the small banks.

right. Many were well managed. But for many the more remote the cross-roads, the deeper the forest, the more desolate the swamp, the more attractive the location. For a remote or obscure address diminished the likelihood that the notes issued by the bank would ever find their way back for collection. There was state regulation but it was far from reliable. In Michigan, where the history is better than elsewhere, the banks were required to maintain a minimum reserve of gold and silver against their notes. Boxes of coins were sent around through the forest just in front of the commissioners who were sent out to enforce the law. As an act of economy, a thin layer of gold was once found to be covering a thick deposit of broken glass. In conservative Massa-chusetts in these years a bank failed. Against notes of $500,000 outstanding, it had cash reserves of $86.48. By the time of the Civil War some 7000 different kinds of bank notes were in circulation in the United States; to these, nu-merous artists with access to a printing press had added another 5000 that were counterfeit. Legal or bogus, the purchasing power was often about the same, meaning nil.

It was too confusing, and in 1865, a few weeks before Appomattox, the right of the small banks — those chartered by the states — to issue notes was finally abolished. But by then bank deposits and bank checks were taking the place of hand-to-hand money. Nothing prevented the banks from creating money by making loans and creating deposits. This they continued to do. Often it was in the same open-handed way that they had made the loans that were taken away in bank notes.

Gold

The United States in the last century was, or seemed on money to be, a maverick case. While wildcat banking flourished, especially on the American frontier, the major countries of Europe were accepting the lessons of Britain and the Bank of England on how banking should be regulated. They were also resolving, it seemed for all time, the question of the kind of metal into which bank notes, bank deposits and government notes would be converted. Silver and gold had for centuries been in competition. It was confusing to have two metals; they changed in value in relation to each other, and the one that was cheaper always got passed on. The one of more value people held. In 1867, the leading nations of Europe met in Paris and resolved that, henceforth, their business would all be done in gold.

The course of events in the United States was different. The Civil War, like the Revolutionary War, had been financed (though much less extensively) by paper money. When prices fell after the war, there were powerful demands, particularly from the farmers, that the Greenbacks be retained. And when great deposits of silver were later discovered in the West, the miners joined with the farmers in a crusade to keep silver. William Jennings Bryan, in memorable oratory, invoked Jesus and the Crucifixion against gold.

But eventually even the United States conformed. By the turn of the century the Greenbackers belonged to history. Bryan had been defeated on the issue of free coinage of silver. Then in the United States, as in Europe, gold became the only metal into which other money, if good, could be converted, and this convertibility was now general. In Western countries the gold standard, as such convertibility is called, was almost everywhere the rule.

Although the impression is now to the contrary, the gold standard was in effect only for a few years. World War I swept the gold out of Europe to buy munitions. This destroyed the gold standard there. It brought gold to the United States in such plenitude that it was far too abundant to serve as money here. The gold standard never functioned effectively again. It too was a prime casualty of the great ungluing.

Uncertainty: Old and New

A world in which all money could be exchanged into gold coins or their equivalent has always seemed marvelously certain. Whatever its defects, there was, indeed, a high certainty about what such money could buy. Over the whole of the last century prices fell, the purchasing power of gold or gold-based money increased.

This certainty, a sadly neglected point, was always greatest for those with money. When the Bank of England raised the Bank Rate or moved otherwise to restrain the banks and ensure that they would have the gold to meet the demands of their depositors, business firms were denied loans. In further consequence, prices fell and jobs were lost. For the farmers and workers so affected, the gold standard was a source of insecurity. The purchasing power of the money was maintained; it was only that they now had less or none. The difference was that, unlike the rich, these citizens were inarticulate and usually innocent of the causes of their misfortune. (On this matter American farmers were much less innocent than most.) Latter-day admirers of the gold standard, and of stern monetary management in general, have but rarely understood that its success in the last century owed much to the helplessness of those who were subject to its discipline. As economic life expanded in Britain and elsewhere in Europe, so did the number of workers who were subject to the uncertainty of employment and income that went with sound central-banking practice. So did the unwillingness to accept it. To the consequences of this I will return.

The United States, we have seen, rejected central banks and opted instead for giving the local banker the right to create the bank notes and the bank deposits that put the local farmers and merchants in business. This too had its

William Jennings Bryan. He invoked Jesus and the Crucifixion against the gold standard.

uncertainties, and these too were severe. Banks would be created; the loans of the new banks and the old would finance a euphoric speculation in land, canals, railroads, commodities or industrial shares. Then would come the crash, and the banks would fail by the score. This cycle continued on into the present century with increasing severity. From crash to crash was usually around twenty years — just time for the memory of the last disaster to fade. Each boom was duly heralded as the response to a new era; doubters were invariably dismissed as men incapable of appreciating the opportunities for gain by which those of true vision were being enriched. After each crash politicians called for confidence. Things were much better than they seemed. Men of financial wisdom counseled patience and, on occasion, prayer. In the panic of 1907, J. P. Morgan took an even more forthright step. He called together the Protestant clergymen of New York City and adjured them to tell their congregations the next Sunday to leave their money in the banks. It was a time for affirming faith, and that included faith in the banking system.

Despite such calming counsel, when panic struck, prices fell, men lost their jobs and banks failed. The bank failures added greatly to the severity of the crash. For then deposits in failed banks were no longer usable money; people no longer had it to spend. This had an astringent effect on business. And the surviving banks, now suffering badly from fright, ceased making the loans that created money. The monetary system was thus superbly arranged to cancel or reduce the money supply precisely when this would do the most to make things worse.

The culminating crash came in 1929. In the next four years around nine thousand banks bit the dust, a third of all the banks in the country. With each failure individuals and companies lost money they would otherwise have spent, loans they would otherwise have received. And the surviving banks battened down against the day when their depositors would come. Then, on March 6, 1933, all the banks in the United States were closed. Except for what little was in hand, the money came to a full stop. Ten years before, Germany had been buried in an avalanche of reichsmarks in an inflation that is not forgotten to this day. Finally it stabilized at a thousand billion of the old currency to one of the new. Now the United States, for practical purposes, had no money. It cannot be doubted that, after 2500 years, there was still much to be learned about the management of money.

The Federal Reserve System

This was a saddening discovery. In 1914, the gold standard had seemed forever. So also in that year it seemed that the uncertainties of the American banking system, those that produced the continuing cycles of boom and bust, had finally been corrected. On almost exactly the day that the guns of August began to sound, the victory of Andrew Jackson over the Eastern financial establishment was finally reversed. The United States set up a central bank. More exactly, in a compromise designed to overcome the old hostility, it established twelve central banks and a co-ordinating body of ill-defined power in Washington. This was the Federal Reserve System.

The Federal Reserve System has always been greatly loved by economists; it even has a nasty but affectionate nickname, The Fed. There was little to be loved in its early performance. No one knew for sure who was in charge — Washington, the regional Banks in Kansas City, St. Louis, San Francisco. Or was it the New York Bank with its special advantage of being in the financial capital?

More serious was an instinct, one that was evident in the earliest days of the Bank of England, for whatever action made things worse. In the years following World War I, there was sharp speculation in farm commodities and farm real estate — the boom of 1919–20. The Federal Reserve Banks looked on tolerantly while banks made the loans that financed this boom. Then came the crash of 1920–21. Now the Federal Reserve clamped down on bank lending and helped to make the resulting depression worse. In 1927, as the great stock market boom was getting under way, it eased credit, an action to which I will return in the next chapter. This helped finance the stock market boom and thus made more severe the crash of 1929, although other factors were more important. After the Crash, during the great deflation of 1929–32, the Federal Reserve continued to worry about inflation. In these years banks were falling like the soldiers on that morning at the Somme. The Federal Reserve was indifferent to their fate, even to that of its own members. The idea of the lender of last resort had not crossed the Atlantic.

However, the prestige of the Federal Reserve remained undimmed. The head of the New York Federal Reserve Bank over much of this period was one Benjamin Strong; he was the first American central banker since Nicholas Biddle whose name was known. Strong owed his high reputation to the elegance of his errors. Men marveled that anyone should have the power to make such sophisticated mistakes. But this is an occupation where standards of performance are pleasantly relaxed. In central banking as in diplomacy, style, conservative tailoring and an easy association with the affluent count greatly and results for much less.

Gradually during the Depression interest rates were brought down; by 1931, the discount rate at the New York Reserve Bank — the rate at which banks could borrow — was 1.5 percent, hardly a usurious charge. The Federal Reserve also bought government bonds on a considerable scale, and the resulting cash went out to the banks — open market operations again. Soon the commercial banks were flush with lendable funds. All that remained was for customers to come to the banks, borrow money, increase deposits and enhance therewith the money supply. Recovery would then be prompt. Now came a terrible discovery. The customers wouldn't come. Even at the lowest rate they didn't think they could make money. The banks wouldn't trust those who were so foolish as to believe they could. That is how it was during the Depression. Cash simply accumulated in the banks; soon they had billions which they were able to lend but couldn't. The banking system had made worse the boom and made worse the crash. Now, when the Federal Reserve decided to act, nothing happened. Yet more remained to be learned about the management of money.

Irving Fisher

That such deficiency remained so late was not the fault of one of the two most interesting figures in the history of American economics. With Thorstein Veblen, whom we've already encountered, that was Irving Fisher. Both were students at Yale at nearly the same time in the last century.

Fisher, a neat, slender, handsome man with a patrician manner and a beautifully trimmed beard, was many things — a learned mathematician, a successful inventor, a disastrous speculator and a committed improver of the human race. He invented a simple card index system which he then manufactured himself and later sold at a handsome price to Remington Rand. His design for improving the race was by better nutrition and more thoughtful breeding — if horses, cattle and wheat, why not people? Also to improve the race, or anyhow its behavior, he was ardently for prohibition, although here economics entered. He argued, no doubt correctly, that men were more productive when off the sauce. In the late nineteen-twenties Fisher went heavily into the stock market and in the Crash lost between eight and ten million dollars. This was a sizable sum, even for an economics professor. When you read that the Consumers' Price Index has gone up, it is Fisher you have partly to thank. He pioneered in the development of index numbers and also in mathematical economics. Though mathematical economics has not yet taught us everything about the economy, it has proved a valuable way of keeping economists occupied.

Fisher's greatest contribution was to our understanding of money. He showed in one simple formula what determines its value. No one, however averse to mathematics, should be put off by it:

$$P = \frac{MV + M^1V^1}{T}$$

P is prices. M is the quantity of ordinary money or cash in circulation. M^1 is also money, being that much larger part which consists of bank deposits. V and

Irving Fisher, 1867–1947.

V^1 are the rate at which each of these two kinds is spent — their velocity of circulation. For centuries a relation had been recognized between prices and the supply of money. This was why prices rose with the issue of the Continental notes and the Greenbacks. Fisher's formula refined and made explicit this relationship. Prices go up as the amount of money, the M's, go up. But money is not merely hand-to-hand cash. Bank deposits subject to spending by check — M^1 — must be added. And, if money is quickly spent, the effect will obviously be greater than if it lies buried in a mattress or is a purely sedentary deposit in a bank. So quantity in each case is multiplied by rate of turnover — the respective V's or velocity of circulation. A particular increase in money supply will have more effect on prices if it is concentrated on a few transactions than if it is spread over many. So you divide by the number of transactions (the T in the equation) to allow for the volume of trade. That is all.

As a description of what determines the value of money, Fisher's equation of exchange is still accepted. Like πr^2, it may well endure.

For Irving Fisher, however, the equation was not merely a description of how things work; he thought it highly operational. By increasing or decreasing the supply of money, you could, he concluded, increase or decrease prices. By reducing or increasing prices, you could suppress the euphoria, offset the depression and thus moderate the cycle of speculation and disaster that had so long been such a blight on economic life. (Fisher was not the first to be captured by this thought.) With his formula in hand, he moved ahead on the remedy. He formed an association to promote the regulation of the money supply and thus to stabilize prices.

In the nineteen-thirties, prices being depressingly low, the obvious step was to increase the supply of money. Prices would then recover, business and employment would be stimulated. In 1933, his idea was adopted, more or less, by Roosevelt. The gold content of the dollar was reduced; for the same gold there would be more dollars. It didn't work. The trial was not wholly fair, for the government kept most of the extra dollars. But Fisher's own formula showed why the effort failed. As money was created, people, frightened as they were in those Depression years, simply held on to it. Low velocity offset the increased quantity. More important, an increase in M, or hand-to-hand money, did not mean necessarily an increase in M^1, or bank deposits. These increased only as borrowers wanted to borrow, bankers wanted to lend. In the Depression, we have seen, neither borrowers nor bankers were willing. The supply of money could not be increased.

Fisher discovered what people, including numerous economists, have been exceedingly reluctant to believe. There are no cheap and easy inventions involving money alone that will solve all, or any, economic problems. Were it so, the inventions would already have been made; we would now all be saved from depression or inflation and be otherwise prosperous and happy.

But Irving Fisher's work was not wasted; it paved the way for a much more complex and imaginative step in economic policy. That was to have the government not only create money but also *ensure* its use — its velocity — by spending it. That was what Keynes now proposed. What is now called the Keynesian Revolution began with Irving Fisher. This Keynes himself affirmed. Writing to Fisher in 1944, he referred to him as one of his earliest teachers on these matters.

John Maynard Keynes. A drawing by Gwen Raverat.

Cambridge and the Cam, 1911. "For him the world was excellent". (Keynes is indicated by the arrow.)

7.
The Mandarin Revolution

The ideas that made revolutions did not originate with the masses, with the people who, by any reasonable calculation, had the most reason for revolt. They came from intellectuals. This was noticed by Lenin: he thought intellectuals disputatious, perverse, undisciplined. But without them, he also believed, the armies of the proletariat would dissolve in purposeless confusion.

Those who are comfortable with things as they are, conservatives in the literal sense, have often and rightly been suspicious of intellectuals and have thought them troublemakers, unable to leave well enough alone, more reprehensible by any measure than the poor or discontented whom so unnecessarily they arouse. Intellectuals have usually thought themselves disliked because others were jealous of their brains. More often it's because they make trouble.

But intellectuals can render conservative as well as radical service. Before and after World War II, their ideas did much, for a time, to save the reputation of capitalism. As the ideas of socialism did not come from the masses, those that saved capitalism did not come from businessmen, bankers or owners of shares whose value had gone with the wind. They came principally from John Maynard Keynes. His fate was to be regarded as peculiarly dangerous by the class he rescued.

Cambridge, England

Keynes was born in 1883, the year that Karl Marx died. His mother, Florence Ada Keynes, a woman of high intelligence, was diligent in good works, a respected community leader and, in late life, the mayor of Cambridge. His father, John Neville Keynes, was an economist, logician and for some fifteen years the Registrary, which is to say the chief administrative officer of the University of Cambridge. Maynard, as he was always known to friends, went to Eton, where his first interest was in mathematics. Then he went to King's College, after Trinity the most prestigious of the Cambridge colleges and the one noted especially for its economists. Keynes was to add both to its prestige in economics and, as its bursar, to its wealth.

Churchill held — where I confess escapes me — that great men usually have unhappy childhoods. At both Eton and Cambridge, Keynes, by his own account and that of his contemporaries, was exceedingly happy. The point could be important. Keynes never sought to change the world out of any sense of personal dissatisfaction or discontent. Marx swore that the bourgeoisie would suffer for his poverty and his carbuncles. Keynes experienced neither poverty nor boils. For him the world was excellent.

While at King's, Keynes was one of a group of ardent young intellectuals which included Lytton Strachey, Leonard Woolf and Clive Bell. All, with wives — Virginia Woolf, Vanessa Bell — and lovers, would assemble later in London as the Bloomsbury Group. All were much under the influence of the philosopher, G. E. Moore. In later years Keynes told of what he had from Moore. It was the belief that: "The appropriate subjects of passionate contemplation and communion were a beloved person, beauty and truth, and one's prime objects in life were love, the creation and enjoyment of aesthetic experience and the pursuit of knowledge. Of these, love came a long way first."[1] With these thoughts, inevitably, Keynes found his interest shifting from mathematics to economics.

The more important instrument of the change was Alfred Marshall, who was not at King's but along the river in the equally beautiful precincts of St. John's, known as John's. Marshall, who combined the reputation of a prophet with the aura of a saint, presided over the world of Anglo-American economics in nearly undisputed eminence for forty years — from 1885 until his death in 1924. When I was first introduced to economics at Berkeley in 1931, it was Marshall's *Principles* students were required to read. It was a majestic book. It was also superb for discouraging second-rate scholars from any further pursuit of the subject.

When he finished with Cambridge in 1905, Keynes sat for the Civil Service examinations and did badly in economics. His explanation was characteristic: "The examiners presumably knew less than I did."[2] But this deficiency was not fatal, and he went to the India Office. Here he relieved his boredom by work on books—a technical treatise on the theory of probability and his later book on Indian currency. Neither much changed the world or economic thought; soon he returned to Cambridge on a fellowship provided personally by Alfred Marshall. It was the economics of Alfred Marshall — the notion, in particular, of a benign tendency to an equilibrium where all willing workers were employed — that Keynes would do most to make obsolete.

War and the Peace

When the Great War came, Keynes was not attracted to the trenches. He went to the Treasury, where his job was to take British earnings from trade, proceeds from loans floated in the United States and returns from securities conscripted and sold abroad and make them cover all possible overseas war

Alfred Marshall. He "combined the reputation of a prophet with the aura of a saint."

purchases. And he helped the French and the Russians do the same. No magic was involved, as many have since suggested. Economic skill does not extend to getting very much for nothing. But an adept and resourceful mind was useful, and this Keynes had. In the course of time Keynes received a notice to report for military service. He sent it back. When the war was over, he was a natural choice for the British delegation to the Peace Conference. That, from the official view, was an appalling mistake.

The mood in Paris in the early months of 1919 was vengeful, myopic, indifferent to economic realities, and it horrified Keynes. So did his fellow civil servants. So did the politicians. In June he resigned and came home, and, in the next two months, he composed the greatest polemical document of modern times. It was against the reparations clauses of the Treaty and, as he saw it, the Carthaginian peace.

Europe would only punish itself by exacting, or seeking to exact, more from the Germans than they had the practical capacity to pay. Restraint by the victors was not a matter of compassion but of elementary self-interest. The case was documented with figures and written with passion. In memorable passages Keynes gave his impressions of the men who were writing the peace. Woodrow Wilson he called "this blind and deaf Don Quixote."[3] Of Clemenceau he said: "He had one illusion — France; and one disillusion, mankind . . ."[4] On Lloyd George he was rather severe:

How can I convey to the reader, who does not know him, any just impression of this extraordinary figure of our time, this syren, this goat-footed bard, this half-human visitor to our age from the hag-ridden magic and enchanted woods of Celtic antiquity.[5]

Alas, no man is of perfect courage. Keynes deleted this passage on Lloyd George at the last moment.

The Economic Consequences of the Peace was published before the end of 1919. The judgment of the British Establishment was rendered by *The Times*: "Mr. Keynes may be a 'clever' economist. He may have been a useful Treasury official. But in writing this book, he has rendered the Allies a disservice for which their enemies will, doubtless, be grateful."[6] In time there would be a responsible view that Keynes went too far — that in calculating the limits on Germany's ability to pay, he was excessively orthodox. Perhaps he contributed to the Germans' sense of persecution and injustice that Hitler so effectively exploited. But the technique of *The Times* attack should also be noticed. It was not that the great men of the Treaty and the Establishment were suffering under the onslaught, although that, of course, was the real point. Rather, the criticism was causing rejoicing to the nation's enemies. It's a device to which highly respectable men regularly resort. "Even if you are right, it is only the Communists who will be pleased."

1919. Lloyd George, Clemenceau and Wilson on the way to sign the Treaty. Keynes called Lloyd George "this syren, this goat-footed bard, this half-human visitor to our age. . . ." But on second thought he deleted the description.

The signing. Allied officers get a peek at the proceedings.

Lydia Lopokova and fellow ballet member.
"Was there ever such a union of beauty and brains
As when the lovely Lopokova married John Maynard Keynes?"

And it is when they are wrong that great men most resent the breaking of ranks. So they greatly resented Keynes. For the next twenty years he headed an insurance company and speculated in shares, commodities and foreign exchange, sometimes losing, more often winning. He also taught economics, wrote extensively and applied himself to the arts, old books and his Blooms- bury friends. But on public matters he was kept outside. He had broken the rules. We saw earlier that, as often as not, the intelligent man is not sought out. Rather, he is excluded as a threat.

Keynes's exclusion was his good fortune. The curse of the public man is that he first accommodates his tongue and eventually his thoughts to his public position. Presently saying nothing but saying it nicely becomes a habit. On the outside one can at least have the pleasure of inflicting the truth. Also, as a free- lance intellectual, Keynes could marry Lydia Lopokova who had just en- chanted London as the star of Diaghilev's ballet. My memory retains from somewhere a couplet:

> Was there ever such a union of beauty and brains
> As when the lovely Lopokova married John Maynard Keynes?

For a civil servant, even for a Cambridge professor, Lopokova would then have been a bit brave. As it was (according to legend), old family friends in Cambridge asked: has Maynard married a chorus girl?

Mostly in those years Keynes wrote. Good writing in economics is suspect — and with justification. It can persuade people. It also requires clear thought. No one can express well what he does not understand. So clear writing is perceived as a threat, something deeply damaging to the numerous scholars who shelter mediocrity of mind behind obscurity of prose. Keynes was a superb writer when he chose to try. This added appreciably to the suspicion with which he was regarded.

But while Keynes was kept outside, he could not, as would a Marxist, be ignored. He was a Fellow of King's. He was the Chairman of the National Mutual Insurance Company. He was the director of other companies. So he was heard. It might have been better strategy to have kept him inside and under control.

Churchill and Gold

The man who suffered most from Keynes's freedom from constraint was Winston Churchill. In 1925, Churchill presided over the most dramatically disastrous error by a government in modern economic history. It was Keynes who made it famous.

The mistake was the attempted return to the gold standard at the prewar gold and dollar value of the pound — 123.27 fine grains of gold and 4.86 dollars to the pound. Churchill was Chancellor of the Exchequer.

In retrospect, the error was not an especially subtle one. British prices and wages had risen during the war as they had in other countries. But in the United States they had risen less and fallen more in the postwar slump. And in France, as elsewhere in Europe, though prices had risen more than in Britain, the exchange value of the local currencies had fallen even more than prices had gone up. When you bought the cheap foreign currencies and then the goods, they were, in comparison with those of Britain, a bargain.

Had Britain gone back to the pound at, say, 4.40 dollars, all would have been well. With sterling bought at that rate, the cost of British commodities, manufactures or services — coal, textiles, machinery, ships, shipping — would have been pretty much in line with those of other countries, given their prices and the cost of their currencies. With pounds bought at 4.86 dollars, British prices were about 10 percent higher than those of her competitors. Ten percent is 10 percent. It was enough to send buyers to France, Germany, the Low Countries, the United States.

Why the mistake? To go back to the old rate of exchange of pounds for gold and dollars was to show that British financial management was again as solid, as reliable, as in the nineteenth century. It proved that the war had changed nothing. It was a thought to which Winston Churchill, historian and professional custodian of the British past, was highly susceptible. Also, only a few people participate in such decisions, and the instinct is strongly conformist. The man of greatest public prestige states his position at a meeting; the others hasten to praise his wisdom. Those who have a reputation for dissent, like Keynes, are not invited. They are not responsible, serious, effective. It follows that financial decisions, like those on foreign policy, are carefully orchestrated to protect error.

The country responded well to Churchill's House of Commons announcement of the return to gold. The *New York Times* said in its headline that he had carried "PARLIAMENT AND NATION TO HEIGHT OF ENTHUSIASM." Keynes wrote instead to ask why Churchill did "such a silly thing." It was because he had "no instinctive judgment to prevent him from making mistakes."[7] And "lacking this instinctive judgment, he was deafened by the clamorous voices of conventional finance."[8] Also, he was misled by his experts. One cannot believe that Churchill read this exculpation with any pleasure.

If British exports were to continue, British prices had to come down. Prices could come down only if wages came down. And wages could come down in only one of two ways. There could be a horizontal slash, whatever the unions might say. Or there could be unemployment, enough unemployment to weaken union demands, threaten employed workers with idleness and thus bring down wages. This Keynes foresaw.

The mine-owners tell their story.

Miners on strike, 1926. After Churchill took Britain back to gold, wages had to come down. Why, Keynes asked, did he do "such a silly thing?"

Charles Rist.

Hjalmar Horace Greeley Schacht (left) and Montagu Norman.

There was, in the end, both unemployment and a horizontal wage cut. As the mines of the Ruhr came back into production after 1924, world prices of coal fell. To meet this competition with the more expensive pound, the British coal-owners proposed a three-point program: longer hours in the pits, abolition of the minimum wage, lower wages for all. (Let Enoch Powell, Ronald Reagan and Milton Friedman take comfort; there was a day when such actions could be urged. Who knows, maybe their sun will shine again.) A Royal Commission agreed that the lower wage was necessary. The miners refused; the owners then locked them out. On the fourth of May, 1926, the transport, printing, iron and steel, electricity and gas and most of the building-trades unions came out in support of the miners. This, with some slight exaggeration, was called the General Strike. For quite a few workers it didn't make too much difference; they were already on the dole, for unemployment, the other remedy, was by then well advanced. In these years unemployment ranged between ten and twelve percent of the British labor force.

The General Strike lasted only nine days. Those who had most ardently applauded the return to gold were the first to see the strike as a threat to constitutional government, a manifestation of anarchy. Churchill took an especially principled stand. The miners remained on strike through most of 1926 but were eventually defeated. Keynes's judgment was redeemed but he was not forgiven. It had happened again: when the men of great reputation are wrong, it is the worst of personal tactics to be right.

The American Impact

After 1925, British prices remained stubbornly too high. Money that might have come to Britain for goods continued to go elsewhere, quite a lot to the United States and later to France. The return to gold was meant to proclaim the strength and integrity of sterling. It demonstrated its weakness and the strength of the dollar instead. In later years A. J. Liebling of *The New Yorker* magazine formulated what he called Liebling's Law. It held, roughly, that if a man of adequately complex mind proceeds in a sufficiently perverse way, he can succeed in kicking himself in his own ass out the door into the street. The return to gold in 1925 was a superb manifestation of Liebling's Law.

By 1927, the loss of gold to the United States was alarming. Accordingly, in that year, Montagu Norman, the head of the Bank of England, in company with Hjalmar Horace Greeley Schacht, the head of the Reichsbank (a man whose reputation for financial wizardry was supported by an exceptionally austere appearance and a notably frozen mind), sailed for New York to try and get it back. There, in company with Charles Rist of the Banque de France, they asked the Federal Reserve to lower its interest rate, expand its loans and thus ease monetary policy. The lower interest rates would discourage the flow of money to the United States. The easier money would mean more loans, more money, higher American prices, less competition in Britain and elsewhere from American goods and easier sales by Europeans in the United States. The Americans obliged. This was the action, as previously told, that is held to have helped trigger the great stock market speculation of 1927–29. The easier money went to finance purchases of common stocks instead.

Everybody Ought to be Rich

The twenties were bad years in Britain, wonderful in the United States for everyone that counted. Farmers were very unhappy. Wages did not rise. But unemployment was low, industrial production rose, and so did profits and so, most of all, did the stock market. All common stocks rose during these years, and especially those that reflected the marvels of the new technology. Radio Corporation of America was the greatest speculative favorite — the electronic miracle, although that word had not yet come into use. For many investors Seaboard Airline was a foothold in the new world of aviation, although, in fact, it was a railroad.

Most exciting of all were the holding companies and the investment trusts. Both were companies formed to invest in other companies. And the companies in which they invested, invested in yet other companies that, in turn, invested in yet others. The layers could be five or ten deep. Along the way bonds and preferred stock were sold. The resulting interest payments and preferred dividends took some of the earnings of the ultimate operating company; the remaining earnings came cascading back to the common stock still held by the promoters. Or this happened as long as the dividends of the ultimate companies were good and rising. When these fell, the bond interest and preferred stock soaked up all of the revenues and more. Nothing was left to go upstream; the stock in the investment trusts and holding companies then went, often in a week, from wonderful to worthless. It was an eventuality that almost no one had foreseen.

The metaphor for all these promotions was Goldman Sachs. There had been nothing like it since the South Sea Bubble; there would be nothing like it again until I.O.S. (Investors Overseas Service) and Bernie Cornfeld.

The golden age of Goldman Sachs was the nearly eleven months beginning December 4, 1928. On that day the Goldman Sachs Trading Corporation was formed. This was an investment trust with the function only of investing in other companies; $100 million of stock was issued, of which 90 percent was sold to the public. This was put in other stock selected in accordance with the superior insights of Goldman Sachs. In February the Trading Corporation was merged with the Financial and Industrial Securities Corporation, another investment trust. Assets were now $235 million. In July the combined enterprise launched the Shenandoah Corporation. Preferred and common stocks to a total of $102.3 million were authorized, again for investment in other stock. The public share of issue was oversubscribed sevenfold so yet more was issued. In August Shenandoah, in turn, launched the Blue Ridge Corporation — for $142 million. A few days later, back at the Trading Corporation, $71.4 million more in securities was issued to buy another investment trust as well as a West Coast bank.

Shenandoah, which had been issued at $17.50 and had risen to $36.00, eventually went down to fifty cents. This was quite a loss. The Trading Corporation did worse. In February 1929, aided by some purchase of itself, it had reached $222.50. Two years later it could be had for a dollar or two. "He took my fortune," said one saddened commentator of his broker, "and ran it into a shoestring." A principal in this vast expropriation — a director of both Shenandoah and Blue Ridge — was John Foster Dulles. A more introspective man might have wondered. Dulles emerged with his faith in the capitalist system unshaken. We shall encounter him again.

Dark Thursday

For Goldman Sachs, as for stocks in general, the day of reckoning was Thursday, October 24, 1929. The market had been weak on the days before. On that morning, a story I've told before, there was a great unrestrained and unexplained headlong rush to sell. This hit the floor of the Exchange with torrential force. The machinery could not adjust to the panic. The ticker fell far behind the market. People across the country could not tell what was happening, only that they had been ruined or would soon be ruined. So they sold and were sold. Inside the Exchange the noise was deafening. Outside in Wall Street a crowd gathered. Perhaps capitalism was collapsing, which would be an interesting thing to see. The police were called; maybe the brokers and bankers would get out of hand. A workman appeared on one of the high buildings to make some repairs. The crowd assumed he was a suicide and waited impatiently for him to jump.

Around noon the Exchange authorities closed the visitors' gallery. It was all too obscene. One who had been watching was Winston Churchill. In the established if unduly simple view, his return to gold in 1925, the subsequent rescue of Britain by low interest rates and easy money in New York had been the cause of it all. It would be good to believe that it was design or guilt that had Churchill on hand but it isn't so. He only happened to be there.

About the time the gallery closed, things took a turn for the better. A little earlier that day the great New York bankers had gathered at Morgan's next door to consider the situation. A rescue operation seemed indicated. Richard Whitney, the Vice-President of the Exchange who was known to all as a

Wall Street on the day of the Crash. A man came to work on a high building. The crowd waited impatiently for him to jump.

Morgan broker, was told to go in and buy. This, with great ostentation, he did. The amounts authorized, though unknown, seem not to have been large. But the rescue worked, and the market turned dramatically around, although later in the day it became soft again. Whitney was a hero, his achievement was widely celebrated and he was made President of the Exchange. Not long thereafter, he was off to Sing Sing for embezzlement. The following Tuesday the real crash came. This time the bankers did not intervene. According to rumor they were unloading the stock they had bought the previous Thursday. With occasional rallies, the market went on down for nearly three years.

The Crash blighted consumer spending, business investment and the solvency of banks and business firms. After the Great Crash came the Great Depression; first the euthanasia of the rich, then of the poor. By 1933, nearly a fourth of all American workers were without jobs. Production — Gross National Product — was down by a third. As noted, around nine thousand banks failed. The government reacted normally: in June 1930, things were bad and getting much worse. A delegation called on President Hoover to ask for a public works relief program. He said: "Gentlemen, you have come sixty days too late. The depression is over."[9]

In Europe, it was World War I that shook the old certainties. The trenches would linger in social memory as the ultimate horror. In the United States it was the Great Depression. This remained in the American social memory for the next forty years and more. When anything seemed wrong, people would ask: "Does this mean another depression?"

Solutions

The effects of the Great Depression spread, and they spread around the world. The richer the country, the more advanced its industry, the worse, in general, the slump. Only Russia was untouched, although this was not an unqualified case for the Soviet system. The time had come for that further stage of the revolution that Lenin saw to be necessary so agriculture was being collectivized. This stage was infinitely more bloody than the first. What was called suffering in the West would have seemed like a miracle of economic affluence in Russia. Stalin himself was later to tell Churchill that these years were the most painful of his life. When Stalin was pained by the pain of others, it was pain indeed.

The first solution that occurred to statesmen was to propose tightening of belts, acceptance of hardship, resort to patience: This is a natural reaction. Few can believe that suffering, especially by others, is in vain. Anything that is disagreeable must surely have beneficial economic effects.

Andrew Mellon: "Liquidate labor, liquidate stocks, liquidate the farmers . . ." Then there would be no way left but up.

Herbert Hoover in the United States and Heinrich Brüning in Germany were the most devoted exponents of this view. Brüning's remedial action in 1931 was especially memorable. Wages were cut; prices were cut; salaries were cut; taxes were raised. All this was done at a time when around a quarter of all German industrial workers were unemployed. Not many have wanted to ask the question which some millions of German workers did ask themselves. If this is democracy, can Hitler be worse? Andrew Mellon, Hoover's Secretary of the Treasury, had a similar proposal: "Liquidate labor, liquidate stocks, liquidate the farmers . . ." After Mellon was finished, there would, it is true, be no way left but up.

Many economists — Lionel Robbins in England, Joseph Schumpeter in the United States — agreed that depression had a necessary, therapeutic function; the metaphor was that it extruded poisons that had been accumulating in the economic system. Others joined in urging patience, a course of action that is easier when supported by a regular income. And many warned that affirmative measures by government would cause inflation. The practical effect in all cases was to come out for inaction. It was not a good time for economists. Britain did abandon the gold standard and free trade. Otherwise Westminster and Whitehall reacted to the Depression by ignoring the steady flow of advice it was receiving from John Maynard Keynes.

Keynes was wholly clear as to the proper action. He wanted borrowing by the government and the expenditure of the resulting funds. This was the essential step on from Irving Fisher. The borrowing ensured the increase in the money supply — in bank deposits or Fisher's famous M^1. What was spent was spent by the government and would then be respent by workers and others receiving the money. The government spending and the further spending by the recipients ensured that there would be no offsetting drop in velocity — in V and V^1. You not only created money but enforced its use.

Keynes in these years did have one notable friend. It was the "goat-footed bard," David Lloyd George. Keynes explained helpfully that he supported Lloyd George when he was right and opposed him when he was wrong. But Lloyd George was by now in the political wilderness with the other winners and losers from World War I. Gradually for Keynes there was compensation. He became a prophet with honor except in his own country. The most successful application of his policies was, in fact, where he was all but unknown.

The Trial Runs

The Nazis were not given to books. Their reaction was to circumstance, and this served them better than the sound economists served Britain and the United States. From 1933, Hitler borrowed money and spent — and he did it liberally as Keynes would have advised. It seemed the obvious thing to do, given the unemployment. At first, the spending was mostly for civilian works — railroads, canals, public buildings, the *Autobahnen*. Exchange control then kept frightened Germans from sending their money abroad and those with rising incomes from spending too much of it on imports.

The results were all a Keynesian could have wished. By late 1935, unemployment was at an end in Germany. By 1936, high income was pulling up prices or making it possible to raise them. Likewise wages were beginning to rise. So a ceiling was put over both prices and wages, and this too worked. Germany, by the late thirties, had full employment at stable prices. It was, in the industrial world, an absolutely unique achievement.

The German example was instructive but not persuasive. British and American conservatives looked at the Nazi financial heresies — the borrowing and spending — and uniformly predicted a breakdown. Only Schacht, the banker, they said, was keeping things patched together. (They did not know that Schacht, so far as he was aware of what was happening, was opposed.) And American liberals and British socialists looked at the repression, the destruction of the unions, the Brownshirts, the Blackshirts, the concentration camps, the screaming oratory, and ignored the economics. Nothing good, not even full employment, could come from Hitler. It was the American case that was influential.

At the close of 1933, Keynes addressed a letter to Franklin D. Roosevelt, which, not seeking reticence, he published in the *New York Times*. A single sentence summarized his case: "I lay overwhelming emphasis on the increase of national purchasing power resulting from governmental expenditure which is financed by loans. . . ."[10] The following year he visited FDR but the letter had been a better means of communication. Each man was puzzled by the face-to-face encounter. The President thought Keynes some kind of "a mathematician rather than a political economist."[11] Keynes was depressed; he had "supposed the President was more literate, economically speaking."[12]

If corporations are large and strong, as they already were in the thirties, they can reduce their prices. And if unions are nonexistent or weak, as they were at the time in the United States, labor can then be forced to accept wage reductions. Action by one company will force action by another. The modern inflationary spiral will work in reverse; the reduced purchasing power of workers will add to its force. Through the National Recovery Administration Washington was trying to arrest this process — a reasonable and even wise effort, given the circumstances. This Keynes and most economists did not see; he and they believed the NRA wrong, and ever since it has had a poor press. One of FDR's foolish mistakes. Keynes wanted much more vigorous

Franklin D. Roosevelt, 1932. The Metropolitan Opera House was packed — with Republicans for Roosevelt.

borrowing and spending; he thought the Administration far too cautious. And Washington was, indeed, reluctant.

In the early thirties the Mayor of New York was James J. Walker. Defending a casual attitude toward dirty literature, as it was then called, he said he had never heard of a girl being seduced by a book. Keynes was now, after a fashion, to prove Walker wrong. Having failed by direct, practical persuasion, he proceeded to seduce Washington and the world by way of a book. Further to prove the point against Walker, it was a nearly unreadable one.

The General Theory

The book was *The General Theory of Employment Interest and Money*. (For some reason Keynes omitted the commas.) He at least was not in doubt about its influence. Shortly before it was published in 1936, he told George Bernard Shaw that it would "largely revolutionise . . . the way the world thinks about economic problems."[13] So it did.

The General Theory was published long before it was finished. Like the Bible and *Das Kapital*, it is deeply ambiguous and, as in the case of the Bible and Marx, the ambiguity helped greatly to win converts. I'm not reaching for paradox. When understanding is achieved after much effort, readers hold tenaciously to their belief. The pain, they wish to think, was worthwhile. And if there are enough contradictions and ambiguities, as there are also in the Bible and Marx, the reader can always find something he wants to believe. This too wins disciples.

Keynes's basic conclusion can, however, be put very directly. Previously it had been held that the economic system, any capitalist system, found its equilibrium at full employment. Left to itself, it was thus that it came to rest. Idle men and idle plant were an aberration, a wholly temporary failing. Keynes showed that the modern economy could as well find its equilibrium with continuing, serious unemployment. Its perfectly normal tendency was to what economists have since come to call an underemployment equilibrium.

The ultimate cause of the underemployment equilibrium lay in the effort by individuals and firms to save more from income than it was currently profitable for businessmen to invest. What is saved from income must ultimately be spent or there will be a shortage of purchasing power. Previously for 150 years such a possibility had been excluded in the established economics. The income from producing goods was held always to be sufficient to buy the goods. Savings were always invested. Were there a surplus of savings, interest rates fell, and this ensured their use.

Keynes did not deny that all savings got invested. But he showed that this could be accomplished by a fall in output (and employment) in the economy as a whole. Such a slump reduced earnings, changed business gains into losses, reduced personal incomes, and, while it reduced investment, it reduced savings even more. It was in this way that savings were kept equal to investment. Adjustment, a benign word in economics, could be a chilling thing.

From the foregoing came the remedy. The government should borrow and invest. If it borrowed and invested enough, all savings would be offset by investment at a high, not a low, level of output and employment. *The General Theory* validated the remedy that Keynes had previously urged. It would have been inconvenient if it had come out the other way.

The University Route

Washington, as noted, was cool to Keynes. So, with *The General Theory* as his weapon, he captured the United States by way of the universities. His principal point of entry was Harvard. It was something I was fortunate enough to see at first hand. I was living as a young tutor at Winthrop House, one of the undergraduate residence units. Winthrop House was an unpretentious place, slightly anti-Semitic like the rest of the university but not anti-Irish as were the more dignified places of residence. It was perhaps for this reason that among our inhabitants were the Kennedy brothers, something that had a considerable effect on my later life.

Resident tutors had free rooms, free meals and as much money as they needed. We met each morning for a leisurely breakfast and to hear of the exceptionally depraved sexual adventures of one of our colleagues on the previous night. He subsequently became a very great social scientist. It was a lovely and tranquil world; the only drawback was that things were so different just outside the university walls. Once in those Depression years I spent Christmas in Los Angeles. The streets were filled with desperate men who pled desperately for a little money; you could sense that they hated what they had to do but they had no choice. When you tried to pass them by, you saw the look of hopelessness and fright in their eyes. That was the contrast with our comfortable world.

Keynes had a solution without revolution. Our pleasant world would remain; the unemployment and suffering would go. It seemed a miracle. In 1936, after the publication of *The General Theory*, there were meetings several times a week to discuss this wonderful thing. One meeting in Winthrop House remains in my memory. Professor Schumpeter presided; he disliked Keynes but loved argument more. Robert Bryce, a brilliant young Canadian, had just come from Keynes's seminar in the other Cambridge, as it was called. When in doubt, as we often were, he told us what Keynes really meant. For the next thirty years Bryce was the pre-eminent figure in Canadian economic policy. More than anyone else he caused Canada to become, even before the United States or Britain, a pillar of the Keynesian faith.

It was the young who were captured. Economists are economical, among other things, of ideas. It is still so. They make those they acquire as graduate students do for a lifetime. Change in economics comes only with the changing generations. The great economists of that day read and reviewed Keynes and uniformly found him wrong.

But so influential was Keynes among the young at Harvard that in later years an association of alumni was formed to combat his influence. They threatened to cease financial support to the university unless his ideas were repressed or expunged, although it is not clear that many had given much before. Conservatives regularly extend their faith to the management of their personal resources. I was singled out for attack as the Crown Prince of "Keynesism." I was greatly pleased and hoped that my friends would be properly resentful.

That was Keynes. You came to him out of conservatism, your desire for peaceful change. And by urging his ideas you won a reputation for being a radical.

To Washington

From Harvard the ideas of Keynes went to Washington — by train. On Thursday and Friday nights in the New Deal years the Federal Express out of Boston to Washington would be half-filled with Harvard faculty members, old and young. All were on the way to impart wisdom to the New Deal. The *Harvard Crimson* once said of the lectures of a noted professor of government that they were what he gave while catching the train to Washington. After *The General Theory* was published, the wisdom that the younger economists sought to impart was that of Keynes.

It was thus that we learned of the Washington reluctance. To spend public money to create jobs might be necessary. But it was not something you urged out of choice. And to urge that a budget deficit was a *good* thing in itself — the heart of the Keynesian remedy — seemed insane. Men of sound judgment were repelled. Even one's best friends, if in positions of responsibility, were cautious in the presence of such heresy. One does not overcome such caution by logic or eloquence but almost always the opposition comes to your rescue. It came galloping in those years.

In 1937, recovery from the Great Depression was slowly under way; production and prices were rising, although unemployment was still appalling. The men of sound judgment now asserted themselves. They moved to cut spending, raise taxes and bring the federal budget into balance. The few Keynesians protested; our voices were drowned out in the roars of orthodox applause. As the budget moved toward balance, the recovery came to a halt. Presently there was a new and ghastly slump, a recession within the De-

Herbert Hoover.

Hooverville.

pression. It was entirely as Keynes predicted. The men of sound judgment had made our case.

The American Keynesians

Where were our allies in Washington? They were, of all places, in the Federal Reserve System. We think of a central bank as a stronghold of myopic, unyielding conservatism. It is not an extravagant view but the Federal Reserve was then headed by Marriner Eccles, a Utah banker of highly original mind. Eccles had seen the lines of depositors form outside his own banks to get their money. He had seen men looking without hope for work. He knew the worried, broken farmers outside town. Why not have the government spend money to provide jobs and help the farmers back to solvency? His experience had caused ideas very similar to those of Keynes to pass through his mind. Roosevelt had brought him to Washington.

Eccles's principal economic aide was Lauchlin Currie, another of the notable Canadians who, in their selfless way, had come south to rescue the Republic. Previously he had been a faculty member at Harvard and had published a book on the supply and control of money that had anticipated some of the important propositions of Keynes. This caused him to be viewed with doubt by the great economists, and he was not promoted. In economics one should never be right too soon. The shrewd scholar always waits until the parade is passing his door and then steps bravely out in front of the band. Eccles and Currie became the leading exponents of Keynes in Washington.

Scholars now speak of the Keynesian Revolution. Never before had a revolution captured a country by way of a bank. No one should worry that it will happen often again.

From the Federal Reserve in the late thirties Currie went to the White House as an assistant to FDR. This was a strategic spot. When an economic post opened in the government or someone was needed for a special economic task, he would see, if possible, that someone with reliably Keynesian views was employed. Several times he called on me. Conservatives always believed that there was a conspiracy to promote the Keynesian ideas. This everyone concerned indignantly denied. Much depends on the point of view. In later years Currie was accused of being a Communist. He was not. But for many people the difference between Keynes and Communism wasn't too great.

Also in the latter thirties, Keynes won his most important influential American recruit; that was Alvin Harvey Hansen, a professor first at Minnesota and then at Harvard and one of the most prestigious figures in the American economic pantheon. Hansen was no youngster whose views could be dismissed by the economic establishment. In books, articles and through his students he propagated the faith. Hansen and two other scholars — Seymour

E. Harris, another diligent evangelist at Harvard, and Paul M. Samuelson, whose textbook, in face of sharp initial attack, instructed millions — made Keynes an accepted part of American economic thought.

Although the recession of 1937 made Keynes's ideas respectable in Washington, action to lift the level of employment remained half-hearted. In 1939, the year war came to Europe, nine and a half million Americans were unemployed. That was 17 percent of the labor force. Almost as many (14.6 percent) were still unemployed the following year.

The war then brought the Keynesian remedy with a rush. Expenditures doubled and redoubled. So did the deficit. Before the end of 1942, unemployment was minimal. In many places labor was scarce.

There is another way of looking at this history. Hitler, having ended unemployment in Germany, had gone on to end it for his enemies. He was the true protagonist of the Keynesian ideas.

Lessons of War

The war revealed two of the enduring features of the Keynesian Revolution. One was the moral difference between spending for welfare and spending for war. During the Depression very modest outlays for the unemployed seemed socially debilitating, economically unsound. Now expenditures many times greater for weapons and soldiers were perfectly safe. It's a difference that still persists.

Also as unemployment diminished, but well before it disappeared, inflation became a threat. Keynes believed himself to have a remedy and so did his followers; it was to put everything into reverse. Raise taxes to keep pace with wartime spending, thus try by all possible means to keep down the budget deficit. Keep the cost of living stable, if necessary by subsidizing the cost of food and other staples. Labor could then be asked to forgo wage increases for the duration. Some price control and rationing might be necessary; it should be applied selectively to essentials in especially short supply. Keynes set it all out in a famous series of letters to *The Times*. In Washington and by now in London the proposals were widely accepted. If Keynes said so, it must surely work.

I circulated a paper with a similar set of proposals in Washington to which I'd been summoned by Lauchlin Currie. It was an inspired action, for, as a consequence, in the spring of 1941, I was put in charge of price control, one of the most powerful economic positions of the wartime years. To say I was overjoyed would be a gross understatement.

I got the news in the Blaine Mansion, a fine Victorian structure on Massachusetts Avenue at Dupont Circle and the first headquarters for wartime price control. James Blaine, like many others, achieved a well-deserved obscurity by running unsuccessfully for the presidency. But his obscurity is less complete than for most. A verse from the campaign, simple, forth-right, good in scan and rhyme, survives to celebrate his character and provenance:

James G. Blaine, James G. Blaine,
Continental liar from the State of Maine.

In a few weeks we outgrew the Blaine house. Three times during the war we burst at the housing seams and had to move. We ended in a sizable acreage previously inhabited by the Census and later taken over by the FBI. The expansion in staff was related to the deeper discovery that, for inflation, the ideas of Keynes as adapted by Galbraith did not work. Long before all the unemployed had jobs, corporations could raise prices—and they did. This led, in turn, to wage demands and on, potentially, to a price-wage spiral. Meanwhile taxes could not be raised fast enough to keep pace with wartime spending. The excess of purchasing power could not, as Keynes had proposed, be mopped up.

The only hope was to go in for price-fixing on a vast scale. This, in the spring of 1942, we did, and rationing followed. That policy did work; prices were kept nearly stable throughout the war.

Previously I had argued against a general ceiling on prices with great conviction; now I argued for it with equal passion. Almost no one noticed this change of mind. No one at all criticized it. In economics it is a far, far wiser thing to be right than to be consistent.

A revisionist view, greatly favored by partisans of the free market, now holds that price increases were only bottled up, to be released after the war. There was, indeed, a bulge when the controls were lifted in 1946, but it was less by far than the increase in the single peacetime year of 1974. Without the controls prices before the war's end would have been doubling and redoubling every year.

With minor exceptions we eventually had control of all the prices in the United States. There could be appeal to higher authority and the courts. No one much did, for higher authority backed us up. If anyone left our offices with a smile, we felt we had not done our job. To be effective, price control had to be painful. To be charged with inflicting such pain, mostly on those who could handsomely afford it, was a psychologically damaging experience for a young man. I was accused of liking it, which, perhaps, I did.

People appealing for price increases came to a large table in the Census Building. Those with the worst case always made the most compelling plea. Knowing that their case was fraudulent, they had rehearsed with the greatest care at the greatest length. We usually had the figures on their earnings; I would look down the row of chairs while someone was pleading his meretricious case and notice that one or more staff members would have a hand resting flat on the table, the index and second fingers moving up and down, each in opposite direction to the other. It was in reference to a fable — the year of the great famine in the land of the ants. One day a patrol from an ant colony on the side of a steep hill found food, a lovely, large, round piece of horse manure. It was directly up the slope from the colony. All the ants were mustered out to bring back the food. They rolled it down the hill, and presently it was rolling faster and faster and threatening to roll right by the ant colony and be lost. The queen ant went up and down the lines encouraging her troops, who were holding against the food, to ever greater exertions. Her antennae were going up and down like the fingers. In ant language it meant, "Stop that horse-shit."

It was while directing price control that I first met Keynes. I had gone to study under him at Cambridge — Cambridge, England, of course — in 1937–38, but it was then that he had his first heart attack, and he did not appear at the university at all that year. He came into my outer office in Washington unannounced one day to deliver a paper. My secretary brought it in and said he seemed to feel he should see me. The name, she said, was Kines. I looked at the paper; there it was, *J. M. Keynes.* The paper was a lucid condemnation of the prices we were setting on corn and hogs. He called them maize and pigs. It was as though St. Peter had dropped in on some parish priest.

With much more emphasis on rationing and less on price control, the British economic policy during the war was otherwise similar to ours. There too it worked. British wartime planning got more from less than that of any other country. As the war ended, I led a group of economists who studied German and Japanese wartime economic management. None doubted that the British management was far more rigorous.

Triumph

After 1941, the economists no longer went to Washington by train. They were already there. All saw the Keynesian remedy for depression and unemployment from, as it were, the front row. The conclusion was inescapable: what would work in war would work in peace. The Keynesian victory was now assured. The failure of the Keynesian system to deal with inflation was not stressed. Inflation was surely peculiar to the war.

Liberal businessmen in these years began to show interest; they formed the Committee for Economic Development to promote the ideas. They were very careful, however, to avoid Keynes's name. And they spoke not of deficits but of a budget balanced only at a high level of employment.

As the war drew to a close, a group of young economists decided to seek Congressional sanction for the idea of government planning to maintain employment. They succeeded, and the Employment Act of 1946 became law. I was one of the many who were surprised at their success. I had thought the idea premature and had not participated in the effort. But, by 1946, it was becoming difficult even for conservative Republicans (or Democrats) to be against full employment, although, in the end, many did rise to the challenge.

Bretton Woods

Meanwhile Keynes himself was completing his last crusade. At Paris he had fought the Carthaginian peace. In 1925, he had fought Churchill and the tyranny of gold. In 1944, representatives from 44 countries had assembled at Bretton Woods in New Hampshire to ensure that the errors on gold and reparations on which Keynes had made his reputation were not repeated. The Bretton Woods Conference was not a conference among nations. It was a conference of nations with Keynes. His only rival was Harry D. White, his friend and disciple at the U.S. Treasury. The result of Bretton Woods was the Bank for International Reconstruction and Development and the International Monetary Fund. The first would guide the minds of the victorious powers to reconstruction, not punishment. The second would give a modicum of flexibility to the rule of gold. A country in trouble could win time by borrowing from the Fund.

When the war was over, Keynes also negotiated the loan — $3.75 billion — that was to see Britain through the postwar years and until exports would again pay for imports. There was now another terrible aberration of the orthodox financial mind — this time it was the Americans. Sterling had been subject to rigid exchange controls during the war. It was made a condition of the loan that it would become fully and freely convertible into dollars (and thus into gold) according to timetable in 1947. This was done. And all who had accumulated wartime hoards of inconvertible sterling — speculators, black-market currency operators, the banks — rushed joyously to change their money into dollars. The loan was used up, literally in a matter of days. In 1925, sterling had been made convertible at an unduly high rate with disastrous results. Twenty-two years later the same error was repeated with infinite precision. This time Keynes was a reluctant participant.

Keynes had always believed that men of self-confessed financial wisdom were wonderfully consistent, especially in their mistakes. He did not live to see this further proof. On April 21, 1946, he died of another heart attack.

The Age of Keynes

After the fiasco of the British loan came the Marshall Plan. This took a far more practical view of the postwar world; with it Europe recovered. The Marshall Plan was a good example of the kind of concerted effort backed by money that Keynes had called for at Bretton Woods.

Germany was a full participant in the Marshall aid. This too was the legacy of Keynes. In the years after 1945, men told each other there must, on no account, be another harsh peace. Keynes's philippic against the Versailles Treaty was now the conventional wisdom. A defeated enemy was now helped, not punished.

In Europe and the United States the two decades following the Second World War will for long be remembered as a very good time, the time when capitalism really worked. Everywhere in the industrialized countries production increased. Unemployment was everywhere low. Prices were nearly stable. When production lagged and unemployment rose, governments intervened to take up the slack, as Keynes had urged. So these were good and confident years, a good time to be an economist, and economists took and were given credit for the achievement. Only the occasional, very mild recessions were still acts of nature or of God.

But these years showed the flaws in the Keynesian miracle as well, although the faults were less celebrated. After the Marshall Plan there was hope that a similar infusion of money — capital — would also rescue the poor countries from their poverty. The rich countries weren't overwhelming in their generosity. But enough was done to show the problem.

In the European countries in the years immediately following the war capital was the missing ingredient. This could be provided and was provided by the Marshall Plan. In the poor countries, on the other hand, industrial experience, industrial skill, industrial discipline, effective public administration, transportation systems and many other things did not exist. These could not be supplied from abroad as was the capital. Nor could anything be done from abroad about the relentless pressure of population on land. Keynes, it was learned, at least by some, was a man for the rich countries, not the poor.

And the great lesson of the war was rediscovered. The Keynesian remedy was asymmetrical; it would work against unemployment and depression but not in reverse against inflation. It was a discovery that was only very slowly and reluctantly accepted, and now, more than thirty years later, there are still some followers of the master who are reluctant to admit the fault. Unemployment, as this is written, is high — in the United States the highest in thirty years. And industrial prices are going steadily, steadily up. What is true in the United States is worse in Britain. But Keynes, once a heretic, is now the prophet of the established faith. One must believe that for his remedies to work.

Inflation can be cured by having enough unemployment. However, with this cure no Keynesian can agree; the essence of the Keynesian system is that it cures unemployment. One can stop the increase in corporate prices and trade-union wages by direct action. (I've long thought such action inescapable.) This does not leave the market system intact as Keynes, the conservative, had intended. It is a portent of radical change that not many wish to face.

There are other problems. Keynesian support to the economy has come to involve heavy spending for arms. This, we've seen, is blessed as sound while spending for welfare and the poor is always thought dangerous. With time, too, it has become evident that Keynesian progress can be an uneven thing: many automobiles, too few houses; many cigarettes, too little health care. The great cities in trouble. As these problems have obtruded, the confident years have come to an end. The Age of Keynes was for a time but not for all time.

8.
The Fatal Competition

[The American people must be on] guard against the acquisition of unwarranted influence, whether sought or unsought, by the military-industrial complex. The potential for the disastrous rise of misplaced power exists and will persist . . . We should take nothing for granted.

—President Dwight D. Eisenhower, 1961

To understand this world you must know that the military establishments of the United States and the Soviet Union have united against the civilians of both countries.

—A high official of the Department of State
to the author, 1974

In his testimony today, Mr. Haughton refused to characterize the payments [to other governments] as bribes, explaining that one of his lawyers . . . preferred to call them "kickbacks."

"If you get the contract," Mr. Haughton said, "it's pretty good evidence that the payments had to be made."

—From the *New York Times* account
of the testimony of Daniel J. Haughton,
Chairman of the Lockheed Aircraft Corporation,
before the Senate Banking and Currency Committee,
August 25, 1975

Politics, in one of the oldest of professional clichés, is the art of the possible. Equally, in its highest development, it is the art of separating the important from the peripheral and then concentrating on what is important, no matter how difficult. No problem in our time is a fraction so important, no source of uncertainty a fraction so valid as the arms competition between the United States and the Soviet Union. This competition has now developed the means for mutual and reciprocal destruction of the two nations, along with the rest of the world, in a matter of hours. Vast technical resources are being invested in the effort to reduce this to minutes. We are concerned in these pages with the ideas that explain our society and guide our behavior. What doctrine and circumstance lie back of this awful effort? There is nothing else that could be so important.

The competition just mentioned rests on two broad currents of thought, both exceptionally ominous in their implications. First, there is the concept of conflict — irreconcilable conflict — between inherently hostile economic, political and social systems. There can be no reconciliation between Communism and capitalism, authoritarian discipline and personal liberty, atheism and spiritual faith. That is the great fact of life.

The second and more recent idea is explicit in the words above of President Eisenhower and the nameless State Department official, only slightly less so in the response of Mr. Daniel Haughton, the since-deposed head of Lockheed. It holds that the arms race is the result of the way we are ruled. It is a manifestation, both in the United States and in the Soviet Union, of the public power of the military establishment and of those who make the arms. It involves a double symbiosis. In the United States the great weapons firms supply the armed services with the weapons they seek. The Air Force, Navy and Army reciprocate with the orders to the corporations that provide the profits and employment by which they function and flourish. The corporations and the services combine to conduct the research and development which make the current generation of arms obsolete and make necessary the next.

This is the first symbiosis. The second is between the United States and the Soviet Union. The same process in only slightly different form exists there. Each power, by its innovations and acquisitions, then creates the need and incentive for the other power to do the same — or more. Thus each works with the other to ensure that the competition is self-perpetuating. The difference between Communism and capitalism, freedom and authority, progress and reaction, Marx and Jesus, is cited but this is liturgical, not real. No faith sustains the arms competition. All who are knowledgeable agree that neither system would survive the conflict. Both countries are caught in a squirrel wheel, a trap.

There are many ways in which the history of the last thirty years could be written. I see no part of that history as so important as the changing vision of the arms race, from its perception as a conflict between systems to the present tendency to view it as a web of power by which we are ensnared. We are all greatly the product of our education in these matters. Mine began in Berlin very soon after the end of World War II.

Berlin: 1945

I knew Berlin rather well before the war; I went there in 1938 to study Hitler's land and agricultural policy. I had just learned that, in academic life, the selection of improbable subjects of study involving extensive travel is taken to suggest an imaginative and inquiring mind and is also a relief from tedium. My next glimpse of the great city was in the summer of 1945. One thought of the landscape of the moon; this was a phrase that came to many lips. When eventually we saw the landscape of the moon, it was more austere and chaste, less broken and much less alarming than Berlin in those summer days.

In 1945, Berlin was literally a city of death, for the bodies were still in the canals and tunnels and under the broken buildings. From Tempelhof air-drome where you came in, one saw burial parties passing into the big cemetery nearby, and also American soldiers with their girls. As a civilian, I had not previously realized that an accomplished warrior could make love with an M-1 rifle slung on his shoulder. Life in Berlin went on.

Half-destroyed buildings are the metaphor of the suffering that goes with war. The experience of horror is by people. But its image does not persist; very soon it cannot be seen at all. Only in structures does it endure. In Nazi times the Haus Vaterland was a famous conglomerate of restaurants and cabarets. Each of the different watering places featured the music, costumes, food and alcohol of a different part of the Reich. In 1945, most of Berlin was a metaphor of destruction. Today the visitor must search out the Haus Vaterland in a wilderness near the Wall to see how the horror of war endures.

In the summer of 1945, I was at a headquarters near Frankfurt with a group that was assessing the effects of the air attacks on the German war economy. One morning one of my fellow directors of the enterprise, George Ball — later Under Secretary of State, Ambassador to the United Nations, a banker and much else — called to remind me that the Big Three — Churchill, Stalin, Truman — would soon be meeting at Potsdam to decide the future of Germany and the world. He thought we should attend. I noted, as a difficulty, that we hadn't been invited. George said that to allow hurt feelings to keep us away would only compound that error. So we flew to Berlin in an old C-47 we'd been given for our work, were admitted immediately to the conference compound on our word that we had come to participate and began operations with an excellent lunch at the senior officials' mess. I was immediately made welcome by the committee that was considering reparations policy; its chairman, Isador Lubin, was an old friend. Ever since, I've wondered how many attending the great summit conferences were self-invited volunteers. In the following months I was concerned with German matters; eventually, in the State Department, I was put in charge of economic affairs in the occupied countries. (There is a lesson here: reticence and modesty ought not to stand in the way of public service.) These responsibilities brought me back to Berlin.

Soldiers, businessmen, civil servants, diplomats, assorted idlers and black marketeers were gathered in the city for the tasks of the occupation. By 1946, two parties were taking form: one party wanted very much to get along with the Russians. They — I should say we, for I was among them — saw little hope for a world in which there was conflict between the two powers. There were

The Brandenburg Gate, Berlin. When the armed representatives of capitalism met the armed might of Communism, the natural tendency was to do a little business. The market was here in 1945.

things to encourage us. When we met socially with the Russians, we learned how grim had been their experience with war, how passionate was their fear of another. Some of our senior army people were similarly moved. They had experienced war and wanted no more of it. We had as symbolic allies our enlisted men. They were meeting regularly with their Russian counterparts for the sale and exchange of merchandise; the market was in the shadow of the Brandenburg Gate which stands between East and West Berlin. Thus they showed that trade was above ideology, that when the armed representatives of capitalism met the armed might of Communism, the natural tendency was not to fight but to do a little business.

There was a second party. It regarded our hopes as ridiculously soft-headed. (There is an interesting point here: political wisdom is thought always to lie with the hard, impervious head and the tough, unyielding mind. One wonders why.) Some members of this group were only concerned to show how tough and hence how intelligent they were. But some, the Foreign Service Officers especially, spoke out of a genuine knowledge of Stalin and the great purges and a genuine concern for his intentions. Also the Soviet activities in Eastern Europe left no room for doubt. It was easy to assume that these would be the same in Western Europe as well.

Present too were the pathologically belligerent, those who even more than the poor are always with us. And there were a few for whom the war had been an exciting thing, a blessed escape from dull jobs, dull wives, deadly routine. Better another war than going back to Toledo, Ohio, or Nashua, New Hampshire.

On occasion, the debate became rather intense. We met in the late afternoons and evenings in the houses of the former Nazis and the German bourgeoisie. The bombs had wrecked the working and middle-class sections of Berlin but largely spared the affluent suburbs. Now the rich had their turn. They were summarily evicted to make way for those who were guiding the occupation. Not many of the latter had ever been housed so well before. All visitors to Berlin remarked on how easily and graciously Americans accommodated to the management of a complement of servants.

In these rather grand surroundings the talk turned regularly to Marx and Lenin. Not all who spoke of their design remembered much of their texts but they were confident of their purpose. It was world revolution, a world Communist order. Everyone in Berlin was a potential hostage to this effort.

The Bureaucratic Interest

These were the heroic thoughts. There was a deeper practical interest. The war had brought great prestige and influence to the armed forces. It had also done wonders for American business. In the previous Depression years businessmen, along with the banks, had been a favorite target of abuse. Then, during the war, the achievement in increasing production and supplying arms had been excellent. Profits had also been good. And a new and close relationship between industry and the armed services had been forged.

This was the beginning of the political alignment, the symbiosis of which I earlier spoke. The Air Force, in particular, had expanded wonderfully in power, prestige, men and airplanes. And a whole new industry had come into existence to provide the equipment and technology and share the gains. There followed a very simple, very practical point, far too obvious to be ignored. If there were a continuing menace, these gains would be continued. If not, they would be lost. The Soviets, not the French, not the British, not the Germans, were obvious candidates to be the new menace.

No one — certainly not many — argued that the gains of war should be preserved by the invention of a new menace. This is not the kind of thing that is said openly; the world has little to fear from forthrightly cynical men. Not many admitted this motivation even to themselves. Personal interest always wears the disguise of public purpose, and no one is more easily persuaded of the validity or righteousness of a public cause than the person who stands personally to gain therefrom. Those who perceive the underlying role of self-interest often hesitate to cite it. Nothing so interrupts the flow of polite conversation and so badly repays an invitation to drink and dine.

The doctrine of inevitable conflict had on its side the businessmen but there were others. It pleases the slightly insecure intellectual to agree with a down-to-earth man of affairs or a general. He proves to himself that he too can function in the world of practical action.

One felt, as time passed, that the practical and respectable men would prevail. So they did.

The Blockade

But one cannot discount the support the doctrine of inevitable conflict had from the Soviets. This, intended or otherwise, was comprehensive and superbly timed. In 1948, land and water communications with Berlin through the Soviet zone were interrupted. The barriers were closed. The ostensible cause was the currency reform in West Germany and its application to West Berlin. But, as read, the Soviet intention was to force the Allies out of Berlin. An heroic gesture was called for; it would be shown that a great city could be supplied, if necessary, entirely through the air. There followed the Berlin airlift.

Time has altered the earlier view of this event. The Soviets were certainly seeking to harass, discourage and protest. Not many historians now think they were seeking a final showdown. They may well have been surprised by the

The Airlift. Its proud statistics on display at the Rhein–Main base near Frankfurt.

reaction. General Lucius Clay, the American commander at the time, has always believed that an Allied convoy presenting itself firmly at the checkpoints would have been let through.

But we had airplanes. Having air power, air power must be a solution. More often than imagined, this has been the basis of military policy. However, it is not easy to criticize men who wished, at whatever cost, to minimize the risk of the armed confrontation that the airlift seemed to avoid. I do not do so. By the spring of 1949, eight thousand tons of freight were being landed each day in Berlin by the primitive piston planes of the time. That was enough, though barely, to sustain the life of the city.

Then agreement was reached, communications were resumed, the airlift came to an end. Coal, the principal cargo, had for a brief moment enjoyed the prestige of air passage; now it was returned to the trains and barges. But by this time a further chain of events was proclaiming the inevitability of conflict. In May 1948, Communist power was fully consolidated in Czechoslovakia. By the end of 1949, the Communist victory was complete in China. On Sunday, June 25, 1950, the United Press dispatch began: "The Russian-sponsored North Korean Communists invaded the American-supported Republic of South Korea today." Two years later, in the presidential campaign of 1952, Dwight D. Eisenhower promised, if elected, to go to Korea to seek an end to the conflict. Adlai Stevenson said in response: "The General has announced his intention to go to Korea. But the root of the Korean problem does not lie in Korea. It lies in Moscow."[1]

In retrospect, each of these events had its separate logic. The Czech takeover was the final step in the consolidation of the Soviet position in Eastern Europe. Earlier steps had not been seriously resisted. Some had been sanctioned in wartime agreements or in Churchill's wartime conversations with Stalin. Like Lenin in Russia, Mao in China moved into a vacuum — again the rotten door. He was then thought a Soviet instrument; this seems now an impossible fantasy. That the North Koreans invaded South Korea is not in doubt; the subsequent efforts to portray it as a riposte to South Korean aggression proves only that, with enough faith, some will believe anything. But that the Soviets sponsored the action as part of the larger strategy of Communist expansion is very much in doubt. Far more likely, as with much since in that part of the world, it was an act of local initiative; were it to happen now, this would be believed. But together the effect of these events was devastating. Those who hoped for accommodation were silenced.

Henceforth the Cold War was the reality. Those who questioned were no longer defeated in argument. They were suppressed. Searching out the doubters became for some an industry and for Joseph McCarthy a career.

McCarthy, however, was a mindless aberration, soon to be struck down by alcohol and his inability to distinguish his friends from his enemies. The basic ideas of the period came from a far more reputable figure: John Foster Dulles. They were not doctrines of great sophistication or depth. Even at the time they were regarded by many with doubt. Dulles was never an object of instinctive popularity or trust. But ideas do not need to be deeply right to be deeply influential. Better that they fit the prevailing mood and need.

John Foster Dulles

Once war could be justified in its own terms — a brave participant sport with medals to the contestants and land and lesser spoils to the winner. This is no longer so. The justification must now be fully above economic interest. One cannot say that war is good for the Air Force, for the supplying industries or even that it sustains employment or output in the economy at large. As with war, so it was with mobilization of energies short of war — the Cold War. Even the defense of free enterprise against Communism by then raised questions. The passion for free enterprise was too obviously related to the revenues therefrom. And those who were most likely to suffer in its defense were those who were paid the least.

Defense of freedom was a much better case and one that was much used. But this was an argument with which those who most disliked the Soviet Union were not completely comfortable. Radicals defended Roosevelt, Mrs. Roosevelt, unions, a better distribution of wealth and the emerging welfare state in the name of freedom. Freedom could obviously be abused, be damaging. It was accepted in the early fifties that some had misused their freedom by espousing Communism, by holding pro-Communist thoughts or by being insufficiently passionate in their Americanism. By those who were most impressed with the Soviet menace this was deemed highly inimical. Freedom, clearly, was not an unqualified good. It was not, in consequence, the best case against Communism.

It was John Foster Dulles who came up with the completely acceptable doctrine on which to base the Cold War, one that avoided all embarrassment. The Cold War had nothing to do with economics; indeed, an excessive preoccupation with material values was a basic fault of the other side. Freedom was mentioned but was not central. The Cold War was a crusade for moral values — for good against bad, right against wrong, religion against atheism. It was the defense of the faith of the average, neighborly, God-fearing American — one's own beliefs and those of the people next door.

For this Dulles could turn to the faith of his fathers. He grew up with it in the small city of Watertown in far northern New York where his father was the

John Foster Dulles. At Princeton, 1907.

"Where MacCrimmon sits is the head of the table." John Foster Dulles and Douglas
MacArthur.

Presbyterian minister. The countryside was a step away. As a boy Dulles sailed on the waters of Lake Ontario. His companion was his younger brother, Allen Welsh Dulles, his partner at law and in the Cold War battles to come.

From Watertown Foster went to Princeton and was intended by his parents for the ministry. However, early on he persuaded them he could do God's work almost as adequately were he a lawyer. So, after going as a young assistant to The Hague and Versailles Conferences and seeing the great in diplomatic discussion, he settled down to the practice of corporation law. By the age of thirty-eight, he was the senior partner of Sullivan & Cromwell, the most prestigious of the great Wall Street law firms. There he made his career.

This involved a certain wandering from his faith. Wall Street is not the epitome of church-going, small-town America. People do not think of corporation lawyers as being primarily concerned with God's work. They are believed, no doubt accurately, to have more remunerative clients. This was especially so of Dulles. In 1929, as I've earlier told, he was a director of the Shenandoah and Blue Ridge Corporations, the classic aberrations of that larcenous year. Hundreds of millions of dollars were lost. Governor Thomas E. Dewey, who launched Dulles in politics, explained later that Dulles took a temporary leave of absence from religion during this period.

However, almost everything about John Foster Dulles remains a trifle ambiguous. Almost all historians, friendly or otherwise, speak of his brilliant mind. But Harold Macmillan, who saw much of him, was reminded of a statesman of whom it was said, ". . . his speech was slow, but it easily kept pace with his thought."[2] Most believed him paranoiac where Communism was involved. But others held that he got along well with the Russians, for he was what they expected a capitalist to be. In the Suez crisis of 1955–56, he lined up with the Soviets against the British, French and Israelis.

It is certain that Dulles had an instinct for command. There is a kind of person who, out of the very certainty of his purpose, right or wrong, both assumes leadership and is conceded leadership. No quality so assures public success. Douglas MacArthur was such a man. So was Charles de Gaulle. So, though with slightly less inner certainty, was Winston Churchill. So, we have seen, was Lenin. An old Scottish saying celebrates this leader: "Where MacCrimmon sits is the head of the table." To be a MacCrimmon is far better than to have brilliance of mind, eloquence of speech or charm of personality.

In the years following World War II, bored with the law and even with making money, Dulles prepared himself for command. He returned to religion and took an active part in the affairs of the National Council of Churches. He resumed his earlier interest in foreign policy and helped negotiate the peace treaty with Japan. For a few months, by appointment, he was in the Senate but he was defeated when he sought election on his own. His power of command did not extend to the average voter. In 1953, Eisenhower made him Secretary of State. He came to office, and so did his moral sanction for the Cold War.

John Foster Dulles was not a very popular figure with liberals of my generation. Many of us agreed with the judgment of Reinhold Niebuhr, the liberal theologian, who said that "Mr. Dulles' moral universe makes everything quite clear, too clear . . . Self-righteousness is the inevitable fruit of simple moral judgments."[3] So it is only fair to let him speak for himself. This he did at his father's church in Watertown on October 11, 1953, nine months after he became Secretary of State. It is the clearest statement we have or would wish of the ideas underlying the Cold War:

> The terrible things that are happening in some parts of the world are due to the fact that political and social practices have been separated from spiritual content.
>
> That separation is almost total in the Soviet Communist world. There the rulers hold a materialistic creed which denies the existence of moral law. It denies that men are spiritual beings. It denies that there are any such things as eternal verities.
>
> As a result the Soviet institutions treat human beings as primarily important from the standpoint of how much they can be made to produce for the glorification of the state. Labor is essentially slave labor, working to build up the military and material might of the state, so that those who rule can assert ever greater and more frightening power.
>
> Such conditions repel us. But it is important to understand what causes those conditions. It is irreligion.[4]

He added:

> But it is gross error to assume that material forces have a monopoly of dynamism. Moral forces too are mighty. Christians, to be sure, do not believe in invoking brute power to secure their ends. But that does not mean that they have no ends or that they have no means of getting there. Christians are not negative, supine people.
>
> Jesus told the disciples to go out into all the world and to preach the gospel to all the nations. Any nation which bases its institutions on Christian principles cannot but be a dynamic nation.[5]

The Cold War was a moral crusade. It was also a religious crusade. And it came close to being a Christian crusade. There was more than a hint that a strong, even militant policy, so long as it avoided "brute power," would have the endorsement of Jesus.

There was a corollary here. Christians were as numerous east of the Iron Curtain as west. Their case, if religion was the issue, could not be less urgent than that of their coreligionists in Western Europe or the United States. Christians were as entitled to rescue as to defense. The Dulles case for the Cold War thus became a case for liberation, for rolling back the Iron Curtain. This Dulles at first proclaimed. However, in 1956, when the Hungarians rose in revolt, that promise was revoked.

Thus the setting. On the Soviet side was the proclaimed commitment to world revolution and a sequence of actions that could easily be interpreted as

Launching the U.S.S. Richard B. Russell. A recent Secretary of Defense suggested that President Eisenhower might have spoken of the Military-Industrial-Congressional complex. Senator Russell was long a major voice on military affairs.

affirming it. In the West was the matching moral and religious commitment to liberation from Communism, or much language that could be so interpreted. The world was set for a dangerous passage.

The Cold War in Washington

The nineteen-fifties in Washington were the years not of Eisenhower but of Dulles. The idea of the irrepressible conflict went virtually unchallenged. The questioning to which, in a democratic society, every important action of the state should be subject was almost completely in abeyance. I saw this, in a minor way, at first hand. I was cochairman with Dean Acheson in the latter fifties of one of the subsidiary organs of the Democratic Party, the Democratic Advisory Council. Acheson was chairman for foreign policy, I for domestic policy. The Council was, by common agreement, the most liberal wing of the opposition — the leading edge. At our meetings Acheson attacked Dulles lucidly, brilliantly and with resourceful invective for being too soft on the Soviets. The debate on his draft foreign policy resolutions consisted almost exclusively of efforts — by Adlai Stevenson, Averell Harriman, Herbert Lehman and other moderate members — to tone down his declarations of war. That was the opposition to Dulles.

At the more practical level, the Pentagon in these years developed weapons systems that were often duplicating or competitive and which were routinely approved. The word Pentagon itself now became a synonym for military bureaucracy and power, and a large and growing weapons industry responded to its will. Men moved with ease from managing the procurement of weapons in Washington to managing their development or manufacture in California. Few spoke against their decisions. The Armed Services Committees of the Congress endorsed all. In 1945, Robert Oppenheimer, the architect of the atomic bomb, was the most heroic figure in the history of American science. A reference to "Oppy" was the highest American achievement in the art of name-dropping, superior if anything to a British reference to Winston, though hardly as imaginative as a French allusion to Charles. In 1953, Oppenheimer's security clearance was lifted; he was excluded from all Washington deliberation and meditation. His substantive sin was in expressing doubts about the wisdom and desirability of the H-bomb. The Oppenheimer case showed as nothing else could have shown that no one in official position, however prestigious, had the right of dissent.

The questioning and dissent outside the government were equally unimpressive. The best scholars in the universities studied Cold War strategy. So with particular prestige did the new Think Tanks. To have spent a summer in the fifties at the Rand Corporation, the special intellectual instrument of the Air Force, established the position of an economics, mathematics or political

Before the Fall. Robert Oppenheimer at Alamogordo after the first nuclear test. With him is General Leslie R. Groves, military head of the Manhattan Project.

science professor for all the coming year. A sociologist so favored might not even return to his university. The intelligence agencies were seen as central to all Cold War strategy, and the most central of all was the Central Intelligence Agency. In these years the CIA was a convocation of intellectuals to the point of being mildly suspect.

The License for Immorality

The controlling doctrines of the CIA, on which as a former ambassador I can speak with firsthand knowledge, involved an important modification of the Dulles conception of the Cold War. The CIA accepted that the Soviets were bent on world revolution. This involved a selective response to Soviet propaganda. When Soviet leaders affirmed this goal, they were believed. When, as later happened, they spoke of peaceful coexistence, they were held to be dissembling.

In addition to ambitions in all non-Communist countries (which more than incidentally required that countering force be deployed in all countries), the Communists were brilliantly and relentlessly unscrupulous. This was in keeping with the Dulles doctrine of a battle between morality and immorality, right and wrong, with the Communists always immoral.

But here a problem arose, as often it does when action seeks the sanction of universal rules. Although the battle was between morality and immorality, you could not fight immorality and remain pure. Once it might have been imagined that Christian principles were a weapon of independent force. The CIA was more practical. So, to fight Communism, it was given a specific exemption from the Dulles ethic; its scholarly members were given a special license for immorality. They were then placed under the direction of Allen Dulles.

There was no danger that this juxtaposition to his brother's principles would cause Allen embarrassment. As noted, there was a difference of opinion on the speed and subtlety of John Foster Dulles's mind. Allen's mind presented no such problem.

Intellectuals, we have seen, yearn to prove that they can be tough-minded and very tough. So it was with those who manned the CIA. The license for immorality was greatly exploited and much enjoyed. Not many gave thought to a day when, the Cold War having abated however slightly, the license for immorality would be revoked and the Foster Dulles-Watertown morality restored with retroactive effect. This happened. For the former licensees it would be an unhappy time.[*]

[*]The reader has a right to ask whether on such matters an author writes from foresight or the wonderfully greater advantages of hindsight. Without claiming always to eschew the latter, I

Khrushchev

As always, we know much less about what went on in the Soviet Union. That Soviet policy in the postwar years was founded on the idea of irrepressible conflict is also certain. This would be plausible if only as a response but it was more than that. And that any such policy must build if not a military-industrial power, then a military-bureaucratic power can also be assumed. Some consequences of the same circumstances will be the same.

But in both the Soviet Union and the United States events were in train in the fifties which would change the perception of the conflict — which would cause it to be seen ever less as a conflict of systems, ever more as a manifestation of power, military, industrial and bureaucratic, within the two countries. I attribute prime importance to five influences. They were Khrushchev, Cuba, the Vietnam war, the increasingly sharp and visible divisions within the Communist world and the persistent unwillingness of the human mind to accept persuasion that is in conflict with evidence. All who exercise power find this latter obstinacy by far the most annoying tendency with which they have to contend.

After nearly thirty years of rule, Stalin died in 1953. Five years later Nikita Khrushchev emerged as his successor, and he held power for the next six. He was then suddenly and summarily discharged from office. By any calculation he was one of the decisive men of the midcentury.

He had been, as he fully acknowledged, an undeviating supporter of Stalin. Had he been otherwise, he would not have kept well. The nearly inescapable instinct of any man so situated is to continue things as before. Such is the whole tendency of bureaucratic interest and inertia, the most powerful of influences in our time. Khrushchev, incredibly, committed himself to a reversal of Stalinist policies. And in this he had major success. He publicly condemned the Stalinist terror and greatly reduced the role of fear in the government of the Soviet

can say that, when I went to India in early 1961, I was profoundly impressed by the political unwisdom, adventurist tendency and amateurism of the CIA operations. And I was even more impressed by the embarrassment the Ambassador of the United States would suffer when, as inevitably would happen, these operations were known. (All involved the participation of enough Indians to ensure that, one day, some or all of their cover would be blown.) Drawing on the support of President Kennedy and Lewis Jones of the State Department, a principled conservative who then presided over South Asian Affairs, and also on powers recently accorded an ambassador over his mission, I abolished all of the nonintelligence operations of the CIA in India. (They were not thereafter restored, or so I've been told.) In Washington a senior CIA official was so angry and distressed that he came to tears. In India the competent officers engaged in intelligence reporting — whose functions were known to the Indians — were, in the end, I always thought, relieved.

Nikita Khrushchev. He traveled with obvious enjoyment to argue that existence and peaceful coexistence were identical.

Union. He enlarged perceptibly the scope for debate, liberalized appreciably the intellectual and cultural life of the country and proclaimed the obvious truth that, after an atomic exchange, little would distinguish the Communist ashes from the capitalist ashes. He recurred repeatedly to the resulting foreign policy theme that there must be peaceful coexistence with the non-Communist world. He traveled with obvious enjoyment to other countries to make his case.

Stalin, he once told Jawaharlal Nehru (who told me), had made the name of the Soviet Union a stench in the nostrils of the civilized world. His task was to see that this was changed. The effort included two visits to the United States — unrequited pilgrimages which somewhat resembled later journeys of American presidents to Peking. In Moscow, with a certain genius for the opportunity, he engaged in impromptu debate with Richard Nixon. He seems to have sensed, if he did not fully know, that millions of Americans would believe that anyone who argued with Nixon could not be wholly wrong.

The defenders of the idea of irrepressible conflict did not give up easily. They warned solemnly against Khrushchev: a typical Communist trickster; an infinitely devious man; a very clever peasant. Khrushchev had promised that socialism would bury capitalism. Better be literal and believe that he meant The Bomb. There could be no reconciliation with a man who took off his shoes in public. There can be no doubt that Khrushchev's diplomacy, including his visits to the United States and the United Nations, was a major turning point in the Cold War.

It also, much later, provided a flash of insight into the way the Cold War was coming to be perceived on both sides. In 1971 and 1974, Khrushchev's memoirs were published. Although there were then questions as to their authenticity, that he was the ultimate source is not now seriously in doubt. In the United States and possibly also in the Soviet Union any writer with the talent and imagination to bring off the fraud would be writing more profitably on his own. Khrushchev tells of his visit in 1959 to President Eisenhower at his "dacha" at Camp David. In the course of informal conversation one evening, Eisenhower told him of the pressure from his generals for weapons expenditure. In the end, the intention of the Soviets being cited and the security of the United States being at risk, he found himself giving in. He asked Khrushchev if he had had similar experience. Khrushchev replied that he had. He was subject to similar pressure. He, however, talked back firmly to his generals. True, he added, they went on to say that if denied the requisite resources, the security of the Soviet Union against the United States could not be guaranteed. And then he too gave in. Khrushchev, perhaps fortunately, was in power in Russia when Cuba came onto the stage.

Cuba

There are countries, which in consequence of size, location and, though more rarely, the wise belief of their people that nature did not intend them to be heroes, are meant for historical neglect. One of these is Cuba. Another is Vietnam. Both, in these years, had a decisive effect on the ideas with which we are here concerned.

Cuba's first impact was in the spring months of 1961. In the previous year there had been the inspired journey of Gary Powers across the Soviet Union as the nations were meeting for a summit at Paris. That the moment called for caution was well beyond the mental reach of Allen Dulles. Next came the Bay of Pigs. This too was conceived, planned and executed by the CIA. Members of the new Kennedy Administration had accepted and even admired the boldness of the enterprise. Presently it developed that not since Joshua's trumpets at Jericho had there been a military operation in which there was so little rational expectation of success. A helpless band of half-trained refugees was landed from some rusty freighters on a badly selected beach. A few ancient Cuban planes frightened off the ships that were to give them further support. The victims were soon rounded up. The Cuban masses, detesting Communism as did Americans, were expected to rise. Of this there was no sign.

At the United Nations Adlai Stevenson was allowed to identify the pilots of the attacking expedition who had landed at Florida after largely missing the Cuban air force as defectors from Castro. Any other American involvement was indignantly, even aggressively, denied. These untruths unraveled within hours. Nothing in the Cold War years was more striking than the incapacity of the scholarly personnel of the CIA for talented falsehood. Perhaps this was not surprising. They had been well brought up in good families, had gone to good schools and been hired on the basis of character and intelligence. So they were without experience in sustainable mendacity.

These untruths and their exposure were the most consequential single feature of the events at the Bay of Pigs. The unhappy flight of Gary Powers in 1960 had been first described as a badly navigated excursion to look at the weather. Sensing better than most the danger of falsehood in a moral crusade, President Eisenhower had moved quickly to affirm the truth. Now, closer to home, there was mendacity on a much larger scale. And the special license was here being used not against the Communists but against the American people and, as in the case of Stevenson, the American government. It was being used, in other words, against the same people to whom John Foster Dulles's moral crusade was designed to appeal — to whom, in an address to the National Council of Churches, he had said: "But I believe that we can still follow the good American tradition of openness, simplicity and morality in foreign policy."[6]

246

Confrontation (of a kind) at the Bay of
Pigs. Fidel Castro . . .

. . . E. Howard Hunt. "Not since Joshua's trumpets at Jericho had there been a military
operation in which there was so little rational expectation of success."

The contradiction between claim and practice was too great. Cynical men were not bothered but cynics were not the people for whom the Dulles ideas were meant. And while Foster Dulles was now dead, the man in charge of immorality was still his brother Allen. (In the aftermath of the Bay of Pigs he was sacked. So tactfully did the Establishment deal with its own in those days it is doubtful if he ever knew he was a failure.) It should surprise no one that, in later years, discussion of the immorality of the Soviet Union would give way to an extremely intense discussion and investigation of the immorality of the CIA. The problem with an appeal to moral values is that such values can be deeply held.

A Look into the Pit

A year and a half after the Bay of Pigs came the Cuban missile crisis. Cuba again. The effect of this was on the concept of the irrepressible conflict itself. Until then discussion of the conflict had been hypothetical, even academic in tone. Generals made speeches threatening the Communists with nuclear annihilation and calling for its calm acceptance by all patriotic Americans. The response was much as to sermons threatening or promising eternal punishment. The fear is in the sermon, not the prospect. Now for a few tense and terrible days the prospect was faced. People looked directly into the pit. There can be no doubt as to the result: thousands and perhaps millions began to wonder if there was not some slightly less heroic but substantially more pleasant alternative. Though it was little noticed at the time, after the missile crisis the generals ceased to make the speeches.

Something else became evident from this crisis, at least to the President of the United States. It was that men of little moral courage who get caught up in the decisions are afraid to resist the accepted view, however catastrophic it may be. So, paradoxically, out of cowardice, the fear of being in dissent or of seeming to be weak, they urge the most dangerous course. During the missile crisis these were the men who advocated an attack on the missile sites, what was called a surgical strike. No one could say *they* lacked guts, the charge of which they were most afraid. The men of independent courage — Adlai Stevenson, George Ball, Robert Kennedy — urged restraint. Coming back from India a few days after the end of the crisis, I went to the theater one evening with President and Mrs. Kennedy. During the intermission we went out by the curtain and sat on the stairs near the stage. This saved the President from the handshakers and the autograph hunters. "I didn't vote for you, Mr. President, but I certainly admire you." He told me, with much feeling, of the recklessness of the advice he had received during the crisis. The worst, he said, was from those who were afraid to be sensible.

Vietnam

The Cuban education was brief and deep. The education by Vietnam was prolonged and, in the end, decisive. In one fashion or another, all the assumptions of conflict as framed by Dulles were there eroded. Only as this is seen can the Vietnam war be understood as one of the great watersheds of modern history. It was an evil and bitter thing, out of which came much light.

A crusade for moral purpose requires a certain minimal moral tone on the part of those for whom the crusade is being mounted. Armies would not have been dispatched to the Holy Land for the redemption of either Sodom or Gomorrah. The saving of South Vietnam allied the United States with individuals whose moral posture few could defend. The gallery included corrupt and despotic politicians, corrupt and cowardly generals and a vast assortment of independent larcenists. Moral purpose was most strongly manifested by those in opposition to the government. Often, if not invariably, moral purpose in Vietnam brought people into such opposition. Meanwhile the country's common soldiers showed little disposition to die for the indefensible gains and privileges of others. It was a thought to which American warriors were not immune.

Twenty years earlier the same conflict between precept and practice had arisen in China. Chiang Kai-shek and his supporters had also been greatly lacking in moral tone. But in the absence of direct military involvement the contradiction had not been so serious. With President Diem, the Nhu family and the politicians that followed as in a revolving door, the impression of villainy was inescapable. Marx had held that capitalism becomes vulnerable at its most advanced stage. Vietnam, like China, proved almost precisely the reverse. Both countries showed that, as capitalism emerges from feudalism, it is characterized by an anarchic rapacity that the people of the advanced capitalist countries cannot understand.

In the end, the American people reacted, caused a President to retire, placed great pressure on his successor when he showed signs of enlarging the war into Cambodia and Laos and brought the Vietnam conflict to an end. It was a remarkable demonstration of democratically expressed will. It flowed from the very sense of moral outrage that, for the opposite ends, John Foster Dulles had sought to arouse.

The Vietnam war destroyed the moral sanction of the war against Communism. Our allies were too immoral. It eliminated also another prop to the doctrine of irreconcilable conflict. This was the concept of Communism as a unified, centrally-directed world conspiracy. Dulles had spoken of atheistic Communism; Dean Rusk, his equally Cromwellian successor, spoke of monolithic Communism. China was a Soviet Manchukuo. All official references

Opposition to the war became respectable. This decorous gathering is in Madison, Wisconsin, where government bondholders are cashing in their bonds.

during his long and diligent term of office — from 1961 to 1969 — were to the Sino-Soviet bloc.

The conception of Communism as a united world transcending national differences and aspirations was vital. It was what made it seem a new and powerful force in the world. It could then plausibly be presented as many-faced, calculating and conspiratorial, relentlessly probing for weak spots in the armor of the non-Communist world. A Communist world divided along national lines and with conflicts within itself lost much of its power, much of its menace and much of its conspiratorial aspect. Some parts might be led to search for friends in the non-Communist world. Polemics and policies would have to be modified accordingly. The Cold War as a conflict between right and wrong had an appealing simplicity. With division in the Communist world there would be complicating degrees of wrong.

It became evident, as the Vietnam war progressed, that the Vietnamese Communists, however much they might be helped by the Soviets and the Chinese, were fighting very much on their own. And through the nineteen-sixties, evidence accumulated of conflict between the Soviets and the Chinese. Soviet assistance to China was suspended; Soviet technicians were withdrawn or expelled. There was talk of minor fighting along the frontier, fighting that could only be a manifestation of suspicion and hostility, for neither country could be imagined to set much store by the real estate at issue. In early 1972, while the Vietnam war continued, Richard Nixon responded to opportunity in a manner that should be a lesson to more principled men. He made a pilgrimage to Peking. This was followed in May of the same year by a trip to Moscow and the affirmation of the new policy of détente. (The English meaning of détente remained obscure; in 1976, President Ford announced that he was dropping the term but not the emphasis on peace.) At a minimum, the policy signified the end of the doctrine of irreconcilable conflict, of one side seeking the destruction of the other at whatever cost to itself. The justification of the strategic arms race could no longer be found in the old ideas. The arms race itself was now the trap.

The Symbiotic Trap

At Potsdam in 1945, Truman told Stalin about the successful tests and imminent use of the atomic bomb. Stalin, according to the contemporary accounts, reacted calmly; observers thought that he did not appreciate the significance of the news. Soviet scientists have since told that he phoned Moscow the same day to order all possible acceleration in the Soviet development of the same weapon.

The competition followed. Each side develops the weapons that make obsolete those currently in use or on order. In each country scientists, engineers, the armed services and the supporting industries join the effort and are rewarded by the task. An example, spectacular but not atypical, of this broad-spectrum collaboration was Project Nobska at Woods Hole on Cape Cod in Massachusetts in the summer of 1956. Naval officers, scientists and engineers from the defense industries gathered for ten weeks that summer to consider the military opportunities deriving from the recent successful tryouts of the nuclear submarine. Edward Teller was there. So was Rear Admiral L. P. Ramage and Admiral Arleigh Burke. From IBM came James S. Crosby. The Associate Director of Nobska was Ivan Getting, Vice-President for Research of Raytheon Industries; the Director was Columbus Iselin, the head of the Woods Hole Oceanographic Institute. The entire enterprise was under the auspices not of the military but of the National Academy of Sciences.

From such a congregation something remarkable could surely be expected. Something remarkable came — a nuclear missile that could be fired from a submarine while underwater, out of sight and undetectable, to devastate a target up to three thousand miles away. This was Polaris.

Polaris, it later developed, countered a threat that the Soviets, at the time, were only contemplating. But this is unimportant. By the nature of the symbiotic trap, the Soviets would have led if they could. Had they been leading, this would have increased the urgency of the meeting at Woods Hole.

On few matters has the capacity of adults, presumptively sane, for the polemics of the schoolyard been more manifest than in the effort to justify this contest by ascribing blame. The Soviets are guilty; therefore the United States must respond. The imperialists are guilty; therefore the people of the Soviet Union will defend themselves. The debate is precisely on a parity with one between the squirrel and the wheel.

The Economic Consequences

It comes down to this: the armed services of the United States want to exist; to exist they must have weapons. The weapons firms want to exist and make money; to do this, they must produce weapons. The Soviets provide the justification for this existence. We justify the same institutions and the same process in the Soviet Union. It is no longer believed that conflict between the two powers is necessary or inevitable; all know that neither system could survive the conflict. We are reduced to believing that the competition prevents the conflict.

The classical New England scenery at Woods Hole celebrates the highest technological achievement of the contest. To visualize its economic effects one should travel west to Tucson, Arizona, and there visit the Davies-Monthan Air Force Base. Here the economic effects stretch almost to the horizon. Davies-Monthan is the world's largest used-airplane lot.

Project Nobska which created Polaris. In the nature of the arms trap, initiating action, East or West, creates the danger with which it deals. The threat these men countered did not yet exist.

Davies-Monthan Air Force Base in Arizona. The world's greatest junkyard.
The end of the wild blue yonder. B-52's (inset) will one day soon be cut up.

Some of the aircraft on the Davies-Monthan lot will be sold. There are good bargains here for poor countries seeking a small place in the sun, wishing to emulate the destructive tendencies of the more advanced civilizations at low cost. And there are better ones — newer, faster, more complicated — for nations that have just struck it rich in oil. But most of the planes will never fly again; here on the range they are headed for the last roundup. No matter what the original cost, however wonderful the original performance, the paths through the wild blue yonder lead but to the junkyard.

There is agreement even in high military circles that the naked weapons competition cannot go on. Some will ask the hard question, what will take its place? What of the jobs it provides? What will replace the purchasing power it generates? John Maynard Keynes proposed that the British government put bundles of pound notes into disused coal pits and fill the pits up. This would create jobs. And much more employment would be created by men digging out the pounds, and much demand would then be generated by the spending of the notes. The idea was never taken up; instead, in the post-Keynesian world, weapons expenditures — the cycle of design, production, obsolescence, replacement — have served instead. I once called it military Keynesianism.

All candid economists concede the role of military expenditures in sustaining the modern economy. Some have held that expenditures for civilian purposes — health, housing, mass transport, lower taxes leading to more private consumption — would do as well. The transition would be rather easy.

This ignores the entrapment. And it ignores the economic power that sustains the trap and keeps it shut. Behind a new manned bomber is the military and industrial colossus we have been here examining. It is strong and resourceful in defending its interest, and we may assume that it is strong and resourceful in the Soviet Union too. Back of improved housing and cities there is no similar power as there is no similar competition. There is only, by comparison, a vacuum.

One should also observe that there is a problem of magnitudes. For the price of a smallish fleet of manned supersonic bombers, a modern mass transit system could be built in virtually every city large enough to have a serious bus line. What would be built then?

The Beginning of Change

The question is one for a later word. Yet it could be that the economics of the entrapment is changing. And the change, and opportunity for escape, could come more rapidly than most imagine.

In all the industrial countries hitherto-disadvantaged groups are releasing themselves from the convention that they were meant, for reasons of race, class or national origin, to have less. They are asserting their claim to enjoyments — leisure, good housing, vacations, education, more than minimal clothing, cultural activities — formerly considered the prerogatives of the affluent or the rich. Along with this, a point to be noted presently, have come the unimaginably large public costs of a highly urbanized existence.

Similar forces in slightly different form are at work in the Soviet Union. There serious inequity in consumption is even more difficult to defend. So is a standard of living too far below that of the nonsocialist world.

The result in all of the industrial countries, socialist and nonsocialist, is an unprecedented demand on economic resources. This manifests itself in the Western industrial countries in wage claims and resulting inflationary pressures. Military budgets are somewhat more closely examined now than in the days when the planes that are rotting at Davies-Monthan were ordered. That scrutiny will, we must hope, continue and with luck become more severe. In the Soviet Union the pressure of competing claims, by all outward evidence, is even stronger. Popularity there too accrues to those who can offer more civilian consumption.

So there is a chance that, with passing years, the economic question will not be what will take the place of military spending. Rather, it will be how military resources can be economized to make way for the other, more urgent claims of an increasingly classless consumption. The economic pressures will be for agreement on arms limitation, not against it.

That is at least a prospect. But it would be unwise for men of reason in either the United States or the Soviet Union — anyone, indeed, with a concern for survival — to await the day and acquiesce in the present entrapment. That entrapment had better be confronted directly, a need to which I will return.

9.
The Big Corporation

The institution that most changes our lives we least understand or, more correctly, seek most elaborately to misunderstand. That is the modern corporation. Week by week, month by month, year by year, it exercises a greater influence on our livelihood and the way we live than unions, universities, politicians, the government. There is a corporate myth which is carefully, assiduously propagated. And there is the reality. They bear little relation to each other. The modern corporation lives in suspension between fiction and truth.

The corporate myth is of a disciplined, energetic, dedicated but well-rewarded body of men serving under a dynamic leader. He reflects the interests of the owners at whose will he serves. His subordinates carry out his orders or transmit them on to the minions below. This is the organization. Its purpose, like that of all business firms large and small, is to make money by making things — to do well by doing good. It does best when it serves the public best. This is accomplished through the market, to which the corporation is wholly subordinate. What the consumer most wants, the market, in prices and sales, best rewards.

Since the corporation is wholly in the service of the consumer, it cannot be in the service of itself; being subject to the power of the public, it cannot have any significant power of its own. Generations of students have learned their economics from Paul A. Samuelson, an early Nobel Laureate in economics, the pre-eminent teacher of his time. His textbook puts the position with clarity and simplicity: "The consumer, so it is said, is the king . . . each is a voter who uses his money as votes to get the things done that he *wants* done."[1] Anyone subject to sovereign power can have no power of his own.

This is the myth. But Professor Samuelson is a sensible as well as distinguished man. So, like other economists, he reverts to the reality when he leaves the classroom. He recognizes that corporations greatly influence their markets — the prices they charge, the costs they pay — that in the real world, to use his words, they are "price-administering oligopolists."[2] Thus they manage prices to which the not-so-sovereign consumer responds. And the corporation also shapes the tastes of consumers to its products. No one can fail

"There are no great men, my boy — only great committees."
© 1975 The New Yorker Magazine, Inc.

to be aware of this power. The advertising that does it dominates our vision and pre-empts our ears.

The modern corporation also exercises power in and by way of government. This too is agreed. Its payments to politicians and public officials are believed by no one except the recipients to be acts of philanthropy or affection. And less mentioned but more important is the naturally advantageous relationship between the modern corporation and the public bureaucracy — between those who build cars and those who build highways, between those who make fighter aircraft and those who guide the Air Force. Between the modern corporation and the modern state there is a deeply symbiotic relationship based on shared power and shared reward.

The myth that holds that the great corporation is the puppet of the market, the powerless servant of the consumer, is, in fact, one of the devices by which

258

its power is perpetuated. Colonialism, we saw, was possible only because the myth of higher moral purpose regularly concealed the reality of lower economic interest. Similarly here. Were it part of our everyday education and comment that the corporation is an instrument for the exercise of power, that it belongs to the process by which we are governed, there would then be debate on how that power is used and how it might be made subordinate to the public will and need. This debate is avoided by propagating the myth that the power does not exist. It is especially useful that the young be so instructed. By pretending that power is not present, we greatly reduce the need to worry about its exercise.

But not completely, for we do not eliminate entirely the associated unease. We sense that our lives are shaped and that government is guided by the modern corporation. The myth disguises but it does not reassure. It leaves those who head large corporations unhappy in the knowledge that they are not loved, wondering why newspapermen, politicians and intellectuals do not share their sense of their own virtue. In the Age of Uncertainty the corporation is a major source of uncertainty. It leaves men wondering how and by whom and to what end they are ruled. One response to this uncertainty will be obvious. It is to look through the myth at the reality of the modern corporation.

The Esalen Institute

One begins with an Arcadian scene. The modern corporation has power. Men love the exercise of power. And in the corporation power must be shared. All but the most elementary decisions require the information, specialized knowledge or experience of several or many people. It is a world, as Charles Addams has observed, where there are no great men, only great committees. Our instinct in the exercise of power is always to our own appreciation, our own view of what should be done. To adjust to the view of others, to accept their information and experience, requires a sensitivity and a restraint that many do not have.

This is the reason that executives go to Esalen on the California coast below Monterey; Esalen seeks to provide the sensitivity and the restraint that the organized exercise of power requires.

One thinks of the effort of married couples to achieve greater harmony and understanding. And rightly so, for in its intimacy of association corporate life is marriage with love but without sex. There is the same need to understand; to civilize; to perfect an association; above all, to persuade the individual that, at some point in the exercise of power, his purpose must be subordinated, without sense of defeat, to that of another.

Since 1965, major corporations — Standard Oil of California and Memorex, along with the State Department and Internal Revenue Service — have been

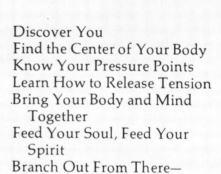

Discover You
Find the Center of Your Body
Know Your Pressure Points
Learn How to Release Tension
Bring Your Body and Mind
   Together
Feed Your Soul, Feed Your
   Spirit
Branch Out From There—
     Blossom

What Esalen could do for you too.

sending their executives to Esalen for sensitivity training, meaning the sensitive exercise of power. On occasion, the results have been astonishing. One communicant at Esalen found himself rejecting the world of shared power and the world as well. He forever abandoned his three-piece business suit, changed to jeans, allowed his hair to grow and remained on as a gardener. How the rest were changed we do not know. The world of corporate power is a carefully protected one. Even social investigators do not intrude. The personal habits of potentates and politicians have always been the stuff of conversation, as they are of history. The psyche, home life, personal hygiene, even the sex habits of the great corporate executive have been little studied. But what Esalen says about the intensely interpersonal exercise of power in the modern corporation is very plain.

From this interpersonal exercise of power, the interaction and resulting purpose of the participants, comes the personality of the corporation. No two are exactly alike. No two exercise power to precisely the same ends. A corporation in which scientists and engineers interact — IBM, ICI, Xerox — will be very different from one which, like Revlon or Unilever, survives by its skill in mass persuasion or even public bamboozlement. Some corporations will measure success primarily by earnings, others by their growth. In yet others technical achievement is a partial measure of accomplishment. Some corporations use the language of service and public responsibility. If men speak often enough of their virtue, they may well persuade themselves to its practice. Others see their corporation as the continuing shadow of the hard-boiled, moneymaking capitalist. Let the Boy Scouts and the do-gooders worry about truth and the public good.

Because corporations differ, no single enterprise fully exemplifies corporate history and personality. All, when studied, revert, except in unguarded moments, to their myth. The exercise of power so central to corporate personality is at least partly concealed. So the solution here has been to synthesize — to draw from the realities of numerous corporations the history that best illustrates corporate development and the modern corporate personality. Our corporation will be Unified Global Enterprises — UGE. Since UGE exists but does not exist, there was no one to defend its myth. Everything having to do with UGE, inside and out, could be seen without censorship.

The Founder

James B. Glow came to Chicago from Greenock on the Clyde below Glasgow in 1871. He opened a butcher shop on the South Side and presently went on to curing hams and making sausage. Within the decade he had developed a sizable meat-packing business. It was a time when things went rapidly. Thereafter, in the words of the official history of the firm, "James Ballantyne

Glow never looked back." By the end of the century Glow Packing, along with Swift, Armour, Wilson and Cudahy, was one of the Big Five.

It was big with a difference. The Swifts and the Armours dominated Chicago society; their pork and beef underwrote the cultural life of the city. James Glow and his two sons paid attention only to their business and to their church. They knew many of their men by their first names; they watched over their families' lives. Their rules were firm and implacable. No single worker could board with a married employee. With husbands away on the night shift, that was temptation. All employees were visited regularly by the company social and religious adviser, who was paid a modest salary by the company itself. Glow Packing, as would now be said, was involved.

The Glows were also famous, even in Chicago, for the work they could extract from their men in the course of a standard seventy-two-hour week, twelve-hour day. However, again there were differences. No Glow plant ever worked on the Sabbath. And along with their weekly pay, Glow employees received, all at no expense, Bible lessons and tracts warning against alcohol, tobacco, spendthrift living and immorality. During the great strikes of the eighteen-nineties, Chicago bosses were hanged in effigy. Reflecting the deep religious feeling in his plants, James B. Glow was several times burned at the stake.

In Chicago in those years, it was said, the meat packers found a use for every part of the pig but the squeal. The Glows did better; they found a use for ingredients that had never been near a carcass. Glow sausages were known to a generation of Americans as Glowworms. The company held that it was an affectionate nickname derived from their shape.

In defense of the Glows, it should be said that, at the time, the standards of the meat-packing industry were not high. During the Spanish-American War more soldiers were felled by the embalmed beef than by the Spanish bullets. There is no reason to believe that Glow products were greatly more lethal than the industry average. And no other company learned its lesson so well. Glow Packing never thereafter failed to stress quality in its advertising.

There was also a happy side to this history. The discovery that a wide range of inexpensive vegetable products, suitably disguised, processed and flavored, could be sold as canned meat and sausage was what launched Glow Packing on a path different from Swift, Armour and the rest. For presently it began to develop its own sources of vegetable oils, oatmeal, cornmeal, cottonseed meal, wheat bran and, it was said although never admitted, freshly milled sawdust. From these materials it was a simple step on to breakfast foods, including the famous Corn Husk and Flaked Barley lines, and thence on to canned dog food and biscuits, as well as to glue and adhesives, liver extracts, regenerative drugs and mineral laxatives.

In 1910, James B. Glow, Jr., well trained in the family traditions, took over from his father; in 1922, in a step of far greater significance than even he could have foreseen, he bought the trade name and syrup formula of Uni-Cola. To this he added, a few years later, the companion beverage, Uni-Up. Uni-Cola owed its popularity to its modestly addictive qualities — the syrup contained an operative infusion of cocaine. Eventually Glow dropped the drug. He was troubled both by his religious convictions and the threat of government regulation. Sales did not suffer as had been expected, and the action has often been cited by business philosophers to show the essential harmony between private interest and the public good. In 1929, the name of the company was changed to reflect the wide range of food products and the new importance of the soft drinks. It became Glow Food and Beverage, Inc. The stock, now widely held, was a marked favorite in the boom that summer.

In the Depression, despite what its annual reports always cited as "basic strengths," sales and earnings of the firm were hit by the general slump. And James Glow, Jr., now in his late sixties, was becoming as unapproachable and autocratic as his father had been before him. He suspected all subordinates of wanting a share in his power; he was deeply averse to unions and the New Deal policies of Franklin D. Roosevelt. A memorable photograph of the period shows him being carried from his offices rather than submit to a National Labor Relations Board order requiring a union election in his Chicago plant. There was a long strike; in the end, union recognition had to be accorded. The company was said in the trade to be foundering. James Glow, Jr., came to be known, out of his hearing, as The Last Glow. Arthur Francis Glow, his nephew and only male heir, came briefly into the family firm in these years but soon returned to his art collection and his lifetime interest in Japanese erotic painting. A. F. Glow was always called The After Glow.

With World War II things were much better. Younger men took hold. Demand for the company products expanded. The United States Army marched on C and K rations from Glow Food and Beverage, this time without noticeable peristaltic effect. In a striking departure from its regular operations, the company undertook the management of a large shell-loading plant in downstate Illinois. The operation was eventually successful. After D-day, Glow, Inc. organized logistics support for the Quartermaster's food operations in the European Theater of Operations. There was a glimpse of larger horizons.

UGE Today

James Glow, Jr., was finally hospitalized in 1947; his resignation became inevitable following his attempt to have his personal chauffeur made President of the Company. He died the next year. Harold McBehan became President and Chief Executive Officer, and what has ever since been called the Era of McBehan began. Many phrases have been used to describe the McBehan business philosophy, most of them from McBehan's own speeches: a concept of sustained growth. Professionalized management by professional managers. A partnership with people. Profit with service. Technology in the service of national security. The nation's host. Nutrition for a free people. Constructive acquisitions for balanced diversification. All these mirrored the thinking of the new and dynamic team that McBehan had brought with him from the Pentagon and the Harvard Business School.

In 1955 came the final change of name; Glow Food and Beverage became Unified Global Enterprises — UGE. "The 'H' is silent," the company house organ proclaimed. By now the old exclusive tie with food and beverages was a thing of the past. UGE was big in pharmaceuticals, electronics, missile guidance systems, computer software, modular dwellings, along with its insurance company, UGEAIR and UGEHOTEL.

Harold McBehan left in 1969 to become Assistant Secretary of Defense for Procurement Planning under Richard Nixon. The loss to the company was regretted. But an opportunity for public service in the critical area of national and free-world defense could not easily be refused. And it was recognized, even if not mentioned, that UGE, as a major supplier of equipment and components, would not suffer from McBehan's presence in this key post. No one expected or wanted favoritism. But no one doubted the advantages of a better understanding, a close working relationship between industry and government.

By the time of McBehan's departure UGE was seventh on the *Fortune* list of the 500 largest American industrials. Its Annual Report for that year counted sales offices in sixty-two countries, substantial manufacturing operations in twenty-four. "Your management," the Report said proudly, "directs a closely articulated, internally reinforcing, inherently dynamic enterprise that responds well to the capabilities that are fundamental to modern managerial methodology and systems." In early 1969, the stock of UGE was at its alltime high; earnings, reflecting the favorable effects from the consolidation and subsequent revaluation of intercorporate holdings and other advanced accounting practices, had reflected their sixteenth straight annual gain. Accounting, it was being shown, was a creative art. (In subsequent years the methods of UGE's accountants came under increasingly close scrutiny from both the Securities and Exchange Commission and private analysts. They were shown to have contributed almost as effectively to earnings as the managerial techniques for which the company is justly celebrated.)

Not everything was good in these years. McBehan acquisitions had attracted the attention of the Department of Justice. The company was the subject

Our history is of James Glow, Harold McBehan, Howie Small. Here is a gallery of contemporaries, friends and fellow descendants:

Henry Ford — of Ford.

Henry Ford II.

Thomas J. Watson — of IBM.

Tom, Jr.

Sosthenes Behn — of ITT.

Harold Geneen.

of a suit calling for divestiture of its insurance affiliate and its advanced electronics subsidiary. Liberal economists and lawyers hailed the action as a landmark step in halting the trend toward increased industrial concentration. The issue was resolved after lengthy court action by a consent decree limiting further acquisition and providing for the divestiture of UGE's automobile rental business. The settlement, which attracted little attention, was worked out for UGE by a team of experienced antitrust lawyers, nearly all of whom had previous experience in the Department of Justice. Legal costs were substantial.

Command Post

Since 1965, more than a third of all UGE employees have been in overseas operations; by the late sixties approximately one half of consolidated earnings were from outside the United States. Brussels, the home of EEC, NATO and numerous satellite organizations, is the multinational capital of Europe. Streetwalkers and mendicants address their prospects as Your Excellency. UGE, somewhat exceptionally, operates from Paris. "The intellectual, artistic and quality consumer goods capital of Europe," Harold McBehan said in his speech at the opening of the new headquarters at La Défense. Also, better food, better whores and the Crazy Horse Saloon, a jovial and somewhat alcoholic minor executive was heard to add. There were more substantial reasons, although they were little publicized. UGE has always enjoyed close and mutually beneficial relationships with French political and military leaders. The Paris location was not unrelated to promised tax advantages and anticipated military orders.

Since 1962, the world headquarters of UGE has been not Chicago but New York. The dominant theme of every age is reflected in the grandest of its structures — religion in the cathedrals, the nation state in Versailles, the Industrial Revolution in the railroad depots, modern sport in the Astrodome and its counterparts, the modern corporation in the skyscrapers. The UGE tower dwarfs the lesser structures across Sixth Avenue at Rockefeller Center. Critics described it as "gross, pretentious, in its own way hideous." Harold McBehan is not known to have heard. "This building," he said at the opening, "is our signature. It writes three letters large in the heavens — UGE."

The board of directors meet in the boardroom on the 79th floor — "the command post." Harold McBehan has called it the great room. The board of directors is the voice of the stockholders, the men and women who own the corporation. From their lips come the marching orders; they are the ultimate authority.

That is the myth. When the first James Glow died, a large chunk of stock went to his three daughters. None of this is now in the family. More went into

Architectural convergence:
G.M. in New York.

Comecon in Moscow.

the Glow Foundation which James B. Glow, Jr., and his brother established for the propagation of the essential principles of free enterprise, a philanthropy which also reduced substantially the impact of the inheritance tax. In subsequent diversification moves by the Foundation much of this stock was sold. Arthur Francis Glow — The After Glow — sold some of his stock when he established his gallery; more went for his Institute for Oriental Erotic Art, yet more to his four former wives in alimony. All of McBehan's acquisitions involved new issues and an exchange of these for the stock of the company being acquired. UGE stock holdings were thus further dispersed.

In 1932, the two noted Columbia University professors, Adolf A. Berle and Gardiner C. Means, studied the control of the two hundred largest nonfinancial corporations in the United States. Nearly half, they discovered, were controlled by their management. No power remained with the owners to hire or fire the managers; the management appointed the directors who represented the stockholders. The directors did not appoint the managers. There would now be no question as to UGE's membership on the management-controlled list. No individual stockholder owns as much as one percent of the stock of UGE. None of the directors owns more than the requisite qualifying shares. All the directors were selected by Harold McBehan and were voted in automatically by proxies returned for the management slate. McBehan's tests for selection were high standing in the financial world, past political service in Washington and a reputation for never interfering with management decisions. The average age of the directors was, until recently, sixty-seven. This has now been lowered slightly by the addition of a black, a consumer advocate and a nun. With the others they meet for two hours every two months and ratify decisions that have already been taken and which several of the board members do not understand. Two cannot remain awake. None has ever opposed management on any matter of more than cosmetic importance. All recognize the overwhelming advantage of those whose information is derived from day-to-day involvement with planning and operations. If UGE were losing money or moving into bankruptcy, the directors, prodded by the two bankers on the board, might well be led to question the quality of the management. Nothing short of this, or the suspicion of major fraud, would cause them to act. The board has confidence, on the whole justified, in the honesty of UGE's management.

The Washington Scene

The Washington office of UGE is on H Street. It is modest as compared with those in New York and Paris but by no means obscure. What is called the UGE presence in Washington is considered vital for company welfare. Tax legislation and decisions; food labeling and truth in advertising; drug safety;

product safety and standards; environmental impact statements; Pentagon orders and intentions; intelligence filtering in from countries where UGE does business; all of these and a dozen other matters call for the constant vigilance of the UGE Washington men. For particularly sensitive operations against the public interest, they engage the services of two large Washington law firms famous for their public-spirited assistance to worthy public causes. Neither Harold McBehan nor any other UGE man has ever overthrown a foreign government or would know how to begin. Their men do play a large part in the government of the United States; otherwise the Washington office would not be worthwhile. UGE has come far since James B. Glow, Jr., traveled each year to the Capitol to lobby against imports of Argentine beef. The UGE Washington men govern without being known, without having had the risk or expense of running for office. It is this public role more than any other which makes UGE a source of unease and uncertainty.

The Technostructure

When he went to the Pentagon, Harold McBehan was succeeded by Howard J. Small, previously Executive Vice-President for Corporate Operations. Howie, as he is known in the firm, is in the same salary bracket as was McBehan — $812,000 a year plus deferred compensation and pension rights. He is entitled also to stock options but since the recent slide in the value of the stock, these have not been mentioned. Howie's jet carries as large and attentive an entourage as any sovereign's. But Howie, unlike McBehan, is little known outside the firm. He is a two-pack-a-day smoker, drinks to keep going, and, were he a vital factor in the enterprise, his heart condition would be the source of the gravest concern. The Dow-Jones wide tape would carry his electrocardiogram and also his latest lung X-ray. In fact, no investor gives Howard J. Small's health the slightest thought. McBehan's departure completed a process long under way, the passage of power in UGE from individuals to organization. Howie doesn't matter.

Again the myth and the reality. The myth of modern company management is of a hierarchy in which orders flow down from above. The reality is of a circle. At the center of the circle is the top management — in the case of UGE, Howard J. Small and his staff of executive vice-presidents, financial vice-presidents, vice-presidents, assistant vice-presidents, the controllers, the treasurer, the counsel, the head of the Washington office. In the next circle are the heads of the companies at home and abroad that make up what is still called the UGE family. In the ring beyond are those whose specialized knowledge contributes to decisions in the many constituent companies and divisions — the engineers, scientists, sales managers, advertising specialists, dealer relations men, designers, lawyers, accountants, economists, the men who manage the computers. Next beyond are secretaries, clerks, typists — the white-collar workers. Next are the men who supervise production on the floor, get out the goods. In the final outer ring are the blue-collar workers.

In the inner rings of UGE there is the power that proceeds from position. In the middle rings there is the power that proceeds from knowledge. In the outer rings the power proceeds from numbers and union organization. Power flows in as well as out. Corporate action is the product of an intense interaction between the rings. Reward — higher pay, more power — goes to the man who enlarges his space on one or another of the rings. This he can do by coming up with a product, a label, a slogan, a commercial or a campaign that increases sales. That is why UGE emphasizes growth as a goal; a great many people in UGE are rewarded in pay, power and perquisites when there is growth on their own turf. With so many working for growth, UGE grows, and growth is its test of success. Economists and politicians speak often of the social gains of economic growth. These they often believe to be an abstract good unrelated to pecuniary interest. Growth is also very good for UGE. This may have even more to do with the emphasis it receives.

The Practice: Eindhoven

UGE is an American company but the corporation is worldwide. The corporation's most notable achievement is to diminish national traits and make all industrial countries alike. Americans are blamed for this. In fact, it is a powerful tendency of the corporation, whatever its national origin. For large tasks the socialist countries too use the corporation — an inevitable convergence.

We see this in Eindhoven, a city of 190,000 people, a couple of hours' drive south and east of Amsterdam. Once it had its moment in world history; in 1944, it was taken by Montgomery's armies when the further jump to Arnhem proved a bridge too far. Since 1891, Eindhoven has been the headquarters of Philips Gloeilampenfabrieken, which in 1974 was ranked third in size among the industrial corporations outside the United States by *Fortune* and thirteenth in the world. This came from sales that year of electrical goods and other technical hardware of $9.5 billion and employment, in some sixty countries, of 412,000 people.

The Glows have long since gone from UGE, and nobody weeps. In the more durable Dutch tradition there is still a Philips on the Philips board. James Glow's concern for the chastity of his workers and their wives is remembered around Chicago only as a minor manifestation of a dirty mind. Howie Small's mind turns to his working force only when they want a wage increase or threaten a strike. He then calls for a firm stand on principle by those responsible and later accepts a compromise. In Eindhoven the Philips presence is still a powerful thing; workers and the firm still live in close association with each other. There are only two ways, it is said in Eindhoven, to be fired from Philips — to shoot the chairman of the company or to molest the coffee girl. The first is recommended, for the second is more serious.

But in Eindhoven, too, the trend is the same. Once the company housed its workers, saw to their health, was concerned with their education. Those tasks have now gone or are going to the city or state. Once the company instructed the workers as to its wishes. Now it asks the union. In talking of the power of the modern corporation, an important distinction must be made. Its public power increases. Its parental power steadily diminishes.

Philips, like UGE, is a creature of its technostructure. In this respect, too, all corporations are alike. Whether in Eindhoven, New York or Houston the quality of the corporate performance depends not on individual brilliance but on organizational competence — on the success in choosing and combining the efforts of the men, and the rare woman, who fill the rings.

These men of the technostructure are the new and universal priesthood. Their religion is business success; their test of virtue is growth and profit. Their bible is the computer printout; their communion bench is the committee room. The sales force carries their message to the world, and a message is what it is often called. Alcohol is under interdict as an intoxicant but allowed as an adjunct of communion and as an instrument of friendly persuasion. Recreation is for regeneration of the business spirit, for a widened range of business contacts. Sex is for better sleep. The Jesuits of this austere faith are the graduates of the Harvard Business School.

The Harvard men were the first in the faith. They still are but now there are numerous subordinate orders. One of these trains at a French business school — INSEAD in the Forest of Fontainebleau. The technostructure of the corporation is a design for drawing on the specialized knowledge of different disciplines. In keeping with this, engineers work here with accountants, economists with marketing men. All and more make up what, needless to say, is called a team. From this comes experience of group effort. The word effort deserves emphasis. Neither here nor elsewhere does the business seminary favor the deeply reverenced leisure of the liberal university, the leisure that is assumed to rest and refresh the brain but which also serves excellently as an excuse for pleasurable idleness. In the corporation faith, the most important word is work.

There is little time for speculative theory. Learning is problem-solving. Following the technique pioneered at Harvard, instruction is by the case method, by practice in making the decisions that students hope they will soon be encountering in the executive suite.

The result of Harvard, INSEAD and the rest, still surprisingly unnoticed, is

The Priesthood: Seminarians at Harvard Business School.

The Priesthood: Seminarians in Spain.

a race of men who, no less than the corporations they serve, are the same. National identity has been excised. They are not Dutch, not French, not English, not Belgian but all slightly American. Their first loyalty is to Philips, IBM, Exxon, BP, Nestlé; not to the Netherlands, the United States, Britain or Switzerland. Their uniform in all countries, the occasional eccentric apart, is the same: a quiet suit, a careful tie, decently polished shoes. The best of them can be dropped on a week's notice into Brussels, Geneva or Indianapolis. There, like a coin in a slot, they will immediately produce. The proletarian, Marx avowed, knows no motherland. This has never been quite true. But it is true of his present-day employer, the modern corporate man.

The Corporate World

Harold McBehan coordinated the worldwide operations of what, in one of his more thoughtful moments, he called his empire by airplane. Overseas managers were summoned once a month to La Défense. The heads of the U.S. operating divisions met monthly in New York or in December at the company's depressing hotel and golf club in the Bahamas. The head of each division had a sales and profit goal for the year; at the meetings each explained how, given proper budget support by the head office, a decent break on consumer confidence and some accounting adjustments, the goals would be substantially exceeded.

Howard Small is also often airborne. But now the management team keeps itself current on all operations. The computer printouts are on Howie's desk every morning. Regularly he ratifies actions which he does not understand. They have been, he knows, well staffed-out.

Philips is less centralized. It likes to think of itself not as a corporation but as a federation. The heads of its over sixty national organizations are appointed by Eindhoven; major capital outlays are approved there. Then each of the national companies — some that manufacture and sell, some that only sell — are left to do their best. They are encouraged to become part of the local scene. In every country the Philips sign in neon lights is, indeed, an inescapable feature of the landscape.

Once every twelve months the heads of the national companies come together to report on operations of the past year and on plans for the next five. They assemble in Ouchy, not far from Lausanne in Switzerland — again the conscious denationalization. Not only do corporations plan; they have five-year plans.

There is a further, more important line of command. In Eindhoven and elsewhere in the Netherlands are some thirteen divisions (with one in Italy) concerned with the development and marketing of Philips products — lamps, television sets, radios, appliances, heavy electrical apparatus and the rest. These product divisions deal directly with those who are making or selling their item in the national companies. A board of management keeps their work under review. Engineering, quality control and marketing virtuosity can thus be kept up to the same standard for the whole enterprise. Principals from different countries concerned with a particular line of products meet from time to time. There are scheduled company flights, and a fleet of airplanes stands by at Eindhoven to facilitate this travel. The Philips style is more staid than UGE but it hasn't eliminated executive movement.

Why Is It Unloved?

Why does UGE — or Philips — arouse unease? Why do they contribute so remarkably to the Age of Uncertainty? The things UGE makes are better, safer and, relative to the incomes of the buyers, much cheaper than the adulterated, indigestible and sometimes lethal merchandise of the ineffable Glows. No modern worker would remain for a day in the factory of the saintly James B. Glow. None would tolerate even for a day Glow's intrusive and prurient interest in his religious, alcoholic and sexual preoccupations.

Harold McBehan was a driven man; so is Howie Small. A philosopher from another time or world would marvel at their view of life; wonder why they so sacrifice their time and health; be puzzled by their curious concept of reward — the trivial obeisance of subordinates and money they do not have time to spend. He would wonder why they work so hard. He might think them foolish; he would not think them wicked.

From our view of UGE — and Philips — we can see how great is the conflict between myth and reality in the modern corporation and how this generates unease and suspicion. Where the myth departs so sharply from the reality, it is only natural to suppose that its purpose is to conceal. No one can believe that UGE is the powerless and passive instrument of market forces. No one with the slightest knowledge of UGE's Washington operations can believe that it is without power in the state. No one can believe that its management is the responsive servant of directors and stockholders. Yet all these things the myth affirms. Where so much must be done to conceal power, only one conclusion is possible. The exercise of power must surely be malign.

Some of the unease disappears when the corporation is looked at candidly and without the covering myth. UGE, when so examined, does not appear as a convocation of saints. Some of its achievements, in a rational world, would seem at least mildly insane. But much of its effort, and some of its exercise of power, is for the manufacture and sale of routine, useful and useless things. Thus does the unease diminish when the myth is dissolved. There remain the multinational operations of the corporation, which are regarded with special alarm. And also its relation to governments and the part it plays in the weapons culture.

And of Philips:

Eindhoven.

London.

Brussels.

Vienna.

Madrid.

São Paulo.

The Multinational Syndrome

For the modern great corporation no place is too far away. It's as much in evidence in Hong Kong and Singapore as in New York, Brussels or Madrid. Howie Small's people have recently won a soft drink concession in the Soviet Union. It is intended to cut into the consumption of vodka. They have hopes for business in North Korea. Because it is everywhere, omnipresent and seemingly omnipotent, the multinational corporation is greatly celebrated in our time. On occasions of introspective ceremony the executives of multinational corporations themselves listen to grave lectures from American professors on how they transcend national power and undermine national identity. All who impart such wisdom, without exception, view the multinational corporation with grave concern.

Again we can be a trifle skeptical; were the multinationals as pernicious as their billing, we should hardly have survived until now. In no place does one see the multinational presence so vividly as in the tiny city-state of Singapore. The great international corporations bring in the materials, bring in the fuel, finance the production, make the products, house and feed those who come to buy or sell and take the products away to market. No one can be in doubt as to the result; they have remade the city in the image of the industrial West.

But one must ask if this is so bad. Once it was the pride of Singapore that it was a Little England — a small tropical port that had tennis, cricket, billiards, Scotch, *The Illustrated London News*, Dickens, all the benefits of British civilization. The impact of Philips and Chase Manhattan is different but who can say it is worse.

It is held that the multinational corporation comes in from abroad to influence the decisions of national governments. In consequence, Frenchmen or Canadians are governed, in some measure, by foreign corporations. This is so. But domestic corporations seek, as does UGE, to persuade or even instruct the government of the countries that gave them birth. This is the basic tendency of the large corporation, national or international. It could be that the foreign corporation, conscious of its external origins, proceeds with more tact than does the large domestic firm. UGE can be thrown out of Canada as Canadian Pacific could not. The fact of life in all industrial countries is corporate power, not international corporate power.

Finally, one must ask if the suppression of national identity is to be deplored. The assertion of such identity by Frenchmen, Germans and the British in the first half of this century brought millions of people to their death in two intra-European wars. In the general view the European Common Market came into existence as the result of a sudden access of economic enlightenment after World War II. Miraculously, after two hundred years, statesmen sat down and began reading Adam Smith on the advantages of the division of labor and how production was limited only by the size of the market. More plausibly, the EEC came into being because, for the modern multinational corporation, national boundaries and the associated tariffs and trade restrictions were a nuisance. It had a better way of keeping foreign competition under control. That was to be the competitor.

What Comes After General Motors

The large corporation is here to stay. Those who would break it up and confine its operations within national boundaries are at war with history and circumstance. People want large tasks performed — oil recovered from the North Sea, automobiles made by the million to use it. Large tasks require large organizations. That is how it is.

Nor can the individual decisions of corporations be too extensively second-guessed. There can and must be rules; but within the rules there must be freedom to decide. More than an individual, an organization, if it is to develop and be effective, must have autonomy and ability to act. The one thing worse than a wicked corporation is an incompetent one. The one thing as bad as a wrong decision is a decision that is greatly delayed.

The ultimate answer for the multinational corporation is multinational authority — government that is coordinate in scope with the corporations being regulated. The decline in national identity is paving the way for this solution. There is no danger, however, that it will come too soon. In Europe international authority is distantly in sight. Elsewhere it is not.

Meanwhile for national governments and national corporations the only answer is a strong framework of rules that align the exercise of corporate power with the public purpose. This is not an exercise in hope and prayer. It is one of the dominant trends of the times. What a corporation can do to air, water, landscape, truth and the health and safety of its customers and the public is far more carefully specified than it was a mere decade ago. Ralph Nader didn't bring this regulation. The need brought Nader. It will continue.

Of further reforms there is less discussion. Especially in the United States it is an article of the free-enterprise faith that General Motors — and UGE — are the final work of God and man. Other things can be perfected; these cannot. A divine hand guided the corporate building by the churchly Glows, by the profane and secular McBehan and even by Howie Small. The result is perfect. To suggest the possibility or need for further change is the modern heresy.

Still, there are suggestions. Putting representatives of labor, minorities, women and the public on boards of directors is discussed. The participation of trade unions is very much an issue in Europe. It seems to me, on balance, a dubious reform. Those members of the board of directors who do not participate in day-to-day management are, we have seen, without power. So accordingly will be the representatives of labor, consumers and the public who are added by this change.

A better line of development would be to abolish boards of directors in the large firms now that they have no function. These would then be replaced with a board of public auditors, which would keep out of management decisions but ensure the enforcement of public laws and regulations, report on matters of public interest, otherwise keep management honest and ratify or, in the event of inadequacy or failure, order changes in the top management command.

You will ask who then would represent the stockholder. The answer is that no one does now. The shareholder in the modern large corporation is without power and without function. He (or she) is also obsolete. A further plausible development would be to pay off such functionless stockholders in bonds and have the dividends and capital gains accrue to the public. That, all will say, is socialism. It is so. But it is socialism after the fact. The great corporation, as it develops, takes power away from the owners, from the capitalists. The most profound tendency of the modern corporation, one that is rarely mentioned, is to socialize itself.

It socializes itself in two ways. It takes all power from its owners — disenfranchises the capitalists. It also makes itself socially indispensable. We now know that if a corporation is large enough, it can no longer be allowed to fail and go out of business. The recent history of Lockheed, Rolls-Royce, Penn Central, the other eastern railroads in the United States, Krupp, British Leyland, British Chrysler affirms the point. All have been rescued or are supported by government. Modern socialism is not the work of politicians or college professors. It is the accomplishment of corporation executives and those to whom they owe money. They are the cutting edge. They are the men who appear in Washington or Whitehall on the day when bankruptcy seems inevitable to ask the government to come in.

On this too Howard Small — Howie of UGE — has shown the way. In line of duty Howie makes frequent speeches to groups of concerned citizens. It is something he must do. The speeches are written for him by a Yaleman who was once an Associate Editor of *Time*. They dwell on the tradition of rugged independence in American life; the dangers of big government; the withering effect of welfare on the morale of those receiving it; and they do not fail to mention the omnipresent threat of socialism. This is the way Howie Small put it in his speech to his own stockholders only last year:

> I speak to you now not as a businessman, not as your president but as an American — a deeply concerned American. My message is government — the ever-expanding maze of government regulations, the ever-increasing cost of bureaucracy, the dead hand of government on enterprise, the blighting impact of welfare checks on people, what the handout state is doing to the

work ethic, the belief that all problems can be solved by throwing a little of your and my money at them. In a word, I speak to you of socialism — socialism not as some distant threat but socialism here and now.

My friends, the time has come when we must reverse this deadly trend — when you must work to do it; when I must work to do it; when together we must put our shoulders to the wheel and stand firm against the tide.

Later in his speech Howie called for "an adequate national defense" and spoke of other areas "for constructive cooperation between government and industry." He said:

I am proud to announce such a step today. In keeping with the rest of the airline industry, UGEAIR has been caught between ever-rising costs and stable passenger revenues, problems, I need not tell you, that are not of our own making. As you have read, we proposed a government takeover of the line. Instead, in a constructive step, Washington has promised an increase in the airmail subsidy, an equally constructive support to our short-term debt refinancing and a constructive guarantee of our new equipment financing. This is the kind of constructive association between industry and government which we should welcome in a free society. It is our best guarantee against the march of socialism.

Howie Small is thus strongly opposed to socialism. But, though he does not know it, he makes a distinction between socialism for the profitable firm and socialism for the failing corporation. There is a somewhat similar distinction between socialism for the rich and socialism for the poor.

We are not through with the corporation. What has just been said assumes that it can be made subordinate to the state and that it can thus be made subject to the public interest. But the corporation is powerful in the state — in the very public institution by which it must be controlled. Surely there is a contradiction here. How can the corporation be controlled by the institution it controls? Surely one must inquire if the corporation is not, in fact, an extension of the modern state — an integral part of larger arrangements by which we are governed. To this thought, and to its particular application to the issues of peace and war, we shall return.

10.
Land and People

We have been talking mostly of the few countries, capitalist or socialist, that as the world measures such matters are exceedingly rich. However serious their other problems, they have gone far to solve the one that for most of the people of the world is transcendent. That is poverty — poverty so severe that it faces those afflicted with the stark problem of how to keep on living. Whether or not they will succeed is for most of the world's people still the greatest uncertainty of all. To the ideas that explain poverty we now turn.

Of these there are an abundance. There is no economic question so important as why so many people are so poor. There is none concerning the human condition to which so many different and conflicting answers are given with so much confidence and such nonchalance. The people are naturally lacking in energy and ambition. Their race or religion makes them so. The country is wanting in natural resources. The economic system — capitalism, socialism, Communism — is wrong. There is insufficient saving and investment. Property, profit or the rewards of toil are not secure. Education is inadequate. There is a shortage of technical, scientific or administrative talent. There is a legacy of colonial exploitation, racial discrimination, national humiliation. Every day in every part of the world every one of these explanations is offered. For mankind's most common affliction we have a multitude of diagnoses, each offered with the utmost casualness. Poverty is a painful thing. It would be well if we knew the cause.

There is no one answer — obviously. It is because so many explanations have a little truth that so many are offered. But one cause of poverty is pervasive. That is the relationship, past or present, between land and people. Understand that, and we understand the most general single cause of deprivation.

The reason is simple. Everything that allows of the first escape from privation — food, clothing, elementary shelter — comes from the land. If these cannot be provided, there is poverty. If they cannot be increased in relation to the numbers of the people, it endures.

In India, Bangladesh, the Nile Valley, Indonesia, the people who work the land are exceedingly numerous. Their product, no matter how divided, provides only the merest subsistence, or less. That improved culture — fertilizer, more water, high-yielding hybrid cereals, better cultivation, better plant protection — could increase yields is not in doubt. The increase can be dramatic; the Green Revolution is real. But these cost money. If all that is produced must be consumed to live, there will be nothing left over to invest in fertilization, irrigation or better seed stock. Also there will be nothing left over, and no incentive to invest, in any case, if all of the product above a bare minimum goes to a landlord or in taxes. And there will be no incentive to invest and improve unless there is education in the advantages of the new methods and the required techniques. For some calculations one does not need a professional economist.

But this is not all. Perhaps a benign Providence or, often more improbably, a wise, efficient and benign government aided by oil or the World Bank will provide some of the means for agricultural improvement — the canals, fertilizer, seed and the guidance in their use. And perhaps land reform will give land to the cultivator. In India these things have partly happened. Indian foodgrain production averaged 63 million metric tons annually in the nineteen-fifties. So far in the nineteen-seventies (which have included some very bad years) it has been 104 million metric tons.[1] But when production increases, the ghost of the Reverend Thomas Robert Malthus then walks. The increased food is consumed by the increased population. There is an equilibrium of poverty; when broken, it re-establishes itself. That too is the history of modern India. In 1951, there were 361 million Indians. In 1976, to eat the added food, there are an estimated 600 million. A revolution, it has often been said, devours its children. Green revolutions are different; they devour themselves. We shall know much about poverty if we know the answer to two questions: How does the equilibrium of poverty develop? How can it be broken?

The Punjab

It has, in fact, been broken on one part of the Indian subcontinent. To the outsider the vast population of this area — India, Pakistan, Bangladesh — however diverse in religion, culture and language and however contentious within itself, has always seemed completely homogeneous in its poverty. But those close to the scene have long remarked on a region of substantial and increasing well-being. This is the Punjab, the great plain that stretches across northern India and Pakistan. Here the fortunes of history and development have given the average farmer a sizable plot of land. Farms of fifteen to thirty acres, vast by Indian or Pakistani standards, are commonplace. To this land comes water from the five great rivers that give the Punjab its name. The result, including the land along the Indus to the south, is, incomparably, the

People and land on the Punjab Plain.

world's greatest irrigation project. And the farms that do not draw on the canals have tube wells that tap the vast underground lake which lies below the plain — a lake that until recently threatened to rise as the result of leakage from the irrigation canals, bring up salt and reduce to infertile marsh the cropland on the surface and which, in an agreeable symbiosis, the tube wells now help to keep under control.

The effect of irrigation is to give the family more land in a smaller area. It allows, as well, of the more effective use of fertilizer, which is also a substitute for land. And with water and fertilizer there is an improved response from hybrid grains. From the increased product comes the wherewithal to buy the fertilizer and improved seed and even, on occasion, a tractor. Improvement then continues. There is an incentive to protect the gains, partly by family limitation, partly because well-prepared sons and daughters move readily into urban occupations. It is the Indian Punjab, predictably, that has first moved toward making family planning not permissive but compulsory. It is from the Indian Punjab that much of the increased production of grain which I mentioned a moment ago has come.

So the equilibrium can be broken. Perhaps, as people elsewhere in Pakistan and India believe, the Punjabis work harder than the rest. But this also is made possible by better food. Perhaps, by nature, they are technologically more apt and progressive. This too is widely believed. It could be because their higher income has long sustained better schools. And their more sophisticated farming provides an early acquaintance with machinery and other technology. What is not in doubt is that the good fortune of the Punjabis in India and Pakistan begins in a better relationship of land and people.

The Possibilities

There are, in principle, four ways in which the equilibrium of poverty can be broken. One is to provide more land or its effective substitute in the form of water and fertilizer. For this the cultivator must, as in the Punjab, have a sufficient minimum of land with which to start.

The second possibility is to alter land tenure to reward the efforts of the people with what they produce. For this too there must be enough land.

The third answer is for people to breed less. The fourth is for them to disappear. If land supply is indeed insufficient, only these last two answers will serve.

Birth Control

The control of population always seems the wonderfully obvious solution. It is practiced with ease by the affluent to protect their well-being. For the poor, unhappily, the population increase is part of the equilibrium of poverty.

Land and very few people. Saskatchewan.

People of means *have* a standard of living to protect. The poor — a highly indisputable fact — have not. The affluent get knowledge of contraceptives and the ability to pay for them as an aspect of affluence. The poor do not. Well-to-do people have a diversity of recreation. The poor, a point that religion and romantic fiction unite in ignoring, rely for much more of their limited recreation on sexual intercourse. It is the only moment of brightness and escape to which the worker from the fields returns. It is one of the very few enjoyments on which wealth is not thought greatly to improve.

Because the task is so unrewarding, governments have usually put their most congenitally inadequate minister in charge of family planning. Rats and locusts are controlled and epidemics are prevented by officials who measure their success by results. Births are controlled by people who measure success by the number and eloquence of their speeches and the weight of the pamphlets they distribute.

Many in the poor countries believe that the rich nations urge birth control because it is a painless way of being rid of them, and the remedy becomes even more attractive if the poor are dark, yellow or black. One consequence is a sensitive reluctance by many in the affluent countries to press the case for birth control. This is unfortunate; no one should be so constrained. The affluent practice contraception. They are not offering advice they do not accept themselves. And the consequences of uncontrolled population growth are visited not upon the rich but upon the poor.

These consequences, it should be noted, come not gradually but with terrible suddenness in the season when the rains fail. As we saw with the potato blight in Ireland, this means that it is the weather, not the preceding population increase, that gets the blame.

However, the problem of population control in the poor country is such as to invite sympathy, not reproach. The most penetrating student of national poverty in our time is the Swedish Nobel Prize winner, Gunnar Myrdal. He is also the most eclectic economist of the age. As a young man he anticipated much of the work of Keynes. His *An American Dilemma* is the classic study of race relations in the United States. Myrdal has shown that the competence of the government of the poor country is itself a part of the equilibrium of poverty. Rich countries have the financial resources to govern effectively. They are not subject to the desperate political pressures of the impoverished. They can make mistakes, for they have a margin for error. The governments of poor countries are politically far more vulnerable. They must assume responsibility for poverty that it is not within their power to ease. They do not have the resources, human or material, to sustain a strong, effective civil service. In consequence, in Myrdal's most famous phrase, there is an intimate

Gunnar Myrdal. He identified the inverse association between poverty and the capacity of the government to deal with it.

association between poverty and the soft state. And nowhere is the softness more inhibiting than in dealing with population growth.

There are exceptions to the rule. China is a very poor country. But, perhaps because of thousands of years of experience in organization, it is not a soft state. And there is no doubt as to the energy with which birth control measures are being pressed. There are stories of committed volunteers who visit each birth-susceptible house before bedtime each evening with the obligatory pill. On the statistics on the effect on population, one's hosts — I was there in 1972 — are less forthcoming. One must be content with assurances that progress is being made.

There is also progress in the Punjab. Nearly twice as large a proportion of all couples has been estimated to use contraceptive protection in that state as in the rest of India. And compulsory sterilization after two or three children is being actively proposed. One must hope that the Chinese and the Punjabis will have success and will point the way for all others. For a livable relationship between land and people, control of population is essential.

Expulsion and Migration

The other remedy for overpopulation is for the people to go. This, for centuries, has been the primary solution. It continues to be so. In the last thirty years the need for readjustment between land and people has set in motion great migrations within and into Europe and within the United States. It has attracted only a fraction of the respectable discussion that has been evoked by birth control. That is because the redistribution of people has been from the poor countries or communities to the rich. The rich have not responded with warmth to this remedy. More often, in a mood of some righteousness, they have sought to erect barriers to the tide. They have not wanted to think that a redistribution of population, however logical and effective, is the right answer to the equilibrium of poverty.

It remains, nonetheless, a solution of the greatest social consequence. Neither the pressures in the poor communities nor the tensions in the rich can otherwise be understood. This is most impressively true of the United States. But it is also true of Europe.

In Sutherland in the Scottish Highlands, as we have seen, the equilibrium of poverty was broken by the forthright expulsion of the people and the burning of their villages so they would not return. Agriculture could then be based on wool, not food; this sustained, for the few who remained, a much higher standard of living. Textiles, we saw, worked with double effect. Wool expelled the people; spinning and weaving employed them in the mills to which they went.

The Cotton Equilibrium

It is possible, indeed, that in the last two hundred years the manufacture of clothing has been a greater force for change than the search for food. The textile inventions, along with steam power, made the Industrial Revolution. In 1794, another elementary device changed the social history of the United States. In that year, the Yankee, Eli Whitney, patented a machine, a saw really, for tearing the cotton lint away from the seeds that were imbedded in it. This invention, the cotton gin, and the new spinning and weaving machinery produced both a big supply and a big demand for cotton fiber. Slavery in the Americas had been in decline; it was marginally profitable only for tobacco, sugar and a few other plantation crops. Men who combined compassion with sensitivity to economic need thought it would soon come to an end. Cotton wonderfully restored the slave economy and the slave trade. And, as we saw

Whitney's cotton gin. It made cotton fiber cheap, allowed cotton textiles to be mass-produced. The teeth on the drum raked the cotton lint from the seeds.

earlier, it transformed slavery itself from a slightly abhorrent thing to a profoundly beneficent arrangement for protecting the black bondsman from his own inability to cope with this world and for ensuring his salvation in the next. The impact of economics on moral judgment was never more visible and direct.

As the demand for cotton expanded, so did the supply of land for growing it. This was along and back from the lower reaches of the Mississippi, and there the slaves were brought. In the North by the nature of mixed agriculture the farmer worked on a variety of tasks by himself. The fundamental human tendency to relax when out of sight of others was countered by his being an independent proprietor and thus rewarded for his own effort and punished for his own sloth. (In time, this arrangement for inducing effort, the immortal family farm, would also, in the eyes of those associated with it, acquire a transcendental moral value. "We must, at all costs, preserve the American family farm.") To make a cotton crop — cotton is made, not grown — required, in contrast, a much larger labor force. The basic tasks on the plantation, planting which was then by hand, chopping or thinning the plants and picking the cotton, were all done by gangs. The laggard worker could easily be identified. And he could then be encouraged to greater productivity by the voice of the overseer and his whip. There has recently been a grave dispute between economic historians over how frequently slaves were flogged. One greatly controverted study reduces the per-slave average to less than once a year, which could have proved to exceptionally lazy toilers the extreme unwisdom of relying on averages. All do agree that this punishment was a well-regarded incentive. Cotton and slavery were deeply symbiotic.

To the antebellum planter, as we have seen, the slave was a happy, irresponsible child, protected in his innocence by his owner. To the abolitionist, and many since, he was dehumanized, toiling flesh. His enslavement and exploitation saved the planter from the penalties of his own incompetence and from his resulting inability to survive in a free-enterprise world. In a third view the slave was a valuable piece of property, serving with intelligence in a profitable business. As such, he was fed adequately, treated with some decency and given medical care when sick, for this best preserved the capital that he embodied. Free workers at the time were not much better off. It is this last view, recently advanced with supporting claims to measurement, that has been bitterly contested.[2]

In all views there is common ground. The income to the slave was at least as low as the self-interest of the planter allowed. The cotton economy was a forced equilibrium of poverty for all but the very few.

This equilibrium was not altered by the Civil War. With emancipation sharecropping replaced slavery. Before, peonage had legal force. Now it was

Ultimate mechanization: The cotton picker.

enforced by the absence of alternatives, and also by various and ingenious arrangements for keeping the sharecropper eternally in debt. Though cotton production was quickly restored — by 1877, it was higher than ever before — the great majority of people associated with its production were still poor. Even if all income had been distributed to the sharecroppers, poverty would still have been acute. The basic relation of people to land was wrong.

The true emancipation came only after World War II. Then machinery and chemistry arrived on the cotton plantation as had the sheep in the Highlands — power cultivation, chemicals to suppress the weeds, the flame cultivator, most important of all the cotton picker. And with these came the remedy, the same in all but detail as in Sutherland and Ireland. There it was the factories or the ships, here it was the highway north. There were jobs in the cities and, if not jobs, welfare checks that would allow for survival. Before World War II, there were 1,466,701 blacks in the rural farm labor force in the states of the Confederacy. In 1970, there were 115,303. In Mississippi, the greatest of the old cotton states, there were 279,176 before the war. In 1970, there were only 20,452.[3] Thus the equilibrium of poverty was broken. The migration is now over, for there are few left to go. People say rightly that the South has changed. Not so many mention the cause.

People caught up in the equilibrium of poverty, people who sense the power of its embrace, search for an escape with great ingenuity, vigor and courage and with very little encouragement from the people in the places to which they seek to go. The rural poor in the United States have been more fortunate than most. They have had some place to which, by entitlement as citizens, they could move. And the South was not the only source of such migrants. There was also Puerto Rico. Here, following its takeover from Spain, the relationship of people to land sustained an equilibrium of poverty that was almost as intractable as in India itself. No journalist visited the island without writing of "the poorhouse of the Caribbean." Then after World War II came the change. Here the cause was less the mechanization of sugar production, which in Puerto Rico was relatively slow, than the airplane and cheap tickets to New York. The people could afford to go, and they went. This, and the development of alternative industry in Puerto Rico itself, broke the old equilibrium. Puerto Rico is still poor but far less so than before migration — before the great and unspoken remedy became available.

Mexico

The Puerto Ricans needed only the price of the cheapest air ticket. The field hands from the South needed even less. To see the importance of migration as a modern remedy one need only go a step farther south to look at an equilibrium of poverty in Mexico where such escape is not easily available.

Whence they came.
Kingston,
Jamaica.

Puerto Rican
shanty town.

Turkish Village.

Mexican independence, we saw, left the landlords undisturbed. In the following decades they thoughtfully increased their holdings at the expense of the ancient communal lands of the people. By 1910, 95 percent of the families in agriculture owned no land. The remaining 5 percent of the families owned nearly half of Mexico; seventeen persons owned nearly a fifth. Some holdings reached sixteen million acres — five times the area of Connecticut.[4] The privileged have regularly invited their own destruction with their greed. In Mexico they were especially brave. Prominent still among the big landowners was the Church. It is a strain on faith if the Church is the landlord and the rents are high. Faith in Mexico was put strongly to the test.

In the long revolution after 1910, the communal lands — the *ejidos* — were returned to the people. Mexico is a large and diverse country; no generalization fits it all. But the usual result was still too many people on too little, too barren land. The familiar problem.

Mexico City was an escape, and it grew prodigiously. But too often it offered only unemployment. The better passage was to Texas, New Mexico, Arizona and California. As in New York for blacks and Puerto Ricans, life would be grim. But it was better than in the overpopulated Mexican village.

So, legally or illegally, they crossed the border. They were called wetbacks for the illegal immigrants who once waded across the Rio Grande. They still wish to come. Employers wish them to come. But a higher social conscience holds they should not come. A large border guard seeks to stop the escape. A man is arrested and sent home. He tries again next day or next week. He is arrested again but on the fifth or sixth try he may make it. No one will doubt the social pressure for this remedy.

It is not, in fact, sufficient. In the Mexican villages the equilibrium of poverty continues. The Mexican Revolution restored the land to the people. But, like the Civil War in the United States, it too left unsolved the far more stubborn problem of the balance between land and people.

The Guest Workers

After World War II, in the years of the great migration from Puerto Rico and the rural South, there was a similar movement, similarly motivated, in Europe. People came to the cities of the industrialized countries from the poor rural villages of Eastern and Southern Europe and adjacent Asia Minor. Yugoslav workers came by the tens of thousands, crossing the line that divides the Communist from the non-Communist world. More would have come from the other Eastern European countries to escape poverty rather than to find liberty, had they been allowed. Turks came to Germany from Asia Minor, Italians and Spaniards to Switzerland, Algerians, Portuguese and some Turks to France.

In all countries a myth was carefully propagated. The movement was for a

Where they are.
Liverpool,
England.

Harlem,
New York City.

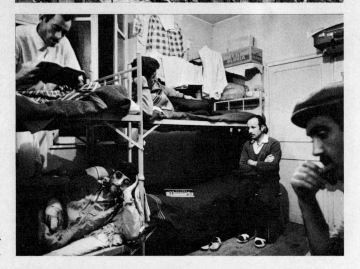

A hostel for Turkish
workers in France.

short time and highly reversible; they were temporary workers, foreign workers, guest workers who would one day go home. No one will now need to be persuaded that something far more fundamental was involved. The guest workers are another chapter in the very long history of the escape from the equilibrium of poverty. Only a determined effort to resist the obvious has kept this from being recognized.

In Britain alone was this great process effectively resisted. West Indians, Pakistanis, Indians, Bengalis, some Africans started to come. But the Empire had been dissolved in the nick of time. One generation had defended it. Their sons defended the home island from its people. Had Britain been protected only by the Rio Grande, they would never have stemmed the tide.

No subject is so lovingly discussed in our time as the economic problem of Britain. No cause is cited with such assurance as the low productivity of her labor force. An obvious explanation goes unmentioned. As compared with Germany and other continental countries, there is no large force of foreign workers impelled to effort by the memory of harder work and greater poverty in the villages whence they came. And impelled also by the fear that, if they relax, they might have to go home. There is satisfaction in Britain over having escaped the social tensions that go everywhere with the migration. Almost no one mentions the economic price. Automobiles must be made, in the main, by Englishmen.

Where It Worked

On the relationship between land and people we have been looking at the hard cases — the dark side of the moon. This is in the established tradition of social study. Only the man who finds everything wrong and expects it to get worse is thought to have a clear brain. (There will be occasion to remark on this again.) Where land and people are involved, there once was a brighter side. It shows, by the contrasting success, the power of this relationship. For me it has also a pleasant, nostalgic value. It allows me to return to a countryside that I know rather well.

The example is on the north shore of Lake Erie. Its focal point is about midway between Detroit and Buffalo or, by Canadian calculations, between Windsor and Niagara Falls. Port Talbot on Lake Erie may well be the most modest center of water-borne commerce in all the world. There are no piers, no berths, no warehouses, no ships, no unions, no dockers, no pilferage and, for that matter, no harbor and no commerce of any kind. But Port Talbot has its claim on history. From a tiny inlet where, on occasion, a creek runs into the lake the settlement of a large and fertile area of Ontario began.

This was in 1803, when a young Irishman fresh from the King's service arrived on this shore. His name was Thomas Talbot — Colonel Talbot. Having been a good soldier, being highly anglicized and having influence in high places, he had been given a substantial grant of land. He had come to supervise its settlement. Migrants were beginning to arrive from the Scottish Highlands, a race of which the Colonel greatly disapproved. "They make the worst settlers . . . English are the best."[5] But the Scotch, as they called themselves here both then and since, were the available talent. The Clearances again.

Each settler coming to Port Talbot was given fifty acres, were the Colonel in a good mood, attracted to his appearance and sober that day. Business was done through a window in the Colonel's house. Those who made an adverse impression had it shut in their face. For surveying the land in 200-acre lots and laying out the roads, the Colonel then got the other 150 acres. This was in addition to his original grant. As the others flocked in, his estate expanded west toward Windsor and Detroit at a wonderful pace.

Here was the potential for terrible trouble — landlordism on a large scale, the beginning of a North American landed elite. As we've elsewhere seen, nothing would have such lasting effect as this initial distribution of the land. Government would be affected. Political power went with the ownership. Political democracy required, above all, democracy in the possession of the land.

But here democracy was saved. Once their own land was cleared, the settlers wanted the acres next door. They clamored for its purchase. The Colonel had rank but no troops. There were none on which he could call. He could not withstand the pressure, and so he sold. At a nominal price the settlers got the rest of the land. Henceforth there was no irreconcilable issue dividing the haves from the have-nots, the kind of issue that would make democratic government impossible.

It was not an exceptional solution. The land problem in the Middle West and Great Plains in the United States — the 160 acres, and later more, of the Homestead Act — was similarly solved. Likewise in the Canadian West. And here the solution was deliberate. The resulting relationship of people to land allowed of general well-being and made political democracy possible and perhaps inevitable. If all have some wealth, all will want and achieve some share in their government.

With the loss of the land the vision of a new landed aristocracy on Lake Erie also evaporated. Colonel Talbot's ambitions were not in doubt. He built himself a feudal retreat on the height of land above the lake, although only the name — Malahide Castle — had grandeur. The castle was of logs. It was a stopover for well-regarded travelers from England who were not impressed by its comforts. In old age Colonel Talbot traveled himself and visited Napoleon III, apparently as an equal. At midcentury, to protect the line, he made the

Port Talbot, Ontario, on Lake Erie. The most modest center of water-borne commerce in all the world. No piers, no ships, no unions, no exports, no imports, no trade of any kind.

estate over to his nephew and heir, Colonel Richard Airey. Then came the accident, one of the most disastrous in the long history of military misfortune. In 1852, Colonel Airey was recalled to the colors for the war in the Crimea. It was Richard Airey's name, and no other, that was on the order that dispatched the Light Brigade. Others were to blame but he did not return.

Five or six miles from Port Talbot, to add a further nostalgic word, is the lovely farm to which the Primordial Galbraiths came from Argyll: in my time we still called it the Old Homestead. The sun shone in on it from the south, and the north wind was kept out by a low ridge, and everything ripened a little earlier than anywhere else to the north of the lake. The apples were famous and lovingly discussed. We came for Sunday dinner with a carefully implanted sense of reverence. It was, we knew, an important place.

The urge to immortality. Early carving by author on door of local barn.

Of those who settled on such farms none became rich but few were poor. All, within a few years of arrival, a generation at most, had property — farms, houses, barns, livestock, a buggy, furniture, clothing — beyond the dreams of any ancestor in Scotland. From our earliest days we were told that our forebears had been men and women of great courage who had suffered great hardship. The hardship was, in fact, for those who remained in the homeland.

Our farm was three miles away. We had a hundred acres, another fifty up the road. Our purebred Shorthorns were modestly famous, of equable disposition and much admired, especially by their owners, and they led me briefly to a career in animal husbandry. It was in this subject that I took my first degree at the Ontario Agricultural College. My first travel into the United States beyond Detroit was as a member of a team especially accomplished in the judging of livestock. We trained at Michigan State, Purdue and the University of Illinois and competed with marked unsuccess at the International Livestock Exhibition in Chicago. Some have since suggested that I should have remained with this field of knowledge.

I remember our farm also as a lovely place. But I remember without pleasure the exceptionally tedious and repetitive toil. If one is born on a working farm, nothing thereafter ever seems like work.

From such farms and others across the border in the United States there began the last of the great adventures in colonization — the settling of the Canadian West. It is surprisingly recent; when I was a youngster, people were still pulling up stakes (as it was still said) and moving to Manitoba, Saskatchewan and Alberta. The Canadian railroads still had colonist cars — bunks and benches and stoves on which to cook. These, at nominal cost, ferried families to the West.

The Canadian westward movement completed the occupation by Europeans of the empty, grain-growing lands of the world. In the United States, Argentina, Australia and on the Canadian prairies, the Europeans took over. Today, though insignificant in number, they produce an estimated one fifth of the world's breadgrains and a much greater share of the exportable surplus.

In a common view of the world, the poor, densely populated countries of Asia, Africa, Latin America till the soil, work the mines, supply food and raw materials for the industrialized lands of Europe and North America. These are the hewers of wood, the haulers of water, the plowmen for the machine civilization. It's a vision which has little relation to reality. Canada and the United States are large producers of raw materials — lumber, pulp, newsprint, coal, cotton, iron ore and a huge variety of other minerals. And in foods, breadgrains in particular, they are pre-eminent. As the Third World is commonly defined, Canada and the United States are the first of the Third World countries. It is another example of what happens when the conjunction of land and people is fortunate. Where the equilibrium is good, there is well-being; there is also the surplus which helps to feed the people who are caught in the equilibrium that is not good.

The City State

Even from the Ontario countryside some people had to go. There were more in a family than the land could use; had all remained, many would have been poor. Detroit (in addition to the Canadian West) was the salvation. We were patriotic. But our passion for King George V did not survive a five-dollar-a-week wage differential. To absorb extra people, to break thus the equilibrium of rural poverty, is one of the major functions of the modern metropolis. Is this possible?

There is an encouraging case, which is Singapore. It is on the edge of the continent where the equilibrium of rural poverty is most visibly extreme. It lacks all resources, including space. The Singapore state is only 27 miles long and 14 miles wide; a moderately ambulatory citizen can easily cross it on foot in either direction in a day. Along with space, Singapore lacks minerals, materials, food, energy, everything indeed except people and a fortuitous location. It is, all agree, on one of the great ocean crossroads of the world. But being on a crossroad has worked no similar miracle for Panama or Suez. Singapore has a per capita income around eight and a half times that of India, six times that of China. As a place of refuge from rural poverty it works — and far better than Calcutta or Shanghai. There must be a lesson here.

Some of the credit accrues, not surprisingly, to the people. The talents of three races — Chinese, Indians, Malays — are united in a harmonious blend. The people work without the fettering traditions to which they would be subject in the countries from which they or their parents came. Migrants and their immediate descendants always work harder and better than people who have been long settled in their surroundings. To put people down in a new place without accustomed support from land or position, give them the challenge of survival and force them to think may be very cruel but it enormously increases their productivity.

The Singapore government's contribution is to make pragmatic use of all ideas and refuse to be the captive of any one. Is Adam Smith alive in Singapore? The answer is: Very much. There can be few places in the world where pecuniary self-interest is pursued more diligently and with more visible satisfaction in the material result.

Is Keynes there? The answer is also yes. Public outlays are balanced as a matter of course against the availability of workers and the current and prospective capacity of the economy.

The post-Keynesian view of inflation — a view which I have long urged — is also treated with respect in Singapore. Wage settlements are controlled, again as a matter of course, to minimize inflation and to keep Singapore's manufacturing competitive in world markets. When others talk of the need for an incomes policy, Singapore economists, businessmen and union leaders are known to yawn. They've had one for years.

Is there planning, even socialism in Singapore? Have the Webbs, Franklin Roosevelt, Clement Attlee been here? Would Enoch Powell and Barry Goldwater be distressed? The answer again is yes. If housing, harbor works, transportation and industrial sites are needed, the government provides. Public apartment blocks control the horizon. Self-interest serves well as a motivation. But it is recognized in Singapore that it does not serve all purposes. And it serves best within a framework of systematic and deliberate planning.

Some of the success of Singapore must be attributed to the rule that nothing is good or bad in principle. The test is whether it works or helps people to work.

The City-State: In Singapore everything except people is lacking.

There can be few countries so little interested in ideological dispute, so free from the rhetoric of both free enterprise and socialism. This is an aesthetic treat.

Singapore has a lively intellectual and university life; the best in the East outside Japan. It is not a place of fear. But it is not a place of perfect freedom. The unions are subject to the wage restraints just mentioned. There is little sympathy for anything that seems to interfere with work. The government gives no encouragement to those who suggest that the Chinese in China have a model that should be emulated. Even travel to China by the young is discouraged. I do not applaud such caution. It seems unnecessary; in any case, there are some principles that all must defend. But the larger point is clear. Singapore shows that there is an urban solution to the problem of land and people. Many people can, indeed, live well on little space.

It is not a secure or easy solution. Singapore must have friendly, well-disposed neighbors, and it must be secure in its trade with the world at large. Much depends also on the continuing tolerant good sense of the people and the ability of the government to adapt. Change anywhere in the world — recession, inflation, alterations in the trade routes — affects Singapore. It cannot influence such changes; being small and without power, it must always adjust. This adjustment must be governed by thought, not formula. It cannot be defeated by narrow political interest or passion. The people must have the confidence, good nature and sense of community to accept change, including when it hurts.

Singapore must also master the increasingly intricate and costly problems of the great metropolis. That is a different and very difficult task.

11.
The Metropolis

So, in the end, almost everyone goes to the city. Whatever the beginning, it is to this that the industrial civilization comes. Better even than the size or composition of the national product, the extent of urbanization measures that development. At the beginning of the present century 38 percent of American workers were employed in agriculture. By 1975, it was 4 percent. In Britain it was 2.5 percent. By contrast, in Italy the agricultural labor force is still around 16 percent of the total; in India some 72 percent are employed, under-employed or unemployed on farms.[1]

Since it is there that people live, the problems of the industrial civilization are seen as the problems of the city. What should be blamed on expanding income and output, the changing composition of product, higher and different consumption, the modern role of unions, the unwillingness of people peace-fully to starve gets blamed instead on the way the city is governed. The modern big-city mayor is a most convenient figure in our time. He gets, and in his innocence largely accepts, the responsibility for the tensions, discomforts, maladjustments and failures of the industrial system.

It follows that to understand that system nothing is so important as an understanding of its urban life. This, like most things, must be examined in some historical depth. For the word city itself, in its singular form, is mislead-ing. There is not one kind of city but several, and all are combined, in varying mix and form, in the great metropolis. Four different types are readily rec-ognizable: the Political Household, the Merchant City, the Industrial City and the Camp. These together make the modern Metropolis.

The Political Household

The Political Household, for most of time, has been the extension of the dwelling of a ruler. Like his palace, it was an expression of his taste and personality and a manifestation of the grandeur of his realm. Visitors spoke of the elegance (or more rarely of the modesty) of the ruler's palace. They spoke as frequently of the magnificence or, on occasion, the squalor of his capital.

Mostly it was the magnificence. Over the centuries nothing has been so thought to enhance royal personality, competence in armed slaughter apart, as the architectural embellishment of the seat of government. Rome, Persepolis,

Angkor, Constantinople, Paris, Versailles, the Forbidden City, Leningrad née St. Petersburg, Vienna, Segovia and literally a hundred other wonders are the result. The late Joseph A. Schumpeter of Harvard, a man who rejoiced in awkward or unpalatable truth, enjoyed remarking on the migration each summer of the tens of thousands of resolutely democratic Americans to see the architectural wonders of the Old World. Their attention during these months, he noted, would be centered exclusively on the monuments to past despotism.

The ruler imposed his will and therewith his order on the Political Household. The order itself was important. Symmetry, even without taste or imagination, has some claim upon the eye. Disorder, a point of importance when we come to the Industrial City, has none. But also, and more often than might have been imagined, there was a conjunction between power, imagination and taste. One of the most remarkable results of that combination has been kept intact for four hundred years. Not only has it survived but it is unsullied; unlike Leningrad or Florence or Paris there is no commercial or industrial overlay or extension through which the visitor must peer or pick his way. The city, the archetype of the Political Household in its high royalist aspect, is Fatehpur Sikri. It has rightly been called "the world's most perfectly preserved ghost town."[2]

Fatehpur Sikri

It was built by Akbar the Great on a low rocky ridge twenty-four miles from Agra, one of the inspired capitals of the Moghuls. (Delhi and Lahore were yet others.) The legend, possibly more trustworthy than most, is that the site was chosen because there in a village lived a holy man, Shaikh Salim Chishti, whom Akbar the Great had visited when he was in despair because he had no son and heir, his near infinity of wives notwithstanding. A son, named Salim for the saint and later to succeed his father as Jahangir, was then forthcoming. In gratitude Akbar, around 1571, quarried the ridge, made a lake some twenty miles around and built a new capital. Visitors coming from Europe in the next years found a city larger than London and in its public buildings by a wide margin more elegant. Fourteen years later Akbar moved on. There are various solemn explanations for this — a failure of the water supply, a strategically unsatisfactory location. The explanations overlook the most plausible reason: other rulers tired of a palace and moved on; the Moghuls, as a legacy perhaps of their nomadic antecedents in central Asia, tired of a city and left.

When Akbar left, so did the people. The private dwellings and shops decayed and disappeared. The walls, mosques, mint, treasury, caravansary, palaces and other public buildings remained. No commerce, no industry has since come near. The ridge that Akbar converted to his capital was of rich salmon-red sandstone. This became the palaces and walls; frequently it was

Fatehpur Sikri: Archetypal city of the princes, "the world's most perfectly preserved ghost town."

Peking: Forbidden City . . .

. . . And modern Canberra.

Temple at Angkor Wat . . .

. . . And National Assembly, Islamabad.

Versailles . . .

. . . And Brasilia.

cut and assembled as though it were timbers and boards so that one thinks of wood structures made of stone. In the clean, dry air and hot sun this marvelous material mellowed but did not crumble or decay. So at Fatehpur Sikri we can see in the purest possible form the city that I have called the Political Household.

Almost everything that survives — the single and double columns that make up the basic design, their massive capitals, the medley of great and small domes, the mosque, the tolerant combination of Hindu and Islamic decoration in the quarters of the Hindu queen, the towering Victory Gate with its enigmatic quotation: "The world is a bridge, pass over it but do not build upon it" — is symmetrically a part of the larger whole. That this city was the extension of one man's personality is not in doubt.

The elegance and symmetry of the Political Household are important for the pleasure they give. This is important also because from the Political Household, along with the Merchant City, comes the image we still retain of what a city should be. From it also has come an important convention in modern urban architecture and design. It is the belief that government has a special claim to architectural and urban magnificence. Industrialists are expected to work, even though they do not themselves live, in cities of routine squalor. Their office buildings may be tall but they must be functional. Executive offices may be large and expensively furnished but only because cost/benefit analysis shows that the resulting impression pays off. Politicians and public officials are believed to need elegance for its own sake. The capital in which they work should be planned and its buildings embellished, even though in a depraved way, as were the royal palaces. What rejoices the eye must, at a minimum, be balanced with what distresses the taxpayer. Aberration at great cost — the Rayburn Building on Capitol Hill, the new FBI fortress on Pennsylvania Avenue, the Woolworth-Gothic towers of the Stalin era in Moscow, the Rockefeller elephantiasis in Albany — is briefly deplored and then forgiven.

The Political Household places its stamp on the city hall and civic center of the modern city. But its influence is most strongly reflected in the modern planned capital — Washington, New Delhi, Canberra, Brasilia, Islamabad, all cities that reflect a ruling conception and design. It deserves a thought that these are almost the only wholly modern cities that the present-day tourist ever believes worth a visit.

The Merchant City

The Merchant City had also a unity of conception and design. This was less the result of central authority than unity of taste. Merchants must be sensitive to fashion. At any given time in architecture, as in dress, manners or crime, there is a ruling style. This gave unity to the houses of the merchants. Also the merchant communities in the mercantilist era before the Industrial Revolution had a strong sense of their collective interest. This led to a meticulous regulation of the terms and conditions of trade and the antecedent manufacture. The regulation extended naturally to the plan of the towns, the design of the houses. Within this larger framework there was then a rewarding competition. The quality and style of the house was an advertisement of the quality and style of the merchant therein, the merchandise therefrom. In consequence, the Merchant Cities — Venice, Genoa, Amsterdam, the Hansa towns that survived the bombers of World War II — rival in order and elegance the Political Households.

The architecture and design differed not in quality but in its reflection of the central purpose of the city. Its supreme expressions in the older Political Household were the palaces of the ruler. In the Merchant City it was inevitably the houses of the merchants, the guild hall and the town hall. To these, on occasion, were added the cathedral or church, for these advertised, legitimized and, in some measure, sanctified the gains from trade.

Two great Merchant Cities survive, as does Fatehpur Sikri, with little modern clutter. One, of course, is Venice, the greatest and by far the best-preserved of all museums of civic design. The other, less well known but more easily encompassed and comprehended, is Bruges in Belgium. It was a member of the Hanseatic League, which was also a source of common ideas in civic design, and in the fourteenth century it was considered the northern counterpart of Venice itself. It is intact because of two accidents — the silting up of the river Zwin which separated it for four hundred years from the sea and thus from the ravages of progress, and the heaven-sent accident in 1914–18 which left it a mere twenty miles removed but totally untouched by the guns of the bloodiest battles of all time. Bruges and its beautiful companions of the mercantile era have also left a deep imprint on our thinking about the city.

We still assess the quality of a city by the elegance and glitter of its principal shopping streets. We do not accept that department stores and shops can be strictly functional; the first must have a certain residual grandeur and the second a modicum of style. Somewhat similar standards are brought to bear on the modern shopping center; its distinction increases if not with its beauty, then with its size, ostentation and apparent cost. When the shops of the central city decay or close up, even though branches are burgeoning on the traffic exchanges on the edge of town, the whole city is said to be in decline. Our tendency to test the quality or distinction of an urban community by its shopping districts is one of the continuing legacies of the Merchant City.

The Merchant City is now part of the Metropolis. Only in a subdued and degraded form, related not to ships and the sea but to agriculture, can the modern Merchant City be found in pure form. It is the onetime crossroads in

The Merchant City. Once: Bruges . . .

. . . And now: Frankfort, Kentucky.

Iowa, East Anglia and Normandy to which farmers repair for fertilizer, farm machinery, building materials, clothing and the education of their young. Its most ubiquitous mercantile establishment is the automobile service station. Merchants still live in the largest houses back from the road and behind a wall or lawn. But there is an aspect of shabby impermanence about these retreats — flaking paint, loose shutters, unraked leaves. It is because the occupants are now civil servants, the current managers of J. C. Penney, Sears, Marks & Spencer. One day soon they will be moved along. The modern Merchant City in its pure form is a depleted and trivial reminder of its great precursors.

The Industrial City

With the Industrial Revolution the Industrial City became synonymous with the city. In consequence, the very connotation of the word city changed. Before 1776, the word had an overtone of grandeur. Dick Whittington's first glimpse of London was of the promised land. Dr. Johnson was even more affirmative: "No, Sir, when a man is tired of London, he is tired of life; for there is in London all that life can afford." The American Republic was launched in Philadelphia, then the second largest city in the English-speaking world. It was regarded by all as beautifully planned and admirably built, and what was then built is so regarded today. This was near the end of urban beauty; soon thereafter a reference to a city became a reference to something not grand, not beautiful, not even solid but something mean, ill-built and dirty. The Industrial City became the characteristic city, and all cities came to be thought somewhat sordid.

There was much about the Industrial City which helped assure this reputation. The Political Household housed courtiers, courtesans, civil servants, soldiers and servants. In the Merchant City were clerks, petty officials, tradesmen. In both of these pre-Industrial Cities there were craftsmen, artisans, small shopkeepers and an abundance of mendicants. But, with the exception of the mendicants, most of those who lived in these cities were required to be generally presentable. That was because they served people of professed gentility who might be repelled by unduly crude appearance, manner or aroma. With the different occupations went a pleasing variety in dress, speech and personal style.

The Industrial City, by contrast, made no such demands. People were now a servo-mechanism. That service was not diminished in the slightest by their being shabby, unwashed, rough of manner and ripe of smell. On the whole, these characteristics were approved, for they minimized the expense of maintenance. In the Industrial City men sought, above all, the lowest cost. The reasons were not entirely to be deplored; the Industrial City, unlike its predecessors, served cheaply those who were also poor.

The Industrial City. A place to shelter the work-stock: This is Halifax, England.

The people of the Industrial City were not beautiful. Nor were their dwellings. Nor, a commonplace point, were the processes by which their goods were made. These all but uniformly involved much smoke and grime. Coal had to be dug and washed; ore had to be smelted; locomotives had to be fired; steam engines had to be fueled; these were all necessary even for processes that otherwise were clean. So almost all industrial operations nurtured or spread filth. Amidst the valuable modern concern over the effect of industrial growth on the environment few note that the course of industrial progress has involved a remarkably steady march from the foul process to the relatively pure one — from dirty coal to clean gas, oil and electricity; from smoke-filled foundries to automated processes and air-conditioned control rooms; from belching steam engines to cleaner internal combustion engines and the wholly antiseptic electric motor, the ultimate power plant of which is far more carefully monitored for pollution than the multitude of chimneys it replaced. Indeed, we take it for granted that the older the industrial community or the more obsolescent the factory, the dirtier it all will be. The early processes firmly established the reputation of the Industrial City as a dirty place.

Finally, among the constants of the Industrial City were the industrialists. While a merchant had to be a man of style and taste, not so a manufacturer. His concern was with methods and machines and efficiency; for coal, steel, chemicals, machinery, the buyer was concerned not with charm, only with performance and cost. And the early consumer products of the Industrial City — cloth and more cloth, cheap tin trays — made no demands on taste. So the early manufacturer was like his product, solid, efficient and graceless, where not crude. He built his house above the mills. Unlike the merchant's house it was expected to be ungainly if not hideous. Economic determinism is omnipresent and extends itself strongly to art.

The Birminghams

Not all Industrial Cities were alike. The leading industrialists impressed themselves strongly upon the life of the city, and sometimes to its advantage. Retiring in 1874 as the world's most eminent manufacturer of screws, Joseph Chamberlain was thrice mayor of Birmingham, England. There followed a remarkable burst of civic pride and enthusiasm. Slums were cleared, parks established, a library and art gallery created, the water and gas supply taken into municipal ownership, sanitation and health made a civic concern. The city that, after Manchester, epitomized English industry became a model of urban development and administration for all the kingdom.

It was, alas, the exception. By the turn of the century in the United States its namesake in Alabama was on its way to becoming the leading Industrial City of the South. It was much nearer the mode.

Coal, iron ore and limestone were all there in close proximity. They were brought together by the Tennessee Coal and Iron Company which, in 1907, was brought by J. P. Morgan into the United States Steel Corporation. The result was absentee management twice removed. The Steel Corporation was operated for Morgan by Elbert Henry Gary, of whom it was said that he never saw a blast furnace until after his death. This Birmingham was merely a place of work. In the early nineteen-twenties, as elsewhere in the American steel industry, men worked a twelve-hour day and a seven-day week, and Christmas like Sunday was just another day of toil. The Alabama Birmingham still bears the simple imprint of its industrial origins. Until recent times its principal expression of civic pride was in its firm resistance to racial integration. However, nothing, even when bad, is forever. Of late, this Birmingham too has moved on to pride in its hospitals, its other civic facilities and its athletic teams.

In one extreme variant of the Industrial City the industrialist took full responsibility for inception, design and administration. He laid out streets, built and owned the houses, built and operated the store or stores where people shopped and sometimes were required to shop. And he laid on water supply and sewerage, if any. This, as in the cities of the princes, was an imposed order, an industrial household. It was, however, designed not for grandeur but for economy and to ensure that the inmates, however sullen, would not be mutinous. A rewarding calm was enforced by keeping them permanently in debt to their employer who could expel them on demand from their houses. It seems possible that no experiment in controlled social design was ever so uniformly reviled as this, the company town. When all was quiet, the employer-landlord would sometimes be celebrated by his sycophants as a Christian idealist or a genial and wise paternalist, and sometimes he would believe his notices. Then, in moments of truth and high ceremony, he would be hung in effigy by people who deplored only the need for the substitution.

The Economics of the City

The government of the Industrial City reflected admirably the dominant economic ethic — the belief in self-interest and classical laissez-faire. There was a city government; it was operated on loose leash from the local capitalists. Since city services added to taxes and living costs and led ultimately to the diminution of profit or the enhancement of production expense, they were kept to the minimum. The filth of the industry was mingled with the offal of the inhabitants. Streets need not be lighted for toilers who should be asleep. The factories required only an unlettered proletariat so that was what the schools provided. Again the imprint of economics on culture.

London, England: The city as the Industrial Revolution made it.

The Metropolis

The Industrial City in Europe in the last century was better served than its counterpart in the United States. Those elected or appointed to office were usually nonlarcenous. In the United States men were measured in straightforward fashion by the money they made. City officials, not surprisingly, sought also to show their worth; this they did by appropriating public money, sometimes in some decently circuitous fashion, for themselves. In 1888, Lord Bryce, the first great British student of American political institutions and folkhabits, concluded that the "government of cities is the one conspicuous failure of the United States."[3] Two decades later Lincoln Steffens, then the dean of the American muckrakers, a man with a unique capacity for repetition, told at appalling length of the evil association of reputable economic power and disreputable political power in the American metropolis. Neither Bryce nor Steffens should have been surprised. The city that so distressed these observers corresponded precisely to industrial need. The industrialist was free from restraint. He could do as he needed with air, water, landscape. The city sheltered his work stock at the lowest possible cost. Since he owned the politicians, they were reliably in his service. Given that the purpose of the city was to produce goods cheap, nothing more was to be asked or expected.

As the visible face of the industrial civilization in the leading industrial countries — Britain, Germany, the United States — the Industrial City had its sharpest delineation around the beginning of the present century. Sheffield, Essen, Pittsburgh were its purest form. Since then in the older countries the image has again been blurred. A new city — the Camp — has appeared. And this and all of the antecedent cities have melted into the Metropolis.

The Camp

A most important influence for urban change has been money, rising real income. In the Industrial City this, in time, was reflected in the housing and even more in the shops, shopping centers, cinemas and stadia where incomes were spent. The social power of money is great for the rich but also for others as well. With higher income came a much enhanced professional class — doctors, lawyers, accountants. Also a new race of artisans, surgeons to automobiles, television sets, washing machines, electricity and the plumbing. And, as we've seen, the industrial firm itself no longer consisted of only an owner, a few bookkeepers, a few foremen and a large toiling mass. Instead there was a complex superstructure: sales managers, advertising managers, controllers and those who understand the computers. Along with the bankers, lawyers, advertising men and public relations flaks who serve the industrial establishment, these made up a new and sizable layer between workers and owners. They were joined by the expanding white-collar mass who, in the industrial nations, now far outnumber those who run the machines. The servo-

The industrialist need not be a man of taste.

proletariat of the Industrial City has been submerged in the great and growing artisan, clerical, technical, professional and managerial class.

With the Industrial City came a well-founded desire by the few who could afford it to escape its smoke and grime and unlovely landscape and, even more, its inhabitants. So with the Industrial City came the suburb. With the reconstitution of a mercantile class and the appearance of the new managerial elite, the number who could afford this escape increased greatly. In the suburbs the rich or the modestly affluent could live in comparatively clean air with their private trees and grass. And they could have schools, churches and recreational facilities of superior quality, the quality ensured and the cost kept down by their not being shared with the poor. There could also be a rewarding segregation according to income, occupation or race. There were rich suburbs and moderate-income suburbs, those favored by bankers and stockbrokers, those that excluded the Jews. In time, every sizable city was surrounded by these classified enclaves.

Unlike the Political Household, the Merchant City or the Industrial City itself, these settlements had no central political or economic function; they did not govern, sell or make. They were merely places where people found space and lived. Increasingly, given the peripatetic character of the modern organization man, the space was occupied only for a brief time. In the absence of central function and the impermanence of its residents, the modern suburb is often less a city than a bivouac. Thus its name: the Camp. In the United States there is yet another Birmingham, this one a bivouac for the peripatetic affluent from Detroit.

Migration

In the classical Industrial City the working force grew, procreation apart, in response to two forces. One was the attraction of the wages of its mills, however dark and satanic. The second was because of the compelled correction of the imbalance between land and people. The people had nowhere else to go. The Industrial Cities of late-eighteenth-century Britain attracted workers with a wage which, however low, was better than could be had in agriculture. However idyllic, Auburn was a very low-income place. And simultaneously the Acts of Enclosure and in Scotland the already-noticed Clearances, along with an increasing population, were liquidating even that alternative. "Industry was in fact the only refuge for thousands of men who found themselves cut off from their traditional occupations."[4] People, a contemporary petition moaned, are being "driven from necessity and want of employ, in vast crowds, into manufacturing towns, where the very nature of their employment, over the loom or forge, may waste their strength, and consequently debilitate their posterity."[5] English agriculture was substituting the greater intelligence, energy and economics of the large-scale farmer for the inefficient, labor-intensive husbandry of those who worked small plots and shared the common land. Seventy-five years later, as we've also seen, the rural population of Ireland was expelled to the Industrial Cities (and also to mines and railway construction camps) in the United States, again by agricultural change. In the same and subsequent years there was a great and accelerating movement to the United States, Canada and South America from Northern, Eastern and Southern Europe, much of it to the vacant lands but increasingly also to the Industrial Cities. After World War II came the aborted migration from the erstwhile Empire to Britain, from the less to the more industrialized European countries and from south to north in the United States. Of these migrations and their causes the last chapter has told.

With these waves of immigrants the city underwent a further change. Previously it had been taken for granted that its internal tensions were those of the industrial society. The workers confronted the capitalist. The strike was its overt manifestation. The people in the valley went into the streets in angry opposition to the employer on the hill and his housecarls in the police. After weeks, sometimes months of struggle, sometimes with violence, always with deprivation, one side or the other gave in. Work was resumed but the anger persisted. This was the conflict that was thought basic in all industrial society.

With the rise of the new managerial class, negotiations with workers passed from owners to organization men. The organization men could be blamed for strikes; better managers avoided or negotiated out of conflict. Those who bargained did not themselves pay the higher wages that were the cost of the settlement. Not having to pay makes a difference. The modern industrial firm was powerful in its markets so, after some ceremonial acrimony, it could pass higher wage costs along to the public in higher prices. Strikes still occurred. But now they were mostly without rancor. Sometimes they usefully reduced burdensome business inventories.

But with migration a new conflict appeared. That was between the two proletariats of the Industrial City, between the old, established, relatively secure, relatively well-paid working force and the new dark tide which it perceived as being both socially and economically its nemesis. Suspicion and dislike were, as often before, facilitated by differences in color, language or country of origin. For the new migrants the capitalist was no longer the enemy. Many who cleaned the streets, tended the buildings and labored without skill on construction sites wished they had industrial employment. Many others simply wished they had employment. Or housing, schools or transportation or a society that was decently color-blind. Their enemy was the government or the social order which resented their presence and sought their exclusion from schools, politics and social life. When these inhabitants revolted, they did not wish to burn the capitalist; they sought, logically, to burn the city.

In Britain prior to the arrival of the Pakistanis, Indians and West Indians, race prejudice — racial xenophobia — had been thought an American disorder. And, in the Northern United States, it had long been thought a Southern affliction. Following the great migrations it was discovered to be pandemic. It also ran in Switzerland against Italians, in Germany against Turks. This tension and the thought and action it provokes are the most dramatic and debated urban development of modern times. On this I will have a further word presently.

The Metropolis

The diversification of the modern city caused by rising incomes and the changing structure of industry, the arrival of the new immigrants and the growth of the Camps have created the final type of city. As noted, it draws on and unites all the kinds that have gone before. It might be called the post-Industrial City; more simply it is the Metropolis. Industry can still be a major *raison d'être* and often is. But the old class structure of the Industrial City has ceased to exist. So have the physical lineaments of the factory town. Affluence has brought the shops and shopping centers and the ancillary services that are in descent from those of the Merchant City. Around, about and forming a part of the Metropolis are the Camps. All have a governing nucleus, which is the residue of the Political Household. In the greatest of the Metropolises — London, Paris, Rome, Tokyo, New York (with the United Nations) — this still has an important bearing on its character.

When we ask as to the future of the modern Metropolis, we are asking about the future of the modern industrial society, for the Metropolis is its tangible, visible expression.

The assimilation of the new arrivals will be the easiest of the problems of the modern Metropolis. The scale of this movement in modern times has been very large. At least within the United States it will be smaller in the future; a country can only liquidate its agricultural working force once. And much tension that is attributed to race is really the result of the unsettling effects of the inward movement and of the economic and cultural poverty of the countryside in which the people were reared.

In the nineteen-thirties, the movement of a very poor agricultural population from the southern Great Plains into California, the Okies and Arkies of John Steinbeck's great novel, was the source of major social tension. Like the subject peoples of Eastern Europe the Okies and Arkies were, when clean, indubitably white. Nonetheless they were pictured as a race apart. Their children are now indistinguishable from other Californians. So it will be with the children, or at most the grandchildren, of the recent migrants. They will have higher educational and economic aspirations than their parents or grand-parents. These aspirations, in greater or less measure, they will achieve. When this happens, the problems of race and color will diminish and even seem archaic. The rich and the poor of the same language, color and race do not live easily side by side. The affluent of different races usually live quite peaceably with one another.

The more plausible problem of twenty or thirty years hence will be how to arrange a new migration into the cities. For, as the present generation of urban dwellers moves up the ladder, there will be a demand for someone to do the less agreeable jobs that they leave behind.

Where Capitalism Fails

On two other matters the prospect is more grim. First there is the fact that capitalism performs excellently in providing those things — automobiles, disposable packaging, drugs, alcohol — that cause problems for the city. But it is inherently incompetent in providing the things that city dwellers most urgently need. Capitalism has never anywhere provided good houses at moderate cost. Housing, it seems unnecessary to stress, is an important adjunct of a successful urban life. Nor does capitalism provide good health services, and when people live close together with attendant health risks, these too are important. They are made more urgent because, on coming to the city, people no longer accept as inevitable untended sickness and then a quiet death as they would in some lonesome sharecropper's cabin. Nor does capitalism provide efficient transportation for people — another essential of the life of the Metropolis.

In Western Europe and Japan the failure of capitalism in the fields of housing, health and transportation is largely, though not completely, accepted. There industries have been intensively socialized. In the United States there remains the conviction that, however contrary the experience, private enterprise will eventually serve. To assert the inherently public character of these industries, even though the practice affirms it, still seems radical. Nothing is now so important as to agree that the nature of these services *is* public and then to ensure that their performance is not merely a matter of adequacy but of pride. City life will never be good while housing, health care and transportation are poor.

There is a larger need. That is to see far more clearly than at present the essentially social character of the Metropolis. In its days of greatest elegance, the city was a household, an extension of the domestic arrangements of the ruler. No line then separated private from public tasks. Construction, artistic

The Metropolis. All that went before is here.

embellishment and maintenance of the city — what would now be regarded as public tasks — may well have absorbed the larger share of the aggregate public and private income. With the Industrial City it came to be assumed that payment for public tasks — education, police protection, courts, sanitation, recreation, public entertainment, care of the old and impoverished — would be only a small subtraction from total revenue. The private household, no one doubted, had the major claim.

This continues to be the assumption. The consequences all recognize. Among the affluent and even among the poor, services supplied out of private income are far more amply endowed than those provided by the city. Houses are clean, streets are filthy. Personal wealth expands; there are too few police officers to protect it. Television sets are omnipresent; schools are deficient. Bathing is possible in a private bathroom but not safely at a public beach. Where capitalism is efficient, it adds to the public tasks of the city; it increases the number of automobiles that must be accommodated in and through the city, adds to the detritus that must be picked up from the streets and makes progressively more difficult the problem of keeping breathable the air and sustaining a minimum tranquility of life.

This is another way of saying that the social aspect of modern metropolitan life is extremely expensive, far more expensive than we have yet imagined. The notion that these social costs are only a deduction from total public and private expenditure — a view that is a legacy of the attitudes of the Industrial City — is now obsolete. It may well be in the future that, if the Metropolis is to be pleasant, healthy, otherwise agreeable and culturally and intellectually rewarding, public expenditures will have to be higher than private expenditures.

The test is to look at the Metropolis as one would look at a household and, indeed, as the rulers regarded the Political Household. There is no *a priori* case for one class of expenditures, public or private, over another — for street sweepers over vacuum cleaners, schools over television sets. The question is which returns the greatest satisfaction at the margin and serves best the sense of the community as to what is good. If the satisfaction from public services is higher than that from private goods for the typical urban dweller, there will obviously be more social good in accepting the fact than in resisting it. Not ideology but the social character of the Metropolis is the controlling circumstance.

The acceptance of the social character of the Metropolis involves more than questions of bread and butter, of housing, health care, clean streets and safe parks. It also involves another dimension, that of art and design. This is my last point. We've seen that people travel by the millions to view the Political Households and Merchant Cities of the past. And many also go to see Washington, Canberra, New Delhi and Brasilia. They do not visit, even in their present and improved manifestations, any of the three Birminghams. The difference is elementary. The Political Households were conceived as a unity. Their design was envisaged as a whole. The cities which people forswear carry the aesthetic legacy of classical liberal capitalism. There is no proof that people were more sensitive to artistic need in the days of Dresden or St. Petersburg than in the age of Düsseldorf or Pittsburgh. But Dresden and St. Petersburg were faithful to their central conception and their common style. These were enforced as the architect enforces a common conception for a whole house. This concept can be good or bad. But one rule can be laid down as final: whether good or bad, it will be better than when there is no governing order at all.

As a legacy of classical liberalism there is a marked unwillingness to socialize design, to specify overall architectural styles to which the subordinate units must conform. It is an unjust interference with property rights and personal preference. But there is no place where the substitution of social for classical liberal expression is more urgent and where, paradoxically, the result serves better the classical utilitarian goal of the greatest good for the greatest number.

The interference with property rights is real. One solution lies in extending the public ownership of urban land. This too accords with the inherently social character of the city and the inescapably socialist character of housing. I've long wondered why European socialists or American liberals, when gathering on occasions of high ceremony to affirm their faith, give so little attention to the public ownership of urban land. For no other form of property is the public case so clear.

The Tyranny of Circumstance

To speak of the social character of the Metropolis and of the necessarily socialist character of its important services is to arouse instant suspicion. There is advocacy here. A socialist is speaking. The proper discounts should be applied.

To suspect advocacy in such matters is not a bad precaution but it is not appropriate in this case. As often in these matters, we imagine choice — scope for ideological preference — when, in fact, there is little or none. The social character of the Metropolis derives not from preference. It follows, as earlier noted, from the far harder circumstance that millions of people live in close proximity to each other with all the friction, all the antisocial opportunity, all the social needs that this ordains. It is this that forces upon the city its social character. This is not the product of preference. It is, once again, the tyranny of circumstance.

Had one wished to forestall this tyranny, there would have been only one way. That would have been to forestall the people. The Metropolis should have been aborted long before it became New York, London or Tokyo.

12.
Democracy,
Leadership, Commitment

Man, at least when educated, is a pessimist. He believes it safer not to reflect on his achievements; Jove is known to strike such people down. Dangers, uncompleted tasks, failures remain in his mind.

Still, in the last two hundred years some remarkable things have been accomplished. Millions now escape poverty, live more contentedly and much longer than ever before. The decline of religious faith in our time proceeds partly from the fact that so many get so much more out of this world and feel it possible in consequence to repose less hope in the next. White men no longer believe they were meant by nature or sent by heaven to rule those who are black, brown or yellow. No one, two hundred years ago, could have foreseen man's capacity, public, social and corporate, to organize for such vast and intricate tasks as arranging travel to the moon, getting oil from under the North Sea or making a television series. Adam Smith thought the joint-stock company — the corporation, in modern language — doomed to incompetence and failure because it taxed this capacity for cooperation beyond feasible limits. Maybe we even understand war better than in the heroic days. Personal proficiency in killing is no longer praised so fulsomely as in earlier times. Being killed is not thought quite so transcendent a glory. Both are recommended, even for other people, with some slight diffidence.

Our tendency, however, is to reflect on failure. We remind ourselves of the number of people who are still poor in the poor countries and also in the rich. We reflect that, two hundred years after Adam Smith, economists have achieved not the control of inflation, not the prevention of unemployment, but the ability to have both at the same time. Organization — the capacity for cooperative effort — we note, can get us to the moon but not into and around New York. Our perception of war now includes the ability to destroy all life if war comes.

Perhaps this pessimism is good. I certainly think so. It causes us to ask: "Well, what can I do?" It is a good question. Is there anything the individual can do?

But there is a prior question. Social existence, as we have sufficiently seen, is a continuing process. As one of its problems is solved, others emerge, often from the previous solutions themselves. Our habit is to ask for solutions. The very best ones will be only a temporary achievement, although nobody should minimize the importance of that. We need also to spare a thought for the mechanism by which we tackle the flow of problems which, like waves on the beach, will continue to come. How good, in particular, are the mechanisms of democratic government for this continuing task? And what makes them better or worse? That I perceive to be the task to which this small adventure in ideas ultimately comes.

The Swiss Case

More than twenty years ago I was working on a book, and it was going badly. I sought out a small Swiss village in the Bernese Oberland, secluded myself and, out of boredom, thought each afternoon, evening and much of the night of what I would write the next morning. The results by accepted standards were excellent; the book, *The Affluent Society*, was held, not least of all by me, to be useful. I've been returning to Switzerland and to Gstaad to write ever since. I've become a part-time Swiss professor; a librarian at the Swiss national library told me some years ago, to my satisfaction, that I was being reclassified as a semi-Swiss author. I've come to feel that I know this small country moderately well.

The Swiss example has always encouraged me to believe that there is power and effectiveness in democracy. It is the Swiss instinct that problems can be solved by the collective responsibility and intelligence of the people themselves. It is that responsibility and intelligence that count. Accordingly, the solution lies with the citizen, not the leader. The Swiss citizen does not delegate to the great in the belief that they have the answers. He seeks the answers. In a few of the 22 (very recently 23) cantons, all voters still meet as a legislative body. The initiative and referendum — a direct vote on issues — are much used. In consequence, many more elections are to resolve issues than to choose leaders. In further consequence, the Swiss have had few noted leaders, few heroes. The most famous Swiss was Calvin, who was French. After Calvin comes William Tell, whose distinction rests only on a somewhat perilous approach to parental duty.

One winter day a few years ago a telephone message was relayed to me from a man in Bern whose name seemed familiar; he wanted me to come over for lunch to discuss economic problems. I sought out my very intelligent Swiss neighbor to find out who he was. "He might have been last year's President," she said. "Anyway, I'm quite sure he isn't President now."

Small countries are far from being masters of their people's destiny. Inflation and recession come in from abroad. In a nuclear war these countries would be no less the victims than the nuclear powers themselves. But for questions within the power of the Swiss democracy — protection of the environment; ethnic reconciliation between those who speak German, French, Italian; a tolerant relationship between religions; provision of good housing and public services; sensible support to agriculture and industry; education that nurtures the democratic idea — it has found solutions, brilliant solutions on the whole.

It is common, even there, to dismiss this democratic accomplishment by saying that Switzerland is a small country that also has had no wars. Perhaps it was the good sense of Swiss democracy that kept it out of Europe's internecine wars, as some have called them. To say that a small country has no problems shows only an instinct for error. Ulster is a small country. So is Lebanon. So is Chile. The Belgians quarrel dutifully over language. Small countries may feel especially obliged to assert their capacity for self-destruction. It is a form of compensation.

For the task of governing themselves, the Swiss have three sources of strength. Each participant in the democracy has a personal concern for the result. Small size and the continued protection of the authority and autonomy of the canton and the responsibilities of the commune or local government — the celebrated Swiss federalism — is a help. One person's vote and voice can have an appreciable bearing on the outcome. So they are worth using and worth careful thought. Important issues are submitted to the people in referendum. Indeed, as noted, most Swiss elections are to pass on issues (new taxes, new spending, votes for women, limits on the number of foreign workers) and are not, as elsewhere, to select between parties and politicians.

The next source of strength is the Swiss sense of community. The Swiss, one need hardly say, have a keen sense of personal pecuniary interest. But they recognize the greater loss if the community is sacrificed to the special interest. Meeting politicians, businessmen, trade union leaders, even bankers in Switzerland over the years, I've always been impressed by the feeling, implied or expressed, that the interest of the commune, canton or country has precedence over the interest of the individual, party or organization and that this is not generosity but good sense.

Finally, I've always thought that the Swiss were far more interested in results than in principle. In economics and politics, as in war, an astonishing number of people die, like the man on the railway crossing, defending their right of way. This is a poorly developed instinct in Switzerland. No country so firmly avows the principles of private enterprise but in few have the practical concessions to socialism been more numerous and varied. When in Switzerland, we bank at a publicly owned cantonal bank, ride the national railroads, pay our bills through the Post Office *giro*, talk on a publicly owned telephone system, send telegrams over state-owned wires, look at public television, get news from the public radio, which can be heard over public telephone wires.

We do not live while there, as do many deserving Swiss, in clean, bright, publicly owned housing, access to which is considered a public right. But we do not pay private insurance on our house because the local government considers it cheaper for the individual and better for the community just to replace a house in case of fire. This is also thought to discourage arson, a risk that is not extreme. Swiss farmers are massively supported by the government, partly because they are thought cheaper for keeping the countryside in condition than a parks service. No industry is so uniquely Swiss as watchmaking. For around half a century the movements of most Swiss watches, a not unimportant feature, have been made by a firm that initially was sponsored by the Swiss government. Only the cases, watchbands, boxes and advertising have their origins in the realm of strict private enterprise. In other countries such arrangements would be thought inconsistent with the fundamental principles of free enterprise. The Swiss do not worry about such trifles.

The Leadership Instinct

The Anglo-American instinct in government is very different from that of the Swiss. We do not solve problems ourselves; we search instead for the man or woman who will do so. Ours is not the politics of people but the politics of leaders. In Switzerland the word leadership is scarcely known. In the United States and Britain it has a familiar and resonant sound.

It's the cause of a wonderful schizophrenia in both British and American political life. All British political journalists of depth deplore the decline of Parliament. American sages weep ecstatically over the congenital ineffectuality of the Congress. People in both countries unite in pleading for better leaders — stronger presidents, the great prime ministers of the past. They are asking for men who would weaken their legislatures yet more.

There could be more power in the democratic process — in the collective judgment of legislators and citizens — than the political sages imagine. That power does not consist primarily in passing or not passing laws. Presidents worry but little about independent legislative action and prime ministers even less. In both countries, and especially in the United States, the legislative power is the power to inform. From this comes the public response, and this response no political leader can ignore. On the Vietnam war, Watergate, the CIA, the international and domestic political legerdemain of the great corporations, the impact of the power to inform was very great in America. A president who wants to act in conflict with the democratic will has only one thought: How can I keep the people on Capitol Hill quiet? Or in ignorance? This would be affirmed if, with help from heaven, one could poll recent presidents on what American political institution they could have best done without. In the unlikely event of honest answers, all would put congressional committees and their investigations either at the top of their list or right next to the press.

I've spent a good part of my adult life writing in Switzerland. A great deal of the rest, I sometimes think, has been spent before congressional committees. I exaggerate only slightly. My first appearance was forty years ago. At an average of three a year since — a few years none, some as many as twenty — that is 120 days, a third of a year. I can look at a committee and, without thought, divide its members into the three basic categories — those members you might persuade; those you watch, for their questions could be mean and even damaging; those you can safely ignore. "Professor, to get down to the practical level: How would this affect the average guy in my part of Michigan?" But there is merit even in the mentally retarded legislator. He asks the questions that everyone is afraid to ask for fear of seeming simple.

The legislative hearing informs. Along with the legislative debate it also converts the good idea into the human right. Democratic power survives in these institutions. Still, it is with leaders that our politics is concerned. In the United States politics means selecting the president.

Politics as a Spectator Sport

This is a process of which I'm also something of a veteran. In my first campaign I worked on speeches for FDR. I campaigned twice with Adlai Stevenson, and then for John F. Kennedy, Lyndon Johnson, Eugene McCarthy, briefly for Hubert Humphrey and for George McGovern. I have had a growing affinity for lost causes. On occasion, no doubt, I contributed the slight added shove which helped ensure the loss.

Presidential selection for the next campaign begins as the last campaign subsides. In its intensive form it lasts a year, costs hundreds of millions of dollars, has many of the aspects of an endurance contest and, on the record, is erratic. Eugene McCarthy observed that, in the first two hundred years, it brought us from George Washington to Richard Nixon, from John Adams to Spiro Agnew, from John Jay to John Mitchell and from Alexander Hamilton to John Connally. He went on to say, "You have to ask yourself how much more of this kind of progress we can stand."

The convention is a precise clue to the major flaw. It's a great spectacle, and politics in the United States has become a spectator sport. Unlike football or hockey, it's an all-season show. Reporters greatly enjoy it, an enjoyment that is enhanced because they can believe, as they cannot of watching a football game, that their work has redeeming social consequence. When, as sometimes happens, they are assailed by doubt, they remind their audience, and therewith themselves, that history is being made. As in football, it is form that counts, not substance. Points are awarded not for wisdom on issues but for performance in the game. Winning is, of course, the only test of achievement.

All this becomes evident at a national convention. It is covered at vast expense by the television networks. Their most experienced commentators patrol the floor. Their experience is with tactics and strategy; they are not expected to feel deeply about issues or policy. In tense, confidential, condescending tones they tell their audience of history in the making. It is a history that all sensible historians will ignore. Reporters interview the managers of the several candidates, the leaders of the state delegations. These tell of complex designs which will soon be abandoned and hopes presented as predictions that will never be fulfilled. Again I speak from some experience. I've been attending these festivals, off and on, since 1940. I was a floor co-ordinator for Kennedy in 1960, a floor manager for McCarthy in 1968, a McGovern archon in 1972. I've sat through many weary hours as a delegate. My bottom bears a permanent latticework design from the chairs. Once I opposed, and possibly helped to veto, the proposed selection of a vice-president. It was because I was thought to have power in my delegation which I didn't in the slightest possess. There was no chance that its members would necessarily agree with me. With that negative exception, I do not believe that I ever had the slightest influence on the selection of a candidate. Once, in Los Angeles, I did tell Edward R. Murrow, who asked me, that "everything was under control." He went immediately to the booth and reported it to Walter Cronkite. They were both very excited. So, the Kennedy forces were admitting that they had everything under control. They discussed this compelling piece of news for five full minutes.

Once the convention that the commentators believe still to exist did assemble. In the case of the Democrats it was made up of two major groups — semi-literates from the rural South and semi-criminals from the urban North. Both were under the command of those who had selected them. The first were kept in line by playing on their natural awe of their surroundings and the threat of not paying their return fare. Those from Tammany, Jersey City, Boston, Chicago, Kansas City knew they could be deprived of illegal income, even threatened with imprisonment, if they did not conform. These malleable statesmen could, accordingly, be bartered or brokered. They are gone forever. Delegates of intelligence and honesty now assemble with their minds made up. The real decisions on candidates come before, in the primaries and the state caucuses and conventions.

The Equilibrium
Henceforth, when the California primary, the last and the largest, is over, we will almost always know who the candidates will be. This is another giant step toward democracy. The conventions, in their great days, gave power to the

few. The primaries give it to the people. As with many others, my commitment to democracy is an article of faith, and I am not really open to argument on the alternatives. But I do think there is rational ground for believing it to be both stronger and safer than any other form. This is because weakness and danger in the modern state come when there is a rift between governing and governed — when people can feel that government is not theirs. The more democratic the process, the less this danger, the smaller this weakness. When people put their ballots in the boxes, they are, by that act, inoculated against the feeling that the government is not theirs. They then accept, in some measure, that its errors are their errors, its aberrations their aberrations, that any revolt will be against themselves. It's a remarkably shrewd and rather conservative arrangement when one thinks of it.

But what we call democracy is considerably less than that. The limousines at the candidates' headquarters on election night are a clue. Our electoral system gives power to the voter. And, let there be no doubt, it gives power to money. The people are many, the rich are few. But politicians need money. And the well-to-do are far more articulate than the average, which is why their indignation is regularly mistaken for the voice of the masses. The result is an equilibrium between voters and money.

But even here democracy is advancing. Public funds now pay a part of the election costs. The rich are not quite as much needed as before.

The Nature of Leadership

For what do people look in leaders, however selected? For what should they look?

Again I plead some qualification. I've had a distant acquaintance with most of the political leaders of the last half century. I missed Hitler, Mussolini and also Stalin. Hermann Goering, Joachim von Ribbentrop, Albert Speer, Walther Funk, Julius Streicher and Robert Ley did pass under my inspection and interrogation in 1945 but they only proved that National Socialism was a gangster interlude at a rather low order of mental capacity and with a surprisingly high incidence of alcoholism.

All of the great leaders have had one characteristic in common: it was the willingness to confront unequivocally the major anxiety of their people in their time. This, and not much else, is the essence of leadership.

In 1933, the Great Depression was the great and pervading source of anxiety. President Hoover was not a foolish man; few have been trained more comprehensively for the presidency. But he could not face directly the economic disaster of his time. Repeatedly he told people who knew better that the slump was over. Roosevelt, in his Inaugural Address and in the legislation of the first hundred days, left no one in doubt. All his energies would be

Leadership is unqualified commitment to the major anxiety of the people. As it was for
Roosevelt . . .

committed to the economic miseries of the time. The people's concern was his concern. What could be done, he would do. There would be no pretense.

Roosevelt was a captivating speaker. He sustained a sense of intimacy with people; he let them believe they were in his confidence. He had charm — it would now for some reason be called charisma. ("Senator Roman Hruska has charisma." "Sir Keith Joseph has charisma.") These qualities would never have been noticed if Roosevelt had failed to commit himself to the anxieties of the time.

The proof is that these qualities made little impression until he had so committed himself. In 1932, Walter Lippmann looked over the candidates; no one's view was thought to be more acute. Roosevelt, he said, "is a pleasant man, who, without any important qualifications for the office, would very much like to be President." [1] A leader can compromise, get the best bargain he can. Politics is the art of the possible. But he cannot be thought to evade.

Nehru

The leader I knew best was Jawaharlal Nehru. We both had association with the University of Cambridge. Once, when visiting the United States, he expressed amused alarm over the number of Oxford men — William Fulbright, Dean Rusk, numerous others — in high positions. I assured him that, as in India, the decisive posts were held by Cambridge men. He professed great relief.

The issue Nehru confronted, with Gandhi, was the independence of India. India should govern herself. More important was the question of equality and dignity for all the people of India — an end to the belief, accepted as truth for two centuries, that Europeans were superior to Asians. This truth had been proclaimed in the clubs, in the railway stations, on the benches in the parks, in the social life of India.

For Nehru the temptation to equivocate was especially strong. He came from a wealthy, aristocratic, socially conservative family. His father was a pioneer in the Congress Movement but at a time when it met in morning clothes, accepted the Raj and no one needed to be reminded that it had been founded by an Englishman. Nehru himself moved easily among Europeans, often with a poorly concealed sense of his own superior grace and education. Once he told me, again not quite seriously, that he would be the last Englishman to be Prime Minister of India. But he faced the principal issue of his time and accepted fully its personal cost, including the years of imprisonment. This affirmed his right to lead. Had he failed so to commit himself, his charm, his highly informed mind (much more informed than Roosevelt's), his famous sense of community with the Indian masses would have counted for nothing. His name would not now be known.

. . . And Nehru . . .

. . . And Martin Luther King, here marching for civil rights.

When Hitler became the great source of anxiety, Roosevelt faced that fear, as did Winston Churchill and Charles de Gaulle. Nehru did not have a similar capacity for change. After independence was won, poverty and the relentless Malthusianism of the Indian people were the all-embracing problems of India. These Nehru did not similarly confront. Surely there was some socialist magic that would wave them away. Heroes of his English years — Sidney and Beatrice Webb, Harold Laski — had thought so, and it must be true. In his last years his leadership suffered. A leader must be able to confront the anxieties of his time. He must also change as these change.

Leadership and Vietnam

John F. Kennedy once told me, as he told others, that he never wanted to let a day go by without asking what he could do to lift the fear of nuclear annihilation from men's minds. If he had lived, it would have been, perhaps, his claim to leadership. We will never know. In his few years he served only to establish a much lesser commitment. That was to the notion that modern government can be interesting, exciting and a proper concern of the idealistic, the enthusiastic and the young.

I came back from India just before Kennedy's death. For much of the rest of the decade I was concerned with what many consider one of the legacies of his presidency, our involvement in Vietnam. I do not share this view; I do know that he was largely responsible for my own education on the subject. Kennedy sent me to Vietnam in the autumn of 1961. A report from Maxwell Taylor and Walt W. Rostow had urged greater involvement, including troops. (They would be disguised, rather imaginatively, as flood control workers.) Kennedy was distressed and guessed I might have a different view. A short passage, helped perhaps by more knowledge and experience of that part of the world than most of my colleagues possessed, persuaded me of the futility and danger of the enterprise. Given the larcenous incompetence and the inspired selfishness and corruption of those with whom we were allied, we could not succeed. There was a more sobering thought: perhaps we should not succeed.

The Vietnam war showed wonderfully the relationship between leadership and commitment. Eugene McCarthy had never previously been celebrated for strong, uncompromising positions. He was amused, civilized and somewhat lazy. It was a time when almost every other major politician was trying to be against the war in principle, for it was a matter of practical necessity. McCarthy scorned such cant and came out in unequivocal opposition. Millions to whom he had previously been unknown flocked to his side.

I had guessed they might. One day in the late summer of 1967, I went up to Mount Ascutney in Vermont to address a meeting urging the opening of peace negotiations. It was to be held in the ski lodge; a couple of hundred were expected. When we arrived, the mountain top was covered with people. I had a damaging sense of exaltation. A sermon on the mount. People were, indeed, waiting for some leadership, any leadership, on Vietnam. Across the Connecticut River in New Hampshire a few months later, McCarthy came within a few votes of beating Lyndon Johnson in the primary. It was clear that in the Wisconsin primary a few weeks later he would win. Johnson called a halt to the bombing and withdrew as a presidential candidate.

In the next months I marched with Gene, if that is the word, and resisted the thought that Robert Kennedy might be the stronger candidate. Mostly I raised money, an easier thing than might be imagined. People who felt guilty about the war assuaged their conscience with cash. Ours must have been one of the few presidential campaigns in history in which no one worried about finances. I led the McCarthy forces on the convention floor, though without great confidence that I was being followed. I seconded Gene's nomination, and when I returned home, my wife asked what had happened to my speech. The television cameras had all been on the riots downtown. In Chicago I had crossed the police lines to address the more violent protesters. The Chicago police dutifully clubbed others who thought to do so but they recognized a member of the Establishment and escorted me through. It was disconcerting but better than being clubbed.

Of all the men I've known in politics, Eugene McCarthy had the most subtle mind and by far the greatest sense of the music of words. He was, indeed, the first serious poet in the American political pantheon. In speaking for his nomination at Chicago, I said that this might not yet be the age of John Milton but it was no longer the age of John Wayne or John Connally. John Connally was sitting there. New York and California delegates sitting near, with that genius for originality that marks American liberalism, jumped to their feet and proposed sexual violence on Connally. John told reporters, "Where ah come from, it helps to have Galbraith against yoou." We owe the end of the Vietnam war to Eugene McCarthy. If he had not committed himself but had tried like the others to straddle the issue, he too would have remained unknown, with his poetry unheard.

Martin Luther King

One day in the spring of that same year I was to lecture at the University of California at Los Angeles. My lecture was canceled. There was unrest on the campus, and for good reason. Word had come of the killing the day before of Martin Luther King. The Chancellor of UCLA was Franklin Murphy, an old friend. He asked me to speak at a memorial gathering on the campus.

I recalled a meeting with King a year earlier — a long afternoon in Geneva. Andrew Young, now a congressman from Atlanta, was with Dr. King. Like

Chicago Convention, 1968. The police dutifully clubbed these opponents of the war, made way for the author. It's better to be a member of the Establishment.

Gandhi and Nehru whom he greatly admired, Martin Luther King had confronted the issue of justice and equality for his people. This he knew to be the only test of a black leader. He knew also, as did Gandhi, that a civilized leader must eschew violence, for violence evokes other anxieties and repels those supporters who are most needed. Now King felt that he must face another issue. Men, black and white, were dying to no purpose in Vietnam. I was identified with that issue, and thus our meeting. He said that a leader must move on to the next great issue when it comes. Some of the lesson that I am stressing here I learned that afternoon.

Berkeley

Is there an education that serves the democratic purpose, gives democracy both power and the wisdom to use it well?

The answer brings me to familiar and beloved scenes, to the older campus of the University of California at Berkeley. I was here during the nineteen-thirties, and we then thought it the best university in the world. I am happy to say that many since have come to accept our insight.

Undergraduates in my day were not politically very concerned; as elsewhere and over the centuries the principal symbols of student achievement were sex, alcohol and idleness, along with a more modern commitment to intercollegiate athletics. But in the sixties Lyndon Johnson, the Vietnam war and the hot breath of the local draft board succeeded where books and professors had failed; the very word Berkeley became a symbol of student involvement in public issues. A massive questioning of the wisdom of accepted authority, many called it a revolt, began here and spread to universities around the world. If you mentioned Berkeley, men and women began to discuss, often with alarm, the role of education in a democracy.

That education has, I believe, two requisites. Both follow directly from the argument I've just made. Education must seek to develop the needed sense of community — the feeling that, at some point, the special interest, even if it is yours, must give way to the general interest; that what best serves all best serves you. With this must go a shrewd awareness that those who resist the general interest must themselves be resisted. When corporations, trade associations, generals, bureaucrats, trade unions, lawyers, physicians, professors put their own pecuniary or bureaucratic interest ahead of the public interest, people must sense, react and oppose. Democratic education must be a lesson in this recognition and this duty.

Second, education must instill the sense of personal security that causes men and women to make a clear and unambiguous commitment to the task at hand, or to distinguish between those who do and those who do not. The evil in modern spectator politics is in the praise it accords the politician who affirms his commitment to the anxieties of the day and then deftly persuades those who dislike the requisite action that they have nothing to fear from his election. "I am for peace but not at the price of weakness." "Poverty must be eliminated but without placing new burdens on the taxpayer." "I stand for a better distribution of income but without interference with the rewards to individual enterprise."

The leaders I have mentioned — Roosevelt, Nehru, Kennedy and, by the standards of his community, Martin Luther King — had what today would be called an elitist education. Perhaps this gave them the sense of security that allowed of their commitment. There is involved here, we should not doubt, a conflict in goals. We want the largest possible number of participants in democratic discussion, and the tens of thousands that the University of California enrolls are proof of the seriousness of the effort. We want these students to believe that, in a democracy, they are sovereign; they have the right and the responsibility and the power to decide. And we want also to train leaders — men and women who are equipped with the knowledge, self-confidence and self-esteem to decide for others and win acceptance for their will. That is the meaning of leadership. We ask, at the same time, for leaders and for followers who are told that leadership belongs to them. It is possible that some conflicts are irreconcilable in principle but not in practice.

Commitment

To understand the importance of commitment is to see in full perspective the problems we have here been discussing. Few, if any, are difficult of solution. The difficulty, all but invariably, is in confronting them. We know what needs to be done; for reasons of inertia, pecuniary interest, passion or ignorance, we do not wish to say so.

The problem of rich countries and poor cannot be solved except by some redistribution of wealth, present or at a minimum potential, between the two groups. That is not difficult to see. But not many want to commit themselves to *that* solution. They are even less inclined to urge what we have seen is the oldest of the remedies, which is for people to move from the poor countries to the rich.

The relentless population increase in the poor countries cannot be checked except by the control of births. The Chinese, and increasingly the Indians, are concluding that this cannot be purely permissive. Few elsewhere wish to commit themselves to this hard truth.

The poorer the country, the poorer it is in administrative resources — the special case of the Chinese with their ancient organizational skills possibly apart. The less, accordingly, can there be reliance on highly organized effort, of which socialism is the extreme example. The greater the poverty, the more, in general, must the poor countries rely on that release of individual energies that both Adam Smith and Karl Marx believed essential in early economic development. Not many in the poor countries want to confront this seemingly very conservative truth.

In the rich countries there is similar difficulty in confronting the problem of poverty. No solution is so effective as providing income to the poor. Whether in the form of food, housing, health services, education or money, income is an excellent antidote for deprivation. No truth has spawned so much ingenious evasion.

We protect our environment only as we say plainly what can or cannot be done to the ambient air, water, landscape. This is a difficult truth. Better an exception for the energy shortage, to protect jobs, for one's own automobile. We make resources last longer by using less. Also a difficult truth.

No politician can praise unemployment or inflation, and there is no way of combining high employment with stable prices that does not involve some control of income and prices. Otherwise the struggle for more consumption and more income to sustain it — a struggle that modern corporations, modern unions and modern democracy all facilitate and encourage — will drive up prices. Only heavy unemployment will then temper this upward thrust. Not many wish to confront the truth that the modern economy gives a choice only between inflation, unemployment or controls.

The problem of the great metropolis is not complex. Overwhelmingly it is money. For people to live close by or on top of each other in great numbers is exceedingly expensive. If we so live, we must be prepared to pay. And if people can escape payment by moving from the city, some or many will go. The economic base will then be eroded, the problem of money be more severe. But again it is more blessed to evade. Better a speech promising more efficient city government, a clampdown on wasteful spending, a stronger line with the teachers, the police and the sanitation unions.

Skidoo

The greatest support to evasion comes from complexity. The problem seeming difficult, we postpone, compromise, yield to the conveniences of politics. To see how we use complexity as a device, it is good, on occasion, to go to a community or a countryside where things are sufficiently stark so that evasion is not possible. One admirable such place is Skidoo 23. It is in the Panamint Mountains in California, not far from the Nevada border, 5600 feet over Death Valley. Skidoo is a force for clarity.

It flourished as a mining town in the early part of this century. (The 23 refers, apparently, to the distance water was piped over the mountains to the mines.) Its greatest moment came in 1908, the year of my birth. Skidoo's most dissolute citizen, Joe Simpson, shot and killed Jim Arnold, the storekeeper, banker and the most respected member of the Skidoo Establishment. Simpson was strung up on a telephone pole, the wires of which gave the news to the world. Reporters rushed in, and the media-conscious citizens strung Joe up a second time to show them how justice of a sort had been done.

No one can look at the deserted and empty mine shafts of Skidoo and escape the fact that resources are exhaustible and nonrenewable.

Skidoo shows also how fragile is the fabric of modern urban existence. Once it was a thriving community of 700 souls. Now the population is precisely nil. For Skidoo the problem was the economic base, as no one on this desert could fail to see. When that eroded, so did Skidoo.

Self-interest — the release of individual energies — made Skidoo. No one could imagine that any other force could bring people hundreds and thousands of miles to bury themselves in the holes one sees here. No one here could believe there is some collectivist or socialist miracle that would similarly populate the desert.

In Skidoo men mined gold. Everything there shows finally how much energy men can expend for no social purpose. Let all reflect on the idle piles in which the gold, most of it, still resides. This capacity for wasting effort is a useful thought to take to the subject of competitive weapons manufacture.

Death Valley

Down below Skidoo in Death Valley, truth has also a wonderful clarity of line. Again we see that the problem is in confronting it.

No one is poor in this valley. That is because there is an excellent relationship between land and people. There are no people. If anyone tried to make a living from *this* land, he would not be rich.

On occasion in the past, people have come to the valley. They always moved on. If they could not have done so, they would have been miserable indeed. Such movement from poor lands to rich has been, we've seen, one of the great solvents for poverty, and for a long time. No one here can doubt its need.

I exaggerate slightly. There are a few families in this valley. People live on income that flows in to them from outside. One resident earlier in the century, Death Valley Scotty, was subsidized in much style by an eccentric millionaire and built the castle that still stands. Without such external support, the few people in the valley would starve — or have to go. The situation of the poor countries is the same. For them, too, income from outside is an antidote for poverty. It is no less a remedy for poverty when it comes as aid — a gift. It is a fact which people of the rich countries try very hard to forget. .

Death Valley has another and yet more important truth to affirm. It is 140 miles long, from 4 to 16 miles wide. Imagine it to have been urbanized as the

Cheyenne Mountain in Colorado. The command post for nuclear war. Outside. (Below) inside.

Death Valley. After the first nuclear exchange the landscape between New Haven and Philadelphia will look generally like this.

Connecticut-New York-New Jersey-Philadelphia area is urbanized. Or London and the Home Counties. Or the Moscow metropolitan area. Or the Tokyo-Yokohama plain. Imagine that the urban and suburban area covers the whole length and breadth of the valley from the mountains to the mountains. Death Valley is how such a metropolis would look after a mere four twenty-megaton bombs. It is how any metropolitan area of similar extent anywhere in the world would look after a similar weight of bombs. To confront this truth fully we must travel east from Death Valley to the eastern slope of the Rockies to the North American Defense Command — NORAD. It is deep inside Cheyenne Mountain not far from Colorado Springs.

The Nuclear Evasion

The truth that men seek there to evade is that this small planet cannot survive a nuclear exchange; that conflict in support of either national passion or differing ideology is grimly absolute; that those bunkered up within Cheyenne Mountain would last for only a few weeks longer than the possibly more fortunate in the town outside.

We do not yet confront this truth. Asked if we want life for our children and grandchildren, we affirm that we do. Asked about nuclear war, the greatest threat to that life, we regularly dismiss it from mind. Man has learned to live with the thought of his own mortality. And he now has accommodated to the thought that all may die, that his children and grandchildren will not exist. It's a capacity for accommodation at which we can only marvel. I suspect that our minds accept the thought but do not embrace the reality. The act of imagination is too great or too awful. Our minds can extend to a war in some distant jungle and set in motion the actions that reject it. But not yet to the nuclear holocaust.

A commitment to this reality is now the supreme test of our politics. None should accept the easy evasion that the decision is not ours. The Russians are no less perceptive, no less life-enhancing, no more inclined to a death wish than we. Their experience of the death and devastation of war is far more comprehensive than ours. We must believe, for it is true, that they are as willing as we are to commit themselves to this reality, to the existence of this threat to all life and to its elimination.

That, indeed, is the highest purpose of politics in both countries, one that far transcends the differences in economic or political systems. For after the first exchange of missiles, as Khrushchev was moved to warn the world, the ashes of Communism and the ashes of capitalism will be indistinguishable. Not even the most passionate ideologue will be able to speak of the difference, for he too will be dead. In an age when so much is uncertain, there is one certainty: This truth we must confront.

A Major Word of Thanks

These are usually called acknowledgments; for this book it is a grievously inadequate word. Adrian Malone, to whom I have dedicated these pages, was the originator of this enterprise, my companion and mentor throughout. My debt is great to him, and only slightly less to Dick Gilling, Mick Jackson and David Kennard, the three directors who divided and shared responsibility for *The Age of Uncertainty*. Without these four colleagues there would have been no television series and, of course, no book.

Supporting the work of Messrs. Malone, Gilling, Jackson and Kennard and in constant support of me were Sue Burgess, Jenny Doe, Sheila Johns and Sarah Hyde. These are persons of high proficiency in all the myriad functions that go with filmmaking and its associated and notably proliferated paperwork, and extend on to managing travel, running offices, driving automobiles and typing scripts. This proficiency they combine with great charm and even greater good humor. My thanks to all four are deeply tinged with love.

All who watch television should know – as I now know – that merit depends less on the man on the screen than on the people who put him there. (The man who performs gets the most care and attention, has the best hours and gets the most pay. It is a beautiful arrangement, allowing always for the point of view.) Thus for a year while filming the series, I worked with two superb cameramen, Henry Farrar and Phil Meheux, and Phil, who was longest with us, I shall regard always as one of the most amused, amusing and accomplished artists an economist has ever been privileged to encounter. John Tellick and Dave Brinicombe presided more silently but not less valuably over the sound recording. It is their highly defensible position, rigorously enforced, that, in watching television, people need not only to see clearly but to hear clearly. Robyn Mendelsohn handled all details for the BBC in New York, and in London and on location Kevin Rowley, Jim Black, Kevin Baxendale, Tony Mayne, Dennis Kettle, Dave Gurney, Dave Childs, Terry Manning, Sid Morris, Francis Daniel, Doug Corry, Stuart Moser, Michael Purcilly, Douglas Ernst, John Lindley, Richard Brick, Colin Lowrey, Sue Shearman, Hilary Henson, Barbara Lane, Jacque Jefferies and Jeni Kine assisted on the cameras, on the lights, with the sound, in the studio and even on my face. The list continues: Paul Carter, Jim Latham and Pamela Bosworth were the film editors; Charles McGhie and Karen Godson the graphic designers; John

Horton the visual effects designer. On the final programs Peter Bartlett, Elmer Cossey, John Walker and Adam Gifford were the very able cameramen, Chris Cox and Bob McDonnell their assistants.

I must add a special word for Mick Burke who, as assistant cameraman, was a truly good companion through all the early filming. Then he took a leave of absence to join the British team that, in the 1975 season, was to climb Mount Everest. There, a few hundred yards from the top, he walked into the gathering clouds and darkness to complete his passage. He did not return.

Going on from television to this book: Joanna Roll, a family friend, and Ben Shephard of the BBC helped well and diligently on research and checking of facts. Angela Murphy and Paul McAlinden, who also designed the book, searched out and helped select the pictures on these pages. The arrangement of these illustrations, a thoroughly pleasant chore which I shared, was, like all else, under the direction of Peter Campbell of BBC Publications.

Paul M. Sweezy, an old friend, read the chapter on Marx and gave me much help. Adam Ulam, another friend of distinctly contrasting view, helped me similarly on Lenin. To both, thanks, with full freedom from responsibility for the result. Among the many others to whom I turned for help, I would like to mention especially Sir Eric Roll, whose eclectic and thoughtful knowledge of the history of economic thought has helped so many of us over the years.

My immediate associates and relatives in Cambridge remain for my final word of thanks. Londa Schiebinger typed and retyped and then went on faithfully to check and correct my facts. Emmy Davis managed the office and much of my life while the enterprise was in progress, in her spare time also typed and checked, and she journeyed with me during the American filming to provide help, protection and safe movement and to calm the emotions of all concerned. As so often before, Andrea Williams was not my assistant but my full-fledged partner. She worked with the BBC on all the details of the television programs, edited this book, saw it through the press, did everything else I would otherwise have had to do.

I've always been suspicious of authors who use these acknowledgments to proclaim their love for their wives. Most likely it is a cover for secret distaste, occasional beatings and adulterous yearnings, fulfilled or unfulfilled. But there are exceptions to the best rules. Catherine Galbraith joined in on this effort from the first day, accompanied me for all the filming, stood off curious intruders by day and by night, showed herself a competent photographer as these pages attest, performed in the last two programs and kept a journal which will one day tell of the talented people and the improbable procedures with which the BBC produces a television series.

John Kenneth Galbraith
Cambridge, Massachusetts 1976

Notes

Chapter 1

[1] John Maynard Keynes, *The General Theory of Employment Interest and Money* (New York: Harcourt, Brace and Co., 1936), p. 383.

[2] Ibid.

[3] Ibid.

[4] A strong case will be made for F. Y. Edgeworth who, though he spent his life in England, was one of the Edgeworths of Edgeworthstown, County Longford.

[5] Unlike Hume and other men of liberal mind at the time, Adam Smith did not welcome American independence. His vision was of a commonwealth embracing all the English-speaking world. Members from North America would sit in the House of Commons in London; eventually, with increasing population in America, the capital would be moved to a more central location across the Atlantic. Cincinnati, Memphis or, considering the claims of Canada, perhaps Green Bay, Wisconsin. That was the destiny that was missed.

[6] Adam Smith, *Wealth of Nations*, Vol. I (London: Methuen & Co., 1950), p. 412.

[7] Smith, Vol. I, p. 8.

[8] Ibid.

[9] Smith, Vol. I, p. 144.

[10] Smith, Vol. II, p. 264.

[11] Smith, Vol. II, pp. 264–265.

[12] William Pitt before the House of Commons on February 17, 1792, quoted in John Rae, *Life of Adam Smith* (New York: Augustus M. Kelley, 1965), pp. 290–291.

[13] Charles Edward Trevelyan quoted in Dudley Edwards, *The Great Famine* (Dublin: Brown and Nolan, 1956), p. 257.

Chapter 2

[1] Allan Nevins, *Study In Power*, Vol. II (New York: Charles Scribner's Sons, 1953), p. 300.

[2] Peter Collier and David Horowitz, *The Rockefellers: An American Dynasty* (New York: Holt, Rinehart and Winston, 1976), p. 59. From the manuscript of Frederick T. Gates's unpublished autobiography.

[3] Herbert Spencer, *The Study of Sociology* (New York: D. Appleton and Co., 1891), p. 438.

[4] Herbert Spencer, *Social Statics* (New York: D. Appleton and Co., 1865), p. 413.

[5] William Graham Sumner quoted in Richard Hofstadter, *Social Darwinism in American Thought 1860–1915* (Philadelphia: University of Pennsylvania Press, 1945), p. 44.

[6] John D. Rockefeller quoted in Hofstadter, p. 31.

[7] Ibid.

[8] *New York Post*, September 13, 1975.

[9] Henry Ward Beecher quoted in Hofstadter, p. 18.

[10] Thorstein Veblen, *The Theory of the Leisure Class* (Boston: Houghton Mifflin Co., 1973), p. 176.

[11] Veblen, p. 57.

[12] Veblen, p. 64.

[13] Veblen, p. 62.

[14] Veblen, p. 65.

[15] James Gordon Bennett, Sr., quoted in Richard O'Connor, *The Scandalous Mr. Bennett* (Garden City, New York: Doubleday & Co., 1962), p. 82.

[16] James Gordon Bennett, Sr., in the *New York Herald*, May 6, 1835, quoted in Don C. Seitz, *The James Gordon Bennetts: Father*

and Son (Indianapolis: The Bobbs-Merrill Co., 1928), p. 39.

[17] Gustavus Myers in Matthew Josephson, *The Robber Barons* (New York: Harcourt, Brace and Co., 1934), p. 340.

Chapter 3

[1] Joseph Schumpeter, *Capitalism, Socialism, Democracy*, 3rd ed. (New York: Harper's Torchbooks, 1967), p. 21.

[2] Karl Marx in Karl Marx and Friedrich Engels, *Selected Works*, Vol. II (Moscow: 1962), p. 22.

[3] Karl Marx quoted in David McLellan, *Karl Marx: His Life and Thought* (New York: Harper & Row, 1973), p. 14.

[4] McLellan, p. 16.

[5] Friedrich Engels quoted in McLellan, p. 28.

[6] Karl Marx quoted in McLellan, p. 58.

[7] McLellan, pp. 56–57.

[8] Karl Marx quoted in McLellan, p. 56.

[9] Karl Marx quoted in McLellan, p. 60.

[10] *Karl Marx: Early Texts*, David McLellan, ed. (Oxford: Blackwell, 1972), p. 129.

[11] Friedrich Engels quoted in McLellan, p. 131.

[12] Karl Marx in Karl Marx and Friedrich Engels, Vol. I, p. 52.

[13] Eric Roll, *A History of Economic Thought* (London: Faber & Faber, 1973), pp. 257–258.

[14] *Karl Marx: Early Texts*, p. 217.

[15] Karl Marx, *The Communist Manifesto*, in Karl Marx and Friedrich Engels, Vol. I, pp. 108–137.

[16] Karl Marx, *The Communist Manifesto*, in Karl Marx and Friedrich Engels, Vol. I, p. 126.

[17] Karl Marx, *The Revolutions of 1848*, Vol. I: Political Writings. (London: Allen Lane and New Left Review, 1973), p. 129.

[18] A spy for the Prussian government quoted in McLellan, pp. 268–269.

[19] Jenny Marx quoted in McLellan, p. 265.

[20] Sir George Grey, British Home Secretary, quoted in McLellan, p. 231.

[21] Karl Marx, *Capital: a Critique of Political Economy*, Vol. I (Chicago: Charles H. Kerr & Co., 1926), pp. 836–837.

[22] Karl Marx quoted in McLellan, p. 315.

[23] Karl Marx, *The Civil War in France: Address of the International Working Men's Association*, quoted in Karl Marx and Friedrich Engels, Vol. II, p. 208.

[24] Karl Marx, *Address to the Working Classes*, quoted in McLellan, pp. 365–366.

[25] Karl Marx, *The Civil War in France*, quoted in McLellan, p. 400.

[26] Karl Marx, *Critique of the Gotha Programme*, quoted in McLellan, p. 433.

Chapter 4

[1] Adam Smith, *Wealth of Nations*, Vol. II (London: Methuen & Co., 1950), p. 158.

[2] Smith, Vol. II, p. 131.

[3] James Mill quoted in "Biographical Sketch" by Donald Winch in *James Mill, Selected Economic Writings*, Donald Winch, ed. (Edinburgh & London: Oliver & Boyd, 1966), p. 19.

[4] R. Ewart Oakeshott, *The Archaeology of Weapons* (London: Lutterworth Press, 1960), p. 183.

[5] Pope Innocent III quoted in Henry Treece, *The Crusades* (New York: Random House, 1963), p. 229.

[6] Smith, Vol. II, p. 72.

[7] William Hickling Prescott, *History of the Conquest of Mexico*, Vol. I (New York: John B. Alden, 1886), p. 163.

[8] Prescott, pp. 163–164.

[9] Prescott, p. 165.

[10] William Hickling Prescott, *History of the Conquest of Peru* (London: Richard Bentley, 1854), p. 314.

[11] See Chapter VI, pp. 170–174.

[12] *Letters of Marie-Madeleine Hachard, Ursuline of New Orleans 1727–1728* (New Orleans: Laboard Printing Co., 1974), p. 58.

[13] John Beames, *Memoirs of a Bengal Civilian* (London: Chatto & Windus, 1961).

[14] Beames, p. 151.

[15] Rudyard Kipling, *A Choice of Kipling's Verses Made by T. S. Eliot* (New York: Charles Scribner's Sons, 1943), pp. 136–137.

Chapter 5

[1] Hugo Haase quoted in *Verhandlungen des Reichstags*, Stenographische Berichte, Band 306 (Berlin: Norddeutschen Buchdruckerei und Verlags-Anstalt, 1916), p. 9.

[2] *Fireside Book of Humorous Poetry*, William Cole, ed. (New York: Simon and Schuster, 1959), p. 122.

[3] V. I. Lenin quoted in N. K. Krupskaya, *Reminiscences of Lenin* (Moscow: Foreign Languages Publishing House, 1959), p. 258.

[4] N. K. Krupskaya, p. 307.

[5] V. I. Lenin, *Imperialism: the Highest Stage of Capitalism* (Moscow: Foreign Languages Publishing House, 1947), p. 16.

[6] V. I. Lenin quoted in N. K. Krupskaya, p. 323.

[7] V. I. Lenin quoted in N. K. Krupskaya, p. 335.

[8] Christopher Hill, *Lenin and the Russian Revolution* (London: The English Universities Press, 1947), p. 117.

[9] V. I. Lenin, *The State and Revolution* (Moscow: Progress Publishers, 1969), p. 92.

[10] V. I. Lenin quoted in Hill, pp. 208–209.

[11] Adam Ulam, *The Bolsheviks* (New York: The Macmillan Co., 1965), p. 531.

Chapter 6

[1] Herodotus, Book I, *Clio*, Rev. William Beloe, trans. (Philadelphia: M'Carty and Davis, 1844), p. 31.

[2] Charles Mackay, *Memoirs of Extraordinary Popular Delusions and the Madness of Crowds* (Boston: L. C. Page and Co., 1932), p. 55.

[3] A. Andreades, *History of the Bank of England* (London: P. S. King and Son, 1909), p. 250, citing Juglar, *Les Crises Économiques*, p. 334.

[4] Nicholas Biddle quoted in Arthur M. Schlesinger, Jr., *The Age of Jackson* (Boston: Little, Brown & Co., 1946), p. 75.

[5] Andrew Jackson quoted in J. D. Richardson, *A Compilation of the Messages and Papers of the Presidents 1789–1908*, Vol II (Washington: Bureau of National Literature and Art, 1908), p. 581.

Chapter 7

[1] John Maynard Keynes, *My Early Beliefs* in *Two Memoirs* (London: Rupert Hart-Davis, 1949), p. 83.

[2] John Maynard Keynes quoted in R. F. Harrod, *The Life of John Maynard Keynes* (London: Macmillan & Co., 1951), p. 121.

[3] John Maynard Keynes, *Essays in Biography* (London: Mercury Books, 1961), p. 20.

[4] John Maynard Keynes quoted in Harrod, p. 257.

[5] John Maynard Keynes quoted in Harrod, p. 256.

[6] Robert Lekachman, *Keynes' General Theory; Reports of Three Decades* (New York: St. Martin's Press, 1964), p. 35.

[7] John Maynard Keynes, *Essays in Persuasion* (London: Macmillan & Co., 1931), pp. 248–249.

[8] John Maynard Keynes quoted in Robert Lekachman, *The Age of Keynes* (New York: Random House, 1966), p. 47.

[9] Herbert Hoover quoted in Arthur M. Schlesinger, Jr., *The Crisis of the Old Order* (Boston: Houghton Mifflin Co., 1957), p. 231.

[10] John Maynard Keynes quoted in Harrod, p. 447.

[11] Franklin D. Roosevelt quoted in Lekachman, *The Age of Keynes*, p. 123.

[12] John Maynard Keynes quoted in Lekachman, *The Age of Keynes*, p. 123.

[13] John Maynard Keynes quoted in Harrod, p. 462.

Chapter 8

[1] Adlai Stevenson quoted in John Bartlow Martin, *Adlai Stevenson of Illinois* (New York: Doubleday & Co., 1976), p. 743.

[2] Townsend Hoopes, *The Devil and John Foster Dulles* (Boston and Toronto: Atlantic

Monthly Press Book, Little, Brown and Co., 1973), p. 426.

[3] Reinhold Niebuhr quoted in Hoopes, p. 37.

[4] John Foster Dulles, "Faith of Our Fathers," based on an address given at the First Presbyterian Church of Watertown, New York. U.S. Department of State publication 5300, General Foreign Policy Series 84, released January 1954, pp. 5–6.

[5] Dulles, p. 6.

[6] John Foster Dulles, "Freedom and Its Purpose," *The Christian Century* (December 24, 1952), p. 1496.

Chapter 9

[1] Paul A. Samuelson, *Economics*, 9th ed. (New York: McGraw-Hill, 1973), p. 58. The same point, in slightly different words, is made in earlier editions.

[2] Paul A. Samuelson quoted in *Newsweek*, September 8, 1975, p. 62.

Chapter 10

[1] These figures are derived from "Area and Production of Principal Crops," 1960/61 and 1973/74 issues and preliminary reports from Ministry of Agriculture, New Delhi, and IN 6005, 1-21-76, from the U.S. Agricultural Attaché in New Delhi.

[2] Robert William Fogel and Stanley L. Engerman, *Time on the Cross* (Boston: Little, Brown and Co., 1974).

[3] These figures are derived from U.S. Bureau of the Census, Sixteenth Census of the United States: 1940 Population, Vol. II, *Characteristics of the Population* (Washington, D.C.: U.S. Government Printing Office, 1943) and U.S. Bureau of the Census, Census of the Population: 1970, Vol. I, *Characteristics of the Population* (Washington, D.C.: U.S. Government Printing Office, 1973).

[4] Henry Bamford Parkes, *A History of Mexico*, Sentry ed. (Boston: Houghton Mifflin Co., 1969), pp. 305–306.

[5] Colonel Thomas Talbot quoted in Fred Coyne Hamil, *Lake Erie Baron* (Toronto: The Macmillan Co. of Canada, 1955), p. 146.

Chapter 11

[1] Figures for the United States, Britain, Italy and India are from *The Yearbook of Labour Statistics* (Geneva: International Labour Office, 1975).

[2] Bamber Gascoigne, *The Great Moghuls* (New York: Harper & Row, 1971), p. 95.

[3] Viscount James Bryce, *The American Commonwealth*, 3rd ed., Vol. I (New York: Macmillan and Co., 1893), p. 637.

[4] Paul Mantoux, *The Industrial Revolution in the Eighteenth Century*, rev. ed. (London: Jonathan Cape, 1961), p. 182.

[5] Ibid.

Chapter 12

[1] Arthur M. Schlesinger, Jr., *The Crisis of the Old Order* (Boston: Houghton Mifflin Co., 1957), p. 291.

So that books might be available for television viewers while the series was being broadcast, the list of illustrations and the index on the following pages were printed from uncorrected proofs. The name of Senator Muskie is Edmund, not Edward. This and some other slips will be corrected in the next printing.

List of Illustrations

page

14   Adam Smith, by Collopy (*National Museum of Antiquities, National Gallery of Scot-land*).

17   Voltaire receiving visitors at Ferney, by Jean Huber (*Hermitage Museum, Leningrad*).

19   (*top left*) François Quesnay, Musée Carnavalet (*Bulloz*); (*top right*) "Tableau Écon-omique", by François Quesnay (*Archives Nationales*); (*bottom*) "Le Hameau", by Hill, Musée Carnavalet (*Roger-Viollet*).

20–21   Professor Wassily Leontief's economic tabulation, 1965 (*Scientific American*).

24–25   Pin-making, from the *Dictionnaire encyclopédique* of Diderot and d'Alembert (*Mansell Collection*).

28   The road to Gobernuisgach Lodge, Sutherland, Scotland (*Ken Lambert, Barnaby's Picture Library*).

29   David Dale. Portrait on bank note, issued January 23, 1967 (*The Royal Bank of Scotland*).

31   (*top*) Quadrille dancing at the Institution for the Formation of Character, New Lanark, Scotland (*Mansell Collection*); (*bottom*) New Lanark (*Ian Dryden, Ikon*).

33   David Ricardo, by T. Hodgetts (*British Museum*).

34   Thomas Malthus, by J. Linnell, National Portrait Gallery.

39   The fever hospital at Grosse Isle (*Catherine Galbraith*).

41   Hauling trees, Upper Ottawa river, Canada, 1871, photo by Notman (*McCord Museum of McGill University, Montreal*).

47   (*top left*) Herbert Spencer, 1888 (*Mary Evans Picture Library*); (*top right*) William Graham Sumner (*Yale University Library*); (*bottom*) Carl Schurtz, photo by Brady (*Culver Pictures*).

50   (*top center*) Jim Fisk; (*top left*) Jay Gould; (*top right*) Daniel Drew; (*bottom left*) "Boss" William Tweed (all *Culver Pictures*); (*bottom right*) Cornelius Vanderbilt (*courtesy of the New York Historical Society*).

51   Erie Railroad bond, October 16, 1847.

52   (*top*) Edward Stokes shooting Jim Fisk on the stairs of the Grand Central Hotel, New York (*Bettman Archives*); (*bottom*) Jim Fisk's tombstone, Brattleboro, Vermont (*Peter Galbraith*).

54   (*top*) John D. Rockefeller, c. 1900 (*Bettman Archives*); (*bottom left*) John D. Rockefel-ler Jr., 1930 (*Associated Press*); (*bottom center*) Nelson Rockefeller, 1975 (*David Hume Kennerley, Associated Press*); (*bottom right*) David Rockefeller, 1973 (*Associated Press*).

56   Henry Ward Beecher (*Culver Pictures*).

59   Thorstein Veblen (*Bettman Archives*).

63   (*top*) "The Breakers", Newport, Rhode Island (*The Preservation Society of Newport County, Newport*); (*bottom*) The Casino, Monte Carlo (*Mansell Collection*).

64   (*top*) Mrs Stuyvesant Fish (*Bettman Archives*); (*bottom*) cartoon from the magazine *Judge* (*Mary Evans Picture Library*).

66   James Gordon Bennett, Jr. (*Bettman Archives*).

69   (*top*) Consuelo Vanderbilt and her father, William K. Vanderbilt (*Bettman Archives*); (*bottom*) Boniface, Comte de Castellane, and his wife, Anna, née Gould (*Radio Times Hulton Picture Library*).

72–73   Page from the catalogue of the Neiman-Marcus store in Dallas, Texas (*Neiman-Marcus*).

76   Karl Marx, 1867 (*International Institute for Social History, Amsterdam*).

79   Marx's birthplace, Trier, West Germany (*Verkehrsamt der Stadt Trier*).

82   Georg Wilhelm Friedrich Hegel (*Popperfoto*).

87   Jenny Marx, *c.* 1851 (*International Institute for Social History, Amsterdam*).

88   Friedrich Engels, 1891 (*International Institute for Social History, Amsterdam*).

92   The Communist Party Manifesto.

94   (*top*) Paris, 1848; (*center left*) Berlin, March 1848; (*center right*) Vienna, October 1848; (*bottom*) Prague, June 1848 (all *Mary Evans Picture Library*).

99   Marx's house at 41 Maitland Park Road, London NW3 (*Greater London Council Photograph Library*).

101   Reading Room, British Museum (*Mansell Collection*).

104   (*top*) Membership card in the First International (*Popperfoto*); (*bottom*) members of the First International, 1868 (*Marx Memorial Library*).

107   (*top*) The Champs Élysées, Paris, 1871 (*Radio Times Hulton Picture Library*); (*bottom*) Dead Communards, 1871, Musée Carnavalet (*Bulloz*).

113   Acre (*Barnaby's Picture Library*).

115   Page from *The Conquest of Constantinople*, by Count Geoffrey de Villehardouin, (*Bodleian Library*).

119   (*top*) Archivo General de Indias, Seville, Spain (*Jim Black*); (*bottom left*) letter from Columbus to his son, Diego, February 5, 1505; (*bottom right*) letter from Francisco Pizarro to Queen Isabella of Spain, 1539 (all *Archivo General de Indias*).

123   (*top*) Abandoned hacienda in Mexico (*Popperfoto*); (*bottom*) Plantation house, Longwood, Natchez (*Associated Press*).

125   John Beames (*India Office Library*).

126   (*top*) The *jirga*, a tribal council adopted by the British in the North West Frontier Province, Wana, 1929 (*Sir John Dring*); (*bottom*) The Hunt Breakfast on the steps of the Ootacamund Club, Nilgiri Hills (*Mansell Collection*).

128   Vultures in Calcutta, 1946, photo by Margaret Bowke-White (*Colorific/Time-Life*).

129   Civilians at the U.S. Embassy during the evacuation of Saigon, 1975 (*Associated Press*).

125   (*top*) Vladimir Ilyich Lenin (*Camera Press*); (*bottom*) Cracow Castle (*Radio Times Hulton Picture Library*).

140   (*top*) Kitchener's poster appeal for volunteers on a postbox in London; (*bottom*) New recruits taking the oath at the White City recruiting office, December 1915 (both *Radio Times Hulton Picture Library*).

144   Cross-section of a Vickers 303 machine gun from a 1918 army handbook (*National Army Museum*).

146   Leon Trotsky (*Camera Press*).

150   (*top*) George V decorating Lieutenant Yagle, September 1918; (*bottom*) The Kaiser, July 1917 (both *Radio Times Hulton Picture Library*).

153   (*top*) Lenin, Krupskaya and Zinoviev in Stockholm, April 1917, on their way from Switzerland to Russia (*Novosti Press Agency*); (*bottom*) Lenin inspecting troops in Red Square, Moscow, May 1919 (*Camera Press*).

156   (*top*) Fiat factory in Turin (*Fiat SpA*); (*bottom*) Engine assembly shop in Fiat Factory, Togliattigrad (*Novosti Press Agency*).

158   (*top*) Rosa Luxembourg; (*bottom*) Karl Liebknecht (both *Marx Memorial Library*).

162   Senator Edward Muskie campaigning at Dadeland shopping center, Miami, Florida, 1972 (*James Pickerell, Camera Press*).

164   Early engraving of coin-minting (*Fotomas*).

165   The money-changer and his wife, by Quentin Metsys, 1514, Louvre, Paris (*Giraudon*).

168   Amsterdam (*Amsterdam City Archives*).

169   Jan Six, by Rembrandt (*Art Promotion, Amsterdam*).

171   John Law. Engraving by Leon Scherk from *The Great Mirror of Folly*, 1720 (*British Museum*).

173   (*top*) "Change des billets", 1720. Dragoons guarding the bank at the "hotel des Monnoyea", Rennes, July 1970 (*Musée de Bretagne, Rennes*); (*bottom*) An English adaptation of a Dutch broadsheet criticizing Law (*British Museum*).

175   William Paterson. Pen and ink drawing (*British Museum*).

177   "Midas transmuting all into paper", by James Gillray, March 9, 1796 (*Bank of England*).

179   The Court of Governors and Directors of the Bank of England in 1903 and 1974 (*Bank of England*).

185   (*top*) Andrew Jackson, by James Lambdin. Painted in the year of Jackson's death, 1845 (*Pennsylvania Academy of Fine Arts*); (*bottom*) Nicholas Biddle (*The Magazine Antiques*).

186   Roslyn Savings Bank (*Culver Pictures*).

189   William Jennings Bryan speaking during a presidential campaign (*Associated Press*).

193   Irving Fisher sailing for Europe on the *Mauretania*, 1927 (*Irving Fisher Jr.*).

196   (*top*) John Maynard Keynes, by Gwen Raverat, National Portrait Gallery; (*bottom*) Cambridge students and friends on the barge *Adibah* in 1911. Keynes is arrowed; on the prow are Rupert Brooke, Roger Fry and Virginia Woolf (*W. M. Keynes*).

199   Alfred Marshall (*St. John's College Library, Cambridge*).

201   (*top*) Lloyd George, Clemenceau and Wilson on their way to sign the peace treaty on June 28, 1919 (*Syndication International*); (*bottom*) Allied officers peer into the Hall of Mirrors at Versailles (*Radio Times Hulton Picture Library*).

202   Lydia Lopokova and Leonide Massine dancing the can-can at the Coliseum in Diaghilev's "Boutique Fantasque", June 1919 (*W. M. Keynes*).

205   (*top*) Coal strike poster issued by the government on October 18, 1920; (*bottom*) Midland miners during the General Strike (both *Radio Times Hulton Picture Library*).

206   (*top*) Charles Rist (*Radio Times Hulton Picture Library*); (*bottom*) Hjalmar Horace Greeley Schacht and Montagu Norman (*Keystone*).

210   The planked surface of Wall Street, New York, on October 29, 1929 (*Popperfoto*).

212   Andrew Mellon, 1926 (*Radio Times Hulton Picture Library*).

215   Franklin D. Roosevelt at the Metropolitan Opera House, New York, on November 3, 1932 (*Associated Press*).

219   (*top*) Herbert Hoover, March 1932, photo by Erich Salomon (*John Hillelson Agency*); (*bottom*) The waterfront in Seattle, Washington, March 1933 (*Associated Press*).

230   The Brandenburg Gate, Berlin (*Syndication International*).

233   The statistics chart at Rhein-Main airfield, Frankfurt, July 24, 1948 (*Popperfoto*).

236   (*top*) John Foster Dulles at Princeton in 1907; (*bottom*) with General MacArthur (*Princeton University Library*).

239   Launching the U.S.S. *Richard B. Russell* at Newport News on December 1, 1974 (*U.S. Navy Photo*).

241   Robert Oppenheimer and General Leslie R. Groves in the Alamogordo Desert, New Mexico on April 15, 1945 (*Popperfoto*).

244   Khrushchev laughing with reporters during one of his visits to the U.S.A., October 23, 1964 (*Albert Fenn,* © *Time Life Inc. 1976*).

247   (*top*) Fidel Castro, 1960 (*Sergio Larrain, John Hillelson Agency*); (*bottom*) E. Howard Hunt, 1973 (*Associated Press*).

250   Anti-war protesters in Madison, Wisconsin, 1970 (*Associated Press*).

253   Project Nobska, Woods Hole, Massachusetts, 1956 (*National Academy of Sciences*).

254   $6 billion worth of stock, Davies-Monthan Air Force Base, near Tucson, Arizona, March 1975 (*Tony Korody, Sygma; John Hillelson Agency*); (*inset*) B-52's in May 1971 (*H. J. Kokojan, U.S. Air Force*).

258   Charles Addams cartoon from *The New Yorker* magazine.

260   Page from the Esalen Institute brochure.

265   (*top left*) Henry Ford, 1941; (*top right*) Henry Ford II, 1976; (*center left*) Thomas J. Watson, President of IBM, 1937; (*center right*) Thomas J. Watson, Jr., Chairman of IBM, 1964; (*bottom left*) Colonel Sosthenes Behn, Founder of ITT, 1957; (*bottom right*) Harold S. Geneen, President of ITT, 1966 (all *Associated Press*).

267   (*top*) The General Motors Building, New York (*Camera and Pen International*); (*bottom*) The Comecon Building, Moscow (*Tom Blau, Camera Press*).

272   (*top*) Class photo outside the Baker Library, Harvard Business School (*Fogg Art Museum, Harvard*); (*bottom*) A seminary outing in Burgos, Spain, 1953 (*Henri Cartier-Bresson, John Hillelson Agency*).

275   The Philips organization throughout the world (*Philips & Co Ltd*).

282   A village on the Punjab Plain in the Indus Basin irrigation project (*Jacoby, Camera Press*).

284   An aerial view of the Saskatchewan plains (*Canadian Government*).

286   Professor Gunnar Myrdal (*Press Association*).

288   Eli Whitney's cotton gin (*Mansell Collection*).

290   Cotton-picking machine at work in Mississippi (*Delta Council*).

292   (*top*) Kingston market, Jamaica, 1971 (*Penny Tweedie, Daily Telegraph Colour Library*); (*center*) Housing in Puerto Rico, 1968 (*Eve Arnold, John Hillelson Agency*); (*bottom*) Peasants at Selge, Turkey (*Picturepoint*).

294   (*top*) Slum conditions in Liverpool, 1949 (*Bert Hardy, Radio Times Hulton Picture Library*); (*center*) Tenement blocks in Harlem, New York (*Dick Saunders, Camera Press*); (*bottom*) Living quarters of Turkish migrant workers in France (*Gilles Peress, John Hillelson Agency*).

297   Port Talbot, Ontario (*Cliff Maxwell*).

298   The initials of Professor J. K. Galbraith inscribed for posterity at the Galbraith farm (*Cliff Maxwell*).

301 The commercial district, Singapore, 1976 (*Professor Charles A. Fisher*).

305 (*top*) Fatehpur Sikri (*Ian Berry, John Hillelson Agency*); (*1st row left*) The Forbidden City, Peking (*Marc Riboud, John Hillelson Agency*); (*1st row right*) Civic Centre, Canberra, 1968 (*W. Pedersen, Australian News & Information Bureau*); (*2nd row left*) Angkor Wat, Cambodia (*L. Ionesco, Colorific*); (*2nd row right*) National Assembly, Islamabad, Pakistan (*Sassoon, Robert Harding Associates*); (*bottom left*) Louis XIII's château at Versailles, 1664, by Pierre Patel, Versailles Museum (*Cliché Musées Nationaux, Paris*); (*bottom right*) Brasilia (*Joachim G. Jung, Colorific*).

308 (*top*) A street off the main square in Bruges (*Barnaby's Picture Library*); (*bottom*) The main street of Frankfort, Kentucky (*Picturepoint*).

310 Halifax in the late 1930's (*Bill Brandt, from the book* Shadow of Light).

313 "Rainswept Roofs", London, in the early 1930's (*Bill Brandt, from the book* Shadow of Light).

315 Leo Baeck House, Bishop's Avenue, Barnet (*Greater London Council Photograph Library*).

320 An aerial view of Tokyo (*Japan Information Center*).

331 President F. D. Roosevelt delivering his inaugural address, March 4, 1933 (*Associated Press*).

333 (*top*) Pandit Jawaharlal Nehru, 1947; (*bottom*) Martin Luther King leading civil rights marchers from Selma to Montgomery, Alabama, March 24, 1965 (both *Associated Press*).

336 Police manhandling a demonstrator outside the Democratic convention in Chicago, 1968 (*Constantine Manos, John Hillelson Agency*).

341 (*top*) Cheyenne Mountain; (*center*) The Norad tunnels (both *U.S. Air Force*); (*bottom*) Death Valley (*Catherine Galbraith*).

Index

Bold figures indicate illustrations

Acheson, Dean, 240

Acre, **115**; assault on (1291), 114

Adams, Henry, 55

Addams, Charles, 259; cartoon by, **258**

Address to the Working Classes (Marx), 105

affluent class: display of, 61–7; enjoyments, 65, 67–70; God and, 55–7; natural selection of, 44–8, 49; publicity, 65–7; of today, 70–75; Veblen on, 57–62

agriculture: collectivization, 154, 211; economy of, before Industrial Revolution, 12–13; in eighteenth-century France, 16–18; Soviet shortcomings, 155, 211

Airey, Colonel Richard, 298

Akbar the Great, 304

Alaska, 122

Algeria, 131

Alsace-Lorraine, 136, 137

America – *see* United States

American Civil War: financed by paper money, 182, 187; as revolt against colonial society, 122

American Dilemma, An (Myrdal), 285

Amsterdam, **168**; banks and creation of money, 166–70

Angkor Vat, **305**

Armand, Inessa, 152

armed services, and close relationship with industry, 228, 232, 240, 245, 252–5

arms race, 227–8, 251–5

Arnold, Jim (Skidoo storekeeper), 340

assembly line, early, **24–5**

Austria, pre-1914 alliance with Germany, 136

automobile industry, Italian and Soviet, 155

Ball, George, 229, 248

Bangladesh: equilibrium of poverty, 29, 281; famine, 37

Bank of Amsterdam, 167–70

Bank of England: founding of, 174; Court of Directors, 176, **179**; and control of creation of money, 176–8, 183; and lending to clearing banks, 178, 188; capacity for economic innovation, 180

Bank for International Reconstruction and Development, 224

Bank Rate, 178, 180, 188

banks and banking, 164–80, 182–7, 190–2; Amsterdam and, 166–70; central banks, 178, 182–4, 191–2; creation of money, 166–70, 176; Depression, 191–2; failures, 190; regulation of money, 166, 174, 176–8

Banque Royale, 170–4

Barnard, George Gardner, 51–3

Bay of Pigs (1962), 246–8

Beams, John, **125**; his ideal of government, 124–7

Beecher, Rev. Henry Ward, **56**, 80; and Spencer and natural selection, 48, 55–7

Behn, Sosthenes, **265**

Ben Bella, Ahmed, 131

Bennett, James Gordon, 65–7, 184

Bennett, James Gordon, Jr., 65–7, 68; **66**

Berkeley, University of California at, 198, 337–8

Berle, Adolf A., 268

Berlin: Marx and, 81–4; Wall, 84; 1848 revolution, **94**; Brandenburg Gate, **230**, 231; airlift, 232–4, **233**; post-war, 228–34

Index

Bern, Lenin in, 145, 147

Biddle, Nicholas, **185**; showdown with Andrew Jackson over bank power, 184

Birmingham (Alabama), 311–12

Birmingham (Detroit), 316

Birmingham (England), 311

birth control, 42, 283–7, 338

Bismarck, Otto von, 105

Blaine, James G., 221–2

Blanc, Louis, 89, 95

Blanqui, Louis Auguste, 89

Blenheim Palace, 68

Bloomsbury Group, 198

Blue Ridge Corporation, 209, 237

Bolsheviks, 139. *See also* Communism

Bonn University, Marx at, 81

Brasilia, **305**

Brattleboro (Vermont), Kipling at, 130, 132

"Breakers, The" (Vanderbilt mansion, Newport), 62, **63**

Bretton Woods Conference (1944), 224

Britain: landowners and workers' rights, 13; loss of American colonies, 36; expansion of production and trade, 36; and colonialism, 124–7; pre-1914 trade unions, 134; and World War I, 139, 149; ruling coalition of capitalists and workers, 157; banking system, 174–8, 183, 188; return to gold standard, 203–7; unemployment, 207; Great Depression, 213; economic policy during World War II, 223; and immigration, 295, 317, 318; low productivity of labor force, 295; agricultural labor force, 303; race prejudice, 318

British India, History of (Mill), 110

British Museum Reading Room, **101**, 145; Marx and, 100; Lenin and, 145

Brooklyn, Plymouth Church, 55

Bruges, **308**; as Merchant City, 307

Brüning, Heinrich, 213

Brussels, 266; Marx in, 91, 97

Bryan, William Jennings, 55, 184, **189**; opposes gold standard, 188

Bryce, Lord, 314

Bryce, Robert, 217

Burke, Admiral Arleigh, 252

Business Enterprise, Theory of (Veblen), 61

Cadillac Mirage, **72–3**

California: emigration of poor whites into, 318–19; University of, Berkeley, 337–8

Callaghan, James, 15

Calvin, John, 325

Camp city, 314–16

Canada: and World War I, 149, 151, 159; quiet revolution, 159; and variant of paper money, 181; and Keynesian doctrine, 217; settling of West, 299; as first country of Third World, 299

Canberra, **305**

Cap Ferrat, 68

capitalism: coalition with workers after World War I, 157; converging with Communism in business, 155; Marx's theory of, 100–103; motivating influence in change, 90; overthrow of, by proletariat, 83, 102–3, 147–8

capitalism, manners and morals of, 43–75; ceremonials, 62–5; Conspicuous Consumption and Leisure, 60–70; gambling, 70; modern rich, 70–75; natural selection of affluent, 44–8; natural selection and the Church, 55–7; railroad struggle, 49–55; publicity, 65–7; Riviera, 67–8, 70; Veblen on, 57–62

Carey, Henry Charles, challenges Ricardo's view, 40

Carnegie, Andrew, 43

Castellane, Count Boni de, **69**, 70

Castro, Fidel, 121, **247**

Central Intelligence Agency (CIA): and Cold War, 242, 246–8; in India, 243*n*; and Bay of Pigs, 246

Chamberlaine, Houston Stewart, 11

Chamberlain, Joseph, 311

Chase Manhattan Bank, 181

Cheyenne Mountain (Colorado), **341**, 342

Chiang Kai-shek, 249

Chicago Convention (1968), 335, **336**

China, 249; Revolution after World War II, 96, 234; and coinage, 163; enmity with Soviet, 131, 251; birth control, 287, 338

Cholera Bay (Quebec), 40

Churchill family, 68

Churchill, Lord Randolph, 70

Churchill, Lady Randolph, 70

Churchill, Winston, 70, 144, 197, 224, 237; disastrous return to gold standard, 203, 204, 209; and General Strike, 207

city life: Camp, 314–16; Industrial City, 309–18; Merchant City, 306–9; Metropolis, 318–23; migration, 316–18; Political Household, 303–6, 309, 322; race prejudice, 318

city state, 299–302

Civil War in France, The (Marx), 106

class structure, ungluing of in World War I, 133–4

Clay, Henry, 184

Clay, General Lucius, 234

Clearances, 27–9, 287, 316

Clemenceau, Georges, **201**; Keynes on, 200

coinage, **164**, **165**; debasing of, 166; invention of, 163, 180

Cold War, 234–5, 243–51; moral sanction for, 235, 238, 240, 246, 249

Cologne, Marx's journalism in, 84–6, 97

colonialism, 109–32; Britain and, 124–7; as Crusades in Eastern Mediterranean, 112–16; Eastern European form of, 134–6; fiscal aspect, 114–16; France and, 121–2, 170–2; ideas governing, 111–12; Marx on, 110, 148; revolts against, 121, 122; Adam Smith on, 109, 117; Spain and, 116–21; United States and, 121, 127–31

Columbus, Christopher: and colonialism, 116, 118; letter to son, **119**

Comecon, **267**

Committee for Economic Development, 223–4

commitment, 338–9

Communards, **107**

Communism, Communists: American aim to save Vietnam from, 130–1; and Cold War, 234–5, 238, 243–51; converging with capitalism in business, 155; divisions within, 243–5, 251; Lenin's insistence on term, 142; victory in Eastern Europe and Asia, 234; Vietnam war's effect on, 249–51

Communist League, 91, 100

Communist Manifesto, 91–3; **92**

Company of the West (Mississippi Company), rise and fall of, 170–4

Connally, John, 335

Conquest of Mexico, History of (Prescott), 117

Conquest of Peru, History of (Prescott), 117, 120

Conspicuous Consumption, 60–70

Conspicuous Leisure, 61

Constantinople, 114

Continental Congress, and paper money, 182, 194

corporations, 257–79; control of, 268; Esalen Institute, 259–61; future of, 277–9; multinational syndrome, 274–7; myth of, 257–9, 269, 274; Philips, 270–74; power of, 257–9; Adam Smith on, 26, 35, 324; UGE, 261–70; unease over, 259, 274

Cortés, Hernando, 118

cotton economy, 288–91

cotton gin, **288**

cotton picker, mechanical, **290**

Cracow, 134; Castle, **135**; Lenin in, 134, 139–41

Critique of the Gotha Programme (Marx), 108

Cronkite, Walter, 329

Crosby, James S., 252

Crossman, Richard, 27

Crusades, **113**; as colonial enterprise, 112–16, 118; myth of, 112, 114

Cuba, 246–8; break with colonialism, 121; missile crisis, 248

Currie, General Sir Arthur W., 159

Currie, Lauchlin, 221; as exponent of Keynes in Washington, 220

Czechoslovakia, Soviet takeover, 234

Dale, David, **29**; New Lanark experiment, 29

Dallas (Texas), Conspicuous Consumption in, 71

Darien venture, 176

Dark Thursday (1929), 209–11; **210**

Darrow, Clarence, 55

Darwin, Charles, 44; Spencer's debt to, 45; and natural selection, 55, 57

Davies-Monthan Air Force Base, 252–5, 256; **254**

Dead Souls (Gogol), 74

Death Valley (California), 340, **341**

democracy: commitment, 338–9; education

in, 337–8; elections, 328–30; leadership, 327–8, 330–7; Swiss model, 325–7
Democratic Advisory Council, 240
Dewey, Thomas E., 237
Detroit, 299
Diderot, Denis, *Encyclopaedia*, **24–3**
Dominicans, and Spanish colonialism, 117
Drew, Daniel, **50**; and Erie Railroad, 49–53
Dulles, Allen Welsh, 237; and CIA, 242, 246, 248
Dulles, John Foster, 209, 235–8; 236; moral sanction for Cold War, 235, 238, 240, 246, 249; career, 237–8
Dutch East India Company, 167, 170

East India Company: as source of income for economists, 32, 110; condemned by Adam Smith, 109; and colonialism, 109–10, 124
Eastern Europe: pre-1914 aristocratic ruling class, 133; and revolution, 134; rule of Europeans by other Europeans, 134–6; retreat from imperialism, 136; and World War I, 137–9; Soviet consolidation in, 231; emigration to industrialized countries, 293–5, 317
Eastern Mediterranean, Crusades as colonial enterprise in, 112–16
Ebert, Friedrich, 157
Eccles, Marriner, 220
Economic Consequences of the Peace (Keynes), 200, 224
education, role in democracy, 337–8
Edward VII, 184
Eindhoven, as Philips headquarters, 270–4
Eisenhower, Dwight D., 234, 246; on danger of misplaced military-industrial power, 227, 228, 245
emigration, 30–40, 287–99, 316–19
Employment Act (American) (1946), 224
Engels, Friedrich, **88**, 108; on Hegel, 83; as Marx's partner, 89, 91, 98, 103
England – *see* Britain
Equity Funding Corporation, 74
Erie Railroad war, 49–53
Esalen Institute, 259–61; brochure, **260**
European Common Market, 276–7

famine, 35, 37–8
Farm Bureau Federation, 18
Fatehpur Sikri, **305**; as archetype of Political Household, 304–6
Feuerbach, Ludwig, 89
Federal Reserve System, 190–2; and Keynesian Revolution, 220
Filene, Edward A., 141
Financial and Industrial Securities Corporation, 208–9
First Bank of the United States, 183
First International: founding of, 103–5; death of, 105; Marx's final address to, 106; membership card, **104**; leaders, **104**
Fish, Mrs Stuyvesant, **64**, 65; party given by, **64**, 65
Fisher, Irving, **193**; formula to determine value of money, 192–5, 213; influence on Keynes, 195
Fisk, Jim, **50**, **52**; and struggle for Erie Railroad, 49–53
Ford, Gerald, and détente, 251
Ford, Henry, **265**
Ford, Henry II, **265**
Fourier, Charles, 89, 95
France: landownership before Industrial Revolution, 13; Adam Smith's impression of, 16–18; agricultural system, 18; Physiocrats, 18, 22; 1848 Revolution, 93–7; 1871 Commune, 105–6; and colonialism, 121–2, 170–2; pre-1914 workers' political strength, 134; pre-1914 alliance with Russia, 136; and territorial imperative, 137; and World War I, 139, 142, 149; ruling coalition of capitalists and workers, 157; finances under Law, 170–4; Revolution financed by paper money, 182; Turkish workers' hostel, **294**
Franco-Prussian War, 105
Frankfort (Kentucky), **308**
Franklin, Benjamin, 15; exponent of paper money, 180, 182
Franklin National Bank, 167
Funk, Walther, 330

Gandhi, Mahatma, 332, 337
Gary, Elbert Henry, 312
Gates, Frederick T., 43

Gaulle, Charles de, 237, 334

Geneen, Harold, **265**

General Motors, **267**, 277

General Strike (1926), 207

General Theory of Employment Interest and Money (Keynes), 216–17, 218

George V, **150**

George, Henry, *Progress and Poverty*, 60

German-French Yearbooks, Marx's editorship of, 86–9

Germany: workers' political strength after 1870, 108, 134; pre-1914 imperialism, 136; and territorial imperative, 137; and World War I, 138–9, 142, 149, 157; fascism, 157, 214; inflation, 190; reparations, 200; Great Depression, 213; Nazi borrowing and spending to cure unemployment, 213–14, 221; and Marshall Aid, 225

Getting, Ivan, 252

Gide, André, 86

Glow, Arthur Francis, 263

Glow, James B., **265**; and founding of UGE, 261–2

Glow, James B., Jr., 263, 268, 269

Goebbels, Joseph, 11

Gogol, Nikolai, *Dead Souls*, 74

gold standard, 187–8, 190; Britain's return to, 203–7; abandonment of, 213

Goldblum, Stanley, 74

Goldman Sachs Trading Corporation, 208–9

Goodhart, Arthur L., 81

Gotha, working-class parties' programme, 108

Gould, Anna, **69**, 70

Gould, Jay, **50**; and Erie Railroad, 49, 51, 53

Great Crash (1929), 191, **120**, 211

Great Depression, 190–2, 211–13, 330; Keynes's remedy for, 213–26

Great Hunger, 37–8, 40, 110

Greenbacks, 182, 187–8, 194

Griffin, James (Erie engine driver), 53

Grosse Isle (Quebec), 38; fever hospital, **39**

Groves, General Leslie R., **241**

Haarlem (New York City), **294**

Haase, Hugo, 138

Hachard, Marie-Madeleine, 122

Halifax, workers' houses, **313**

Hamilton, Alexander, 183

Hansen, Harvey, as American exponent of Keynes, 220

Harris, Seymour E., 221

Harvard Business School, 271, **272**

Harvard University, Keynes's influence on, 217–18

Haughton, Daniel J., on "kickbacks" in arms race, 227, 228

Hegel, Georg Wilhelm Friedrich, 81–4, **82**; Marx's acceptance of, 83–4

Herodotus, on invention of coined money, 163

Highgate Cemetery, Marx's grave, 77

Hitler, Adolf, 11, 80; economic policy, 213–14, 221; as true protagonist of Keynesian ideas, 221

Hobson, J. A., 147

Hofstadter, Richard, 48

Hoover, Herbert, **219**; and Great Depression, 211, 213, 330

Hooverville, **219**

Hughes, Howard, 65

Hume, David, 15, 27

Humphrey, Hubert, 328

Hungary, revolt (1956), 238

Hunt, E. Howard, **247**

hunt breakfast, **126**

imperialism – *see* colonialism

Imperialism: the Highest Stage of Capitalism (Lenin), 147

India, **128**; landownership by Moghuls, 13; equilibrium of poverty, 29, 281–3; famine, 37; colonialism in, 110, 124–7; result of independence, 127, **128**, 334; American aid, 132; CIA in, 243*n*; agricultural labor force, 303

Indonesia, and equilibrium of poverty, 29

Indus Valley, and coinage, 163

Industrial City, 309–18; as characteristic city, 309–11; class structure, 314–16, 318; economics of, 312–14; migration to, 316–19; suburb, 316

Industrial Revolution, 12, 13, 27, 288, 309

inevitable conflict, doctrine of, 228, 232, 240–2, 243, 245, 249; abandonment of, 251 inflation: Germany, 190; Keynes's remedy, 221–3, 225–6, 300

Innocent III, Pope, 114

INSEAD (French business school), 271

International Monetary Fund, 224

Ireland: Malthus and Ricardo ideas tested in Great Hunger, 37–8; emigrants to America, 38–40, 110, 317

Iselin, Columbus, 252

Islamabad, National Assembly, **305**

Italy: automobile industry, 155; famine, 157; agricultural labor force, 303

Jackson, Andrew, and struggle against Biddle's bank, 184

Jan Six (Rembrandt), **169**

Jefferson, Thomas, 122

Jerusalem, and Crusades, 113, 114, 131

Johnson, Lyndon, 328, 335

Johnson, Dr Samuel, on London, 309

Jones, Lewis, 243*n*

Jordan, David Starr, 60

Kapital, Das (Marx), 100–103

Kapitza, Peter, 155

Kennedy, John F., 61, 243*n*, 328, 329, 338; and Cuban missile crisis, 248; as a leader, 334

Kennedy, Robert, 248, 335

Keynes, Florence Ada, 197

Keynes, John Maynard, 18, **196**, 255, 300; on power of vested interests compared with encroachment of ideas, 11; and shortage of purchasing power, 36; on ideas as motivating force in change, 42, 90; his debt to Irving Fisher, 195, 213; at Cambridge, 197–8; interest in economics, 198; at Treasury during World War I, 198–200; condemns reparations in *Economic Consequences of the Peace*, 200, 224; unpopularity, 203, 207; attacks return to gold standard, 204–7, 224; advocates government borrowing and spending as cure for Depression, 213–14; his *General Theory of Employment Interest and Money*, 216–17, 218; his views in America and Canada, 217–21, 223–4, 225–6; his cure for inflation, 221–223, 226;

at Bretton Woods, 224, 225; negotiates American loan, 224; "legacy" of, 225–6

Keynes, John Neville, 197

Khrushchev, Nikita, 155, **244**, 342; as decisive man of midcentury, 243–5; reverses Stalinist policies, 243–5; and peaceful co-existence, 245

Kienthal, socialists' conference (1916), 148

King, Martin Luther, **333**, 338; and leadership, 335–7

Kingston (Jamaica), **292**

Kipling, Rudyard, 130

Kirkcaldy, birthplace of Adam Smith, 15

Knights of the Hospital of St John of Jerusalem, 114–16; **115**

Korea, 234

Krak des Chevaliers, 116

Kreuznach, 86

Krupskaya, Nadezhda, 139, 145, 152, **153**

labor, division of, 23

labor theory of value, 32, 35, 37, 102

Lahore, 124

landlords: absentee Irish, 37; Malthus and Ricardo theories on revenue of, 36; power of, against workers, 13, 35

Lassalle, Ferdinand, 89

Latin America, colonialism and, 116–21

Law, John, 121, **171**; and Banque Royale, 170–4; and Mississippi Company, 170–4; collapse of schemes, **173**, 174

leadership instinct, 327–8, 330–7

League of the Just (later Communist League), 91

Leisure Class, Theory of the (Veblen), 60–61

Lenin, V. I., **135**, **153**, 211; in Cracow, 134, 139–41; as true revolutionary compared with Marx, 141–2; on role of peasants in revolution, 142–3, 154; in Switzerland, 143, 145–8, 151–2; revolutionary conferences, 145–7, 148; theory of imperialism and capitalism, 147–8; and 1917 Revolution, 151–4; takes power in Petrograd, 152–4; his miscalculation, 154, 157; on intellectuals' role in revolution, 197

Leontief, Wassilly, great tabulation of American industry, **20–21**, 22

Ley, Robert, 330

Liebknecht, Karl, 157, **158**

Liebling, A. J., his law, 207

Lincoln, Abraham, congratulated by Marx, 78

Lippmann, Walter, on Roosevelt, 332

Liverpool, **294**

Lloyd George, David, **201**; on World War I, 136; Keynes on, 200, 213

London: Marx in, 97–108; First International born in, 103; Dr Johnson on, 309

London and County Bank, 170

Lopokova, Lydia, **202**, 203

Los Angeles, 217; modern rich in, 74

Louisiana Purchase, 122

Lowell, Abbott Lawrence, 60

Lubin, Isidor, 229

Luxembourg, Rosa, 157, **158**

Lydia (Asia Minor), invention of coined money, 163, 180

MacArthur, Douglas, **236**, 237

McBehan, Harold, **265**; and UGE, 263–5, 266, 268, 269, 273, 274

McCarthy, Eugene, 328, 329; and Vietnam war, 334–5

McCarthy, Joseph, 234–5

MacDonald, Ramsay, 139

McGovern, George, 328, 329

machine guns, 144

Macmillan, Harold, on Dulles, 237

Madison (Wisconsin), **250**

Malthus, Rev. Thomas, **34**; pessimistic Principle of Population, 32–5, 40, 109–10; on shortage of purchasing power, 36

Manchester, Engels in, 89

Mansfield, Josie, 51, 53

Mao Tse-tung, 234

Marie Antoinette, 18

Marlborough, ninth Duke of, 68

Marshall, Alfred, **199**; his economics rendered obsolete by Keynes, 198

Marshall Plan, 225

Marx, Heinrich, 80

Marx, Jenny (wife), 81, 86, **87**, 98, 100, 108

Marx, Jenny (daughter), 108

Marx, Karl, 35, 42, **76**, 157, 198, 339; "universal man", 77–8; journalism, 77–8, 85–6,

90–91, 97–8; birth and early life in Trier, 78–81; birthplace, **79**; Jewish ancestry, 80; atheism and suspected anti-semitism, 80; at Bonn University, 81; in Berlin, 81–4; and Hegel's ideas, 83–4; continual harassment by police, 84, 89, 91, 97, 98; in Cologne, 84–6; edits *Rheinische Zeitung*, 85–6; marries Jenny von Westphalen, 86; in Paris, 86–91; edits German-French Yearbooks, 86–9; partnership with Engels, 89, 91, 98, 103; forms ideas on Communism, 89–93; edits *Vorwärts*, 90–91; in Belgium, 91, 97; composes *Communist Manifesto*, 91–3; and 1848 revolution, 93, 97; revives *Rheinische Zeitung*, 97; in London, 98–108; one London home, **99**; writes *Das Kapital*, 100–103; and progressive immiseration of workers, 102, 147; helps to form First International, 103–5; and Paris Commune, 105–6; last years, 106–8; on colonialism, 110, 148; compared with Lenin, 142–3; *Address to the Working Classes*, 105; *Civil War in France*, 106; *Critique of the Gothic Programme*, 108

Massachusetts, and development of government paper money, 180, 181

Maxim gun, **144**

Means, Gardiner C., 268

Mellon, Andrew, **212**, 213

Mencken, H. L., on conscience, 74

Menon, Krishna, 132

Merchant City, 306–9

Metropolis, 318–23; capitalism's failure in, 319; race prejudice, 318–19; social character, 319–22

Mexico: revolt against colonialism, 121, 122; hacienda, **123**; equilibrium of poverty, 291–3

Michigan, and bank regulation, 187

Mill, James, 32; and colonialism, 110; *History of British India*, 110

Mill, John Stuart, 32; and colonialism, 110

miners' strike (1926), **205**

Mississippi, 121; plantation house, **123**; migration of rural labor force, 291

Mississippi Company, rise and fall of, 170–4

Index

money, 161–95; banks, 164–80, 182–7, 190–2; creation of, 166–70, 176; function, 163–4; gold, 187–8, 190; government borrowing and spending of, 195, 213–14, 216–18; origins, 163; paper money, 180–4; regulation of, 166, 174, 176–8; value of, Fisher's formula for, 192–4

Monte Carlo, **70**; Casino, **63**

Moore, G. E., 198

Morgan, J. P., 70, 190, 312

Moscow, **153**; Comecon, **267**

multinational syndrome, 276–7

Murphy, Franklin, 335

Murrow, Edward R., 329

Myrdal, Gunnar, **286**; and study of national poverty, 285

Napoleon III, 105, 296

National Recovery Administration (NRA), 214

natural selection: of affluent, 44–8, 49; Church and, 55–7

Nehru, Jawaharlal, 61, 241, **333**, 338; as a leader, 332–4, 337

Neue Rheinische Zeitung, Marx as editor, 97

New Harmony (Indiana), 30

New Lanark: Owen's industrial experiment, 29–30; mills, **31**; Institution for the Formation of Character, 30, **31**

New Orleans, 122

New York: modern rich in, 71; world headquarters of UGE, 266; General Motors, **267**; Haarlem, **94**

New York and Erie Rail Road Company, share, **51**

New York Herald, 65–7

New York Tribune, Marx's journalism for, 78, 98

Newfoundland Park battlefield, 149

Newport (Rhode Island): as monument to conspicuous wealth, 61–2, 65; "The Breakers", 62, **63**

Niarchos, Stavros, 86

Niebuhr, Reinhold, on Dulles, 238

Nixon, Richard, 245, 264; and détente, 251

Norman, Montague, **206**, 207

North American Defense Command (NORAD), 342

Noske, Gustav, 157

nuclear evasion, 342

O'Reilly, Alexander, 122

Old Homestead (Ontario), Galbraith family home, 298

Oppenheimer, Robert, 240, **241**

Orléans, Philippe, Duc d', and Law's plan for national bank, 170, 172

Owen, Robert: and New Lanark and New Harmony, 30; influence on Marx, 89

paper money, 180–4; revolution financed by, 182

Paris: Marx in, 86–91; 1848 Revolution, 93–7, **94**; Commune of 1871, 106, **107**; UGE operations from, 266

Paterson, William, **175**; and Bank of England, 174–6

peaceful coexistence, 242, 245

peasants: decisive class in war, 134; not amenable to slaughter, 151; and power of landlords, 13; role in revolution, 142–3, 154–5

Pentagon, and weapons systems, 240

Peru, Spanish colonization of, 117, 118

Petrograd (now Leningrad), Lenin takes power in, 152, 154

Philadelphia, 309; First International in, 105

Philippines, American colonial experience in, 130

Philips Gloeilampenfabrieken, 270–4, **275**

Physiocrats, 18–22

Pitt, William, 36, 176; on Adam Smith, 32

Pizzarro, Francisco, 118; letter to Queen, **119**

Platten, Fritz, 152

playing cards, as currency, 181

Poland: ruled by other East European countries, 134; Lenin in, 134, 139–43

Polaris, 252

Political Household, 303–6, 309, 322

population explosion, 32–5; control of, 283–7

Poronin, 141, 143

Port Talbot (Ontario), 295–8; **297**

Potsdam Conference (1945), 229, 251

poverty, equilibrium of, 29, 280–1; breaking of, 281–91; city state, 299–302; cotton economy, 288–91; Mexico, 291–3; migration of workers, 293–9; Punjab, 281–3, 287
Powers, Gary, 246
Poznan, 136
Prague, **94**, 134
Pravda, Lenin's contributions to, 141
Prescott, W. H., 117, 120
presidential elections, 328–30
Principle of Population, Essay on the (Malthus), 110
Principles of Economics (Marshall), 57, 198
Principles of Political Economy (Mill), 110
Principles of Political Economy and Taxation (Ricardo), 110
Progress and Poverty (George), 60
Project Nobska, 252, **253**
Proudhon, P. J., 89
Puerto Rico: breaking of equilibrium of poverty, 291; shanty town, **292**
Punjab, 282; British colonization of, 124–7; and breaking of equilibrium of poverty, 281–3, 287; birth control, 287
purchasing power, shortage of, Malthus's idea of, 36

Quebec, and paper money, 180, 181, 182
Quesnay, François, 18–22, **19**; *Tableau Économique*, 18, **19**

race prejudice, 318–19
Radio Corporation of America, 208
railroad struggle, and affluence from, 49–55
Ramage, Rear Admiral L. P., 252
Rand Corporation, 240
reason, men of, 16
Rembrandt, 167; *Jan Six*, **169**
Republican Party, Marx's involvement with, 78
revolution: financing by paper money, 182; Lenin's view of, 142–3, 148; Marx's view of, 148; peasants' role in, 142–3; three conditions for, 96
Rheinische Zeitung, Marx as editor of, 85–6, 97
Rhodes, Knights Hospitallers in, 116

Ricardo, David, 32, **33**, 77, 176; his labor theory of value, 35–6, 37, 40, 102; on landlords' revenue, 36; and colonialism, 110
Richard B. Russell, U.S.S., **239**
right to work, as motive of 1848 Revolution, 95
Rist, Charles, **206**, 207
Riviera, its service to the rich, 68–70
Robbins, Lionel, 213
Rockefeller, David, **54**
Rockefeller, John D., 43, **54**; law of improvement by sacrifice of young, 48
Rockefeller, John D., Jr., **54**
Rockefeller, Nelson D., **54**; on dangers of compassion, 48
Roll, Sir Eric, on motivating influence on capitalist change, 90
Roosevelt, Franklin D., **215**, **331**, 338; puzzled by Keynes, 214; as a leader, 330–2, 334
Rosenberg, Alfred, 11
Rostow, Walt W., 334
Ruge, Arnold, 86, 89
Runnymede, 13
Rusk, Dean, 249
Russia (*see also* Soviet Union): Revolution, 96, 142–3, 151–4, 182; pre-1914 Empire, 134; alliances, 136; and World War I, 139, 151; Lenin takes power, 152

Sachs, Goldman, 208–9
Saint-Simon, Duc de, 89, 95, 174, 180
Samuelson, Paul A., 221, 257
Saskatchewan, 284
Say, Jean Baptiste, 36
Schacht, Hjalmar, **206**, 207, 214
Schumpeter, Joseph A., 77, 213, 217, 304
Schurz, Carl, **47**, 48
Scopes, John T., 55
Scotland, and Clearances, 27–9, 287, 316
Seaboard Airline, 208
Second Bank of the United States, 184
Second International, 105
self-interest, and wealth of nations, 22–3, 30
Seville, Archivo General de Indias, 118, **119**
Shaplen, Robert, 57
Shaw, George Bernard, 216
Shenandoah Corporation, 209, 237
Simpson, Joe (Skidoo murderer), 340

Index

Singapore, **301**; multinational presence in, 276; as prosperous city-state, 299–302

Six, Jan, 167, **169**

Skidoo 23 (California), 339–40

Small, Howard J., **265**; and UGE, 269, 270, 273, 274; on danger of socialism, 278–9

Smith, Adam, 13–27, 46, 77, 300, 339; **14**; as first economist, 13–16, 32; academic career, 15; Grand Tour, 16–22; impressed by France and Physiocrats, 16–22; as man of reason, 16, 42; rejects Quesnay's *Tableau*, 18; on division of labor, 23; on combinations and corporations, 26, 35, 324; his economic model, 32; optimism contrasted with Ricardo and Malthus, 35; and colonialism, 109, 117; *Wealth of Nations*, 15, 22–6, 36

Social Darwinism, 44–8, 55–7

Social Democrats: and World War I, 138–9, 142; Zimmerwald conference (1915), 147

Somme, Battle of (1916), 149

South Sea Bubble, 176, 178

Soviet Union (*see also* Russia): colonialism, 131; agriculture, 155, 211; automobile industry, 155; collectivization, 211; arms competition with America, 117–8, 251–5; consolidation in Eastern Europe, 231, 234; and Berlin blockade, 232–4; and Korea, 234; Cold War, 234–5, 238, 243–51; and Cuba, 249; and Vietnam, 251; and détente, 251

Spain, and colonial achievement, 116–21

Spanish-American War, 130

Spencer, Herbert, **47**, 77; as the great Social Darwinist, 44–8; originator of "survival of fittest", 44; and ascent of privileged classes, 44–5; allows charity, 45; American tour, 46–8; Beecher and, 48, 55–7

Stalin, Josef, 211, 231, 243; policies reversed by Khrushchev, 243–5; and atomic bomb, 251

Steffens, Lincoln, 314

Stevenson, Adlai, 246, 328; on Riviera, 68; on Korea, 234; and Cuban missile crisis, 248

stock-market speculation (1927–29), 208–11

Stokes, Edward, 53

Strathnaver, Highland clearances, 27

Streicher, Julius, 11, 330

Strong, Benjamin, 191

Suez crisis (1956), 237

Sumner, William Graham, **47**, 58, 77; as Social Darwinist, 46, 48

supermarkets, 161, **162**

Sutherland, Highland clearances, 27–9, **28**, 287

Sweezy, Paul M., 78

Switzerland: Lenin in, 143, 145–8, 151–2; as revolutionary capital of world, 145; race prejudice, 318; democratic example, 325–7

Tableau Économique (Quesnay), 18, **19**

Talbot, Colonel Thomas, and settlement of Port Talbot, 295–8

Taylor, A. J. P., 136

Taylor, Maxwell, 334

Tell, William, 325

Teller, Edward, 252

Templars, 114

Tennessee Coal and Iron Company, 312

territorial imperative, 136–7, 138

Teutonic Knights, 114

Texas, the modern rich in, 71, **72–3**

textile revolution, 12, 288

textile town, New Lanark as model, 29–30

Thiers, Adolphe, 106; Marx on, 103

Third World: Marx's standing in, 110; Canada and United States as first countries of, 299

Tilton, Elizabeth, 57

time computer, **72**

Times, The, attack on Keynes, 200

Togliattigrad, automobile industry, 155, **156**

Trevelyan, Charles Edward, 38

Trier, Marx's birthplace, **79**; Marx's early life in, 78–81

Trotsky, Leon, 142, **146**

Truman, Harry S., 251

Turgot, Anne Robert Jacques, 22

Turin, automobile industry, 155, **156**

Turkey, **292**

Tweed, Boss, 50, 53

Ulam, Adam, 154

underemployment equilibrium, 216

unemployment, 204, 207, 225; Hitler's cure for, 213–14, 221; Keynes's remedy, 213, 214, 216, 220–1, 223

Unified Global Enterprises (UGE): as illustration of corporate development, 261–70; founding of, 261–3; changes of name, 262, 263, 264; present-day, 263–6; Era of McBehan, 264–6, 268, 273, 274; overseas operations, 266; control of, 266–8; Washington office, 268–9; technostructure, 269–70; reason for unease, 274; and multinational syndrome, 276

United States of America: emigration to, 38–40, 110, 317; and Social Darwinism, 45–8; railroad struggle, 49–53; high capitalism in, 49–75; reconciliation of natural selection with Christian faith, 55–7; Conspicuous Leisure and Conspicuous Consumption, 61–70; publicity, 65–7; marriages with European aristocracy, 68–70; the modern rich, 70–75; painful colonial experience, 127–31; aid to India, 132; pre-1914 industrial proletariat, 134; and World War I, 149, 151; ruling coalition of capitalists and workers, 157; and invention of paper money, 180, 182; financing of Revolution, 182; banks and the central banks, 182–7, 188–90; struggle between political and banking power, 183–7, 191; and gold, 188, 207–8; stock-market speculation, 191, 208–10; Great Depression, 190–2, 211–13, 214, 330–2; and Keynesian Revolution, 217–21, 223–4, 225–6; recovery and further recession, 218–21; price control, 222–3; aid to Europe, 225; arms race with Soviet Union, 227–8, 251–5; close relationship between industry and armed services, 228, 232, 240, 245, 252–5; Berlin air-lift, 234; Cold War, 234–5, 240–2, 245–51; and Korea, 234; and Cuba, 246–8; and Vietnam, 249–51, 334–5; and big corporations, 261–70, 274–9; cotton economy and equilibrium of poverty, 288–91; as first country of Third World, 299; agricultural labor force, 303; race prejudice, 318; and leadership instinct, 327, 330–2; presidential elections, 328–30, 335

United States Steel Corporation, 312

Urban II, Pope, and real motive of Crusades, 112

Valladolid, 120

Vanderbilt, Consuelo, 68, **69**

Vanderbilt, Cornelius, **50**, 74; and Erie Railroad struggle, 49–53; policy of robbing the public, 49, 53; and Conspicuous Consumption, 62, 68

Vanderbilt, William K., 68

Vanderbilt University (Nashville), 62

Veblen, Thorstein, 57–61, **59**, 77, 192; his view of the American rich, 57, 58–60, 61, 62–4; eccentric life, 60; on distinction between makers and moneymakers, 61; Conspicuous Leisure and Conspicuous Consumption, 61, 62–4, 70; *Theory of Business Enterprise*, 61; *Theory of the Leisure Class*, 60–61

Venice, 307

Verdun, 149

Versailles, **305**; "Le Hameau", 18, **19**

Versailles Treaty, signing of, 200, **201**

Vienna, **94**

Vietnam war, **129**, 249–51; American intervention, 130–1, 159, 334–5; opposition to, **250**; relationship between leadership and commitment, 334–5

Voltaire, **17**; as man of reason, 16

Vorwärts, Marx's work for, 90–91

wages: cuts in, 204, 207; law of, 102, 213

Walker, James J., 216

Wall Street Crash, **210**

Warsaw, 134

Washington: and Cold War, 240–2; and Keynesian Revolution, 218–23; UGE in, 268–9

Washington, George, 183

Watson, Thomas J., **265**

Watson, Tom, Jr., **265**

Wealth of Nations, An Inquiry into the Nature and Causes of the (Smith), 15, 22–6, 36

Western Europe: pre-1914 ruling class and capitalists, 133; industrial proletariat, 134; pre-1914 imperialism, 136; and World War

Index

I, 138–9, 149–51, 157; quiet revolution, 157; coalition of capitalists and workers, 157; failure of capitalism in health and housing, 319

Westphalen, Baron Ludwig von, 81

White, Harry D., 224

Whitney, Eli, 289; cotton gin, **288**

Whitney, Richard, 211

William of Orange, 174

Wilhelm II, Kaiser, **150**

Wilson, Woodrow, **201**; Keynes on, 200

Wood, Charles, 38

workers: coalition with capitalists after World War I, 157; and law of wages, 35; migration to industrialized countries, 293–5, 316–19; overthrow of capitalism, 83, 102–3, 147–8; and power of landlords, 13, 35; pre-1914 political force, 134; support for World War I, 138–9, 142–3, 157

World War I: collapse of political and social systems in, 133–4, 157–60, 163; causes of, 136–8; workers' reaction, 138–9, 142–3, 157; recruiting, **140**; stupidity and slaughter, 143–4, 148–51; heroism a matter of rank not courage, 151; end, 157; Peace Treaty, 200

World War II: as watershed of change, 133; benefit to American business, 231–2, 263

Young, Andrew, 335

Zimmerwald, socialists' conference (1915), 147

Zurich, Lenin in, 151–2